One Woman's Journey to Shamanism

This is not only the amazing story of a scientifically verified psychic healing, it also tells why *you* should be a shaman—and how to do it!

Tayja Wiger's life has taken her through the tortures of physical and sexual abuse, chemical dependency, prostitution, multiple personalities, suspected mental retardation, reform schools, psychiatric institutions and hospitals.

Tayja's unusual travels through A.A., reparenting, reincarnational readings, self-understanding through astrology and psychic healing have led her to a respected position as a healer, an ordained Christian minister and a shaman.

It is not the darkness of the valleys Tayja has experienced that are important; it is the spiritual victory which has taken her beyond the expectations of any who knew her before she was thirty years old.

This story urges all people to do the same: to have great visions, then to live those visions on Earth, for it *is* possible. Out of the change from fear to love in individual lives comes love for each other and our planet.

Not only will you read about Tayja's experience as she learns about becoming a shaman and healer, but you will learn to share in the unity of consciousness, and learn to work with spiritual energies. You will learn to experience your Higher Self. By reading about the ritualistic relationship between the Self and the World, you will learn how to develop all these incredible transforming abilities in yourself!

By using the techniques in this book, you will move toward a new understanding of the universe that can help you achieve *whatever* you desire, and can help YOU to become a modern shaman.

Cynthia Bend and Tayja Wiger

CYNTHIA BEND makes her home in Afton, Minnesota with her husband, horses, cat and dog where they all share a comfortable life. She received her B.A. at Carleton College, Northfield, Minnesota (where Tayja received the healing which released her from blindness). She earned an M.A. in Human Development at St. Mary's College, Winona, Minnesota, and has been involved with helping people ever since, teaching communications with disabled adults, and teaching PSI techniques through Blind Awareness. She has participated in and taught psychospiritual development classes, and currently teaches healing and channeling classes. She is a MariEl healer.

TAYJA WIGER (pronounced Tāy'ă) has experienced many miracles in her life, from blindness to sight, from epilepsy to healing. She is a Native American Sioux who has lived many lifestyles to prepare her for her mission. She is a gifted healer and channeler who lectures on a variety of New Age subjects in the United States and Canada. She is an ordained Spiritualist minister who has lived in Arizona and taught and used the Indian traditions.

To Write to the Author

We cannot guarantee that every letter written to the authors can be answered, but all will be forwarded. Both the authors and the publisher appreciate hearing from readers, learning of your enjoyment and benefit from this book. Llewellyn also publishes a bi-monthly news magazine with news and reviews of practical esoteric studies and articles helpful to the student, and some readers' questions and comments to the authors may be answered through this magazine's columns if permission to do so is included in the original letter. The authors sometimes participate in seminars and workshops, and dates and places are announced in *The Llewellyn New Times*.. To write to the authors, or to ask a question, write to:

Cynthia Bend/Tayja Wiger
c/o THE LLEWELLYN NEW TIMES
P. O. Box 64383-034, St. Paul, MN 55164-0383, U.S.A.

Please enclose a self-addressed, stamped envelope for reply, or $1.00 to cover costs.

About Llewellyn's Spiritual Sciences Series

SIMPLE, PRACTICAL, EFFECTIVE, COMPREHENSIVE, AUTHORITATIVE, INDIGENOUS TO OUR CULTURE

In a world and time that is becoming more complex, challenging and stressful, filled with "over choice" and "cognitive confusion," we are making available to you a unique series of books for self-exploration and growth that have the following distinctive features:

They are designed to be simple, cutting through abstraction, complexities and nuances that confuse and diffuse rather than enlighten, and focus your understanding of your life's purpose.

They are practical; theory always leading to practice to be crowned by devotion when followed through by you as the experimenter. You are the ultimate "laboratory" and "judge."

They are effective, for if you do the work, you will obtain results of psychospiritual transformation and expansion of consciousness.

They are comprehensive because they integrate the exoteric with the esoteric, the sacred traditions of the past with the best insights of modern science.

They are authoritative because they are all written by persons who have actually lived and experienced what they tell you about.

They are part of our Western Culture and philosophical and Mystery Traditions, which must be understood if the synthesis of the Eastern and Western spiritual traditions and Universal Brotherhood is to be realized.

This series will reconcile the fragmented aspirations of ourselves, synthesize religion and science to bring about that psychosynthesis which is the greatest need of our age and its highest aspiration.

Forthcoming book from Cynthia Bend

Channeling Demystified

Forthcoming book from Tayja Wiger

The Maturs Zone

Llewellyn's Spiritual Sciences Series

BIRTH OF A MODERN SHAMAN

A Documented Journey and Guide to Personal Transformation

Cynthia Bend and Tayja Wiger

1988
Llewellyn Publications
St. Paul, Minnesota, 55164-0383, U.S.A.

International Standard Book Number: 0-87542-034-6
Library of Congress Catalog Number: 87-45747

First Edition, 1987
First Printing, 1987

Library of Congress Cataloging-in-Publication Data
Bend, Cynthia, 1925–
   Birth of a modern shaman.

   (Llewellyn Spiritual sciences series)
   Bibliography: p.
   1. Wiger, Tayja, 1954–   2. Shamans—Biography.
3. Indians of North America—United States—Biography.
4. Indians of North America—United States—Religion and mythology.   5. Shamanism.   6. Occultism.   I. Wiger, Tayja,
1954–   II. Title.   III. Series.
E98.R3W633   1987   299'.7'0924 [B]   87-45747

ISBN 0-87542-034-6

Cover Photo: **Brad Armstrong Photography Ltd.**
Illustrations: **Carol Ann Smith**
Book Design: **Terry Buske**
Produced by Llewellyn Publications
Typography and Art property of Chester-Kent, Inc.

Published by
LLEWELLYN PUBLICATIONS
A Division of Chester-Kent, Inc.
P.O. Box 64383
St. Paul, MN 55164-0383, U.S.A.
Printed in the United States of America

Dedication

To all of the spiritual people who have helped me gain clear sight into what's happening in this life for me.

To the Wiger family for all that they have done for me in the last nine years; for bringing forth the spiritual part of my life and helping me to understand my purpose.

To my brother, Chuck Lawrence, who encouraged me to go through the dark to get to the light.

To the social workers in my past who believed I could make it in spite of all those who believed I couldn't.

To my real mother and my real father because I love them both in spite of all the things I went through with them. I know now that it was my choice. It was the rough way, but it was the way I learned the best.

To my friends in Blind Awareness who supported and believed in my vision without sight.

To my friends who supported me for years through the anxiety of the hospitals and all the things I went through.

To the spiritual healers who supported me through accomplishing the miracles of my life.

A special thanks to Cynthia Bend who made this book possible.

Most of all I want to dedicate my book to God. Without his love for me, I would never have made it on this earth plane. I want to thank God for putting His warm loving arms around me and keeping me in the Light and sending His spirit guides to help me through my life.

Tayja M Wiger

Acknowledgments

A special thanks to June Beck, writer, counselor and friend, for her knowledge and assistance in the preparation of this book.

Warm thanks to Rev. Marilyn Rossner for putting her personal life aside and welcoming the power for Tayja's healing.

Heartfelt thanks to those in Blind Awareness who have read this manuscript with a sharp eye for accuracy of detail: Kathy Messetler, Joyce Anderson, Joan Washburn, Sue Knips, Grace McLaughlin, and Bill Mitchell.

Grateful acknowledgment to Tayja's reparenting family, especially Jeanne Wiger for her care and her time in discussing the Creative Learning Center Program with me and for reviewing our manuscript.

Sincere thanks to Tsonakwa for the support he gave to Tayja's healing and to Spiritual Frontiers Fellowship for giving permission to transcribe important passages on shamanism from Tsonakwa's lecture and class given at the Spiritual Frontiers Fellowship Midwest Retreat at Carleton College.

We express gratitude to the medical doctors who have given their time and knowledge in the clarification of medical reports.

A special thanks to Dr. Boris Bagdassarroff, Dr. Nor Hall and Dr. Norman Shealy for taking time from their busy schedules to review this book.

Loving thanks to Meredith for keeping my relationship with the computer on a functional level, and to Dick for the loan of his printer.

—Cynthia Bend

Contents

The Artist

CAROL ANN SMITH is a psychic/sensitive gifted in the art of joining, through her drawing, worlds rich and ever new. Like Tayja, she knows how to take life's fragments and form them into a rich and varied whole. Of her art she says, "Drawing has always been a way to the truth for me. It is a form of meditation, a way of remembering who I am, a way home."

Carol has had one-person shows, won numerous awards, and her illustrations have appeared in many books. Although her successes have been rewarding, Carol's art is far more to her than a profession. As she explains, "Creativity is teacher, friend and lover. It is to consciously participate, bringing forth the highest with reverence for all Life."

Carol has been initiated for work on this book through a network of happenings, beginning with her sharing training with Tayja as a psychic instructor for the blind, and climaxing in her presence at Tayja's healing at the Spiritual Frontiers Fellowship Retreat in June of 1984.

A close contact with the images of Tayja's life and their extension into realms of higher consciousness have added new dimensions to this book. The universe and Carol share their gifts together and with you.

Preface

Serge King, Ph.D.

The Challenge of the Modern Shaman

"You look more modern than I thought you'd be," said the visitor as we sat in my comfortable living room overlooking the ocean that surrounds the island of Kaua'i. He glanced at my large screen TV, the VCR and the Tabora seascape on the wall with a faint trace of disapproval. Clearly I did not fit his model of what a shaman is supposed to look like.

His remark was typical of many visitors who expect—perhaps even hope—to find me wearing some kind of robe or sarong and living in primitive simplicity in a cave or a forest far away from the amenities of civilization. The general idea is that such a setting would somehow make me more authentic. I have even considered finding such a spot, having a ti-leaf skirt and cloak made, and giving all my visitors a nice show that would comfortably fit their preconceptions. Shamanism, however, is not limited to a particular location or style of dress or cultural environment. It is a way of thinking and acting that defies boundaries and limitations of any kind, and yet uses them when it fits a purpose.

In the old and ancient days the shaman—who was a healer of mind, body and circumstances—was right in the midst of tribal or village life. He or she might also play the part of priest/priestess or chief/chieftess if there were no one else to fill those roles, but the primary role was always that of the healer. The shaman took part in the work, play and cultural activities of the village and often used each of those for healing purposes, especially the cultural activities of art, song, dance and ritual. In some cultures the shaman wore distinctive clothing and only engaged in certain activities, while in others it was impossible to tell him or her apart from anyone else unless you were family, friend or acquaintance. When the shaman's services were called upon there was always appropriate compensation in goods or services of some kind, according to the local economic structure. In old Hawaii, for instance, those who made use of the shaman's healing abilities might in return give fruits and vegetables, livestock, tools, mats and/or clothing. Or they might give their services of fishing, farming, handcrafting or cleaning for a certain period. The important point is that the shaman was a part of the community, sharing its life and hopes and dreams and proximity. Isolation of the shaman from the community occurred only in times of religious or political repression, and even then there were links maintained with a few.

Now shamanism is experiencing a revival of interest and freedom. Now the shaman is coming back into the community where he/she belongs in a viable, vital, visible way. It isn't necessarily any easier now, as the story in this book shows, but it is extremely important that the new shamans who are remembering and reviving the ancient skills become fully a part of today's society, become modern shamans in every sense of the word.

A modern shaman (or "urban" shaman, as I often say) is one who uses the ancient knowledge in the context of our present social and cultural environment. I will frequently tell my apprentices that anyone can be a shaman in the woods (where there are no people to get in the way); the tough task is to be a shaman in the city. And yet the shaman belongs where the people are. That does not mean the modern shaman *must* live downtown or in a crowded barrio, or in a fast-growing suburb, but it does mean that he or she integrate with and be accessible to those who are to be helped. The tough task of being a modern shaman is made tougher by the fact that shamanism has only recently begun its revival, and it does not have a strong basis of support in today's culture. In the absence of such support, shamans need to help each other. The success of modern shamans, then, will depend on adaptability, integration, and cooperation.

Shaman knowledge has to do with an awareness of, and the ability to direct, the powers of mind and the forces of nature. Adapting the ancient wisdom to modern society is a fairly simple process because human beings still have the same desires for health, wealth and happiness, and the same emotions of love, anger and fear. And Nature still has the same basic elements of (to use the Hawaiian version) Fire, Water, Wind and Stone. The shaman's healing work is still, as it always has been, to change beliefs and expectations in order to change experience. The wisdom and its application are the same, only the context is different. An ancient shaman in the deep forest of a volcanic island using his hands to heal a wound from a wild boar and a modern shaman in a high-rise apartment building using her hands to heal a wound from a domestic cat use the same wisdom. An ancient shaman diverting a lava flow to save a village and a modern shaman calming the wind to keep a forest fire from burning a suburb use the same wisdom. The shaman skills of telepathy, energy release, manifesting, shape-changing, blessing, belief-change and inner journeying are not affected by time. All they have to do is be adapted to circumstances.

Integration is more difficult in today's society because of its variety and complexity. Most ancient shamans only had one or very few socio-cultural systems to deal with, and therefore a limited number of beliefs to work on. Today, however, there is such a vast mixture of radically different social, cultural, religious and philosophical systems that the modern shaman must constantly expand his or her knowledge and maintain an exceptional awareness of the prevailing beliefs of his or her community and its individuals through heightened development of the intuitive faculties as well as by paying close attention to information supplied by the media.

More than ever, there is the need for cooperation among modern shamans in order to maintain and extend the wisdom, to give each other moral and practical support (even shamans need friends and helpers), and to broaden the application of shamanism to modern problems. My solution has been to form Aloha International, a world-wide network of shaman healers trained in the Hawaiian tradition, but there also needs to be cooperation among the shamans of different traditions. It is truly cooperation that is needed because shamanism is truly a non-hierarchical, democratic philosophy. There is a tremendous amount of healing work to do, on ourselves and for the world in general. Let us do it together in a spirit of real Aloha.

Foreword

Marilyn Zwaig Rossner, Ph.D.

Tayja Wiger is a shaman. By this I mean that she has exhibited in her life and person many of the characteristic traits and extraordinary experiences generally associated by anthropologists with traditional portraits of the shaman.

As a native child she went through difficult trials, social dislocation, alienation from the life of community, and was beset with various "initiatory illnesses." After passing through inner encounters with various demonic and god-like powers on the psychic plane, she finally made peace with the wisdom of her ancestors, learned to "discern the spirits" and harmonize herself with the forces of her inner world so that she could learn to help and to guide others along the path of spiritual reconciliation.

When I first met Tayja, she was just at that point in the evolution of her soul when she was ready to be healed of two of the most debilitating disorders produced by her initiatory illness: blindness and epilepsy.

As it turned out, I was the instrument, or catalyst, through which that healing was to be effected.

The circumstances connected with our meeting are rather interesting, and I shall narrate them here.

Before I do so I should perhaps tell something about myself. In my daily work I am a professional person—a special educator with particular expertise in behavior therapy and children's emotional disorders. But I am also a sensitive by birth; and although it is perhaps unusual, I have managed to arrange a place in my life for roles both as a professor of special education in a community college, as well as a psychic, a Spiritualist medium, and an ordained minister in the interfaith

Spiritual Science Fellowship of Canada, which I founded in 1977.

It was in my latter capacities that I met Tayja, after accepting an invitation from Spiritual Frontiers Fellowship USA to give a workshop in Minnesota during the summer of 1984.

It was early on a very hot evening in June that the healing of Tayja Wiger occurred. The large gothic chapel at Carleton College, Northfield, Minnesota was packed with over 500 people for the concluding event of the Spiritual Frontiers Fellowship USA's Annual Midwest Retreat. This was a Healing Service. A full choir with vocalists and assorted musicians all dressed up for the occasion crowded the platform in the sanctuary. The soft, melodious tones of the giant pipe organ played quietly behind the voice of Ethel Lombardi who gently intoned a guided meditation. The swishing of the large fans placed around the sanctuary gave the faint impression of a cool breeze.

Thirty or more of the teaching staff of the Retreat stood behind several rows of chairs placed in the nave of the chapel in front of the pews. I was one of them, and my husband John, an Anglican priest and university professor who was at the time a National Vice President of S.F.F., stood behind the chair next to mine. We were all waiting for the time in the service when the people—all 500 of them—would begin to file forward from the pews and take their places, for a few moments each, one by one, in one of the 30 or more chairs. Then we were supposed to lay our hands on each person who sat in the chair in front of us and ask for his or her healing, in "body, mind and spirit."

I had done this before, at previous S.F.F. retreats. But this time there was something indefinably different about it all. While standing there behind the empty chair, several times I could feel myself begin to slip into a light trance state—and out of it again. Later, my husband John told me that he was aware of this.

While I am (among other things) a trance medium, it is not my customary practice to go into that kind of state while attempting spiritual healing. And in any case, this was certainly not a deliberate kind of trance. During those fleeting moments while I was in that state, I became aware of the warm and loving closeness of my "spirit control," Master Sivananda talking with me about an approaching healing.

Swami Sivananda of Rishikesh had been—in this world—a medical doctor who went on to become great sage, one of the saints of modern India. In his early life he had been a healer, using the skills of modern medicine to alleviate the pains and ills of the poor. Then he became a renunciate, a swami, and concentrated upon the spiritual ills of mankind. Today he is remembered as "the Saint Francis of modern India."

He has been appearing to me, and guiding me, from the world of spirit since I was four years old. Now Sivananda, in his spiritual body, was with me here in the chapel. I knew it, and knew that something very special was going to happen. But exactly what it was I did not yet know.

At this point the people began coming forward from the pews to take their seats, one by one, in front of the healers. A tall, native Indian girl—who had attended the week-long retreat accompanied on campus by her Seeing Eye dog—came down the aisle escorted by an usher. Rather than take the first vacant seat at the end of the aisle of chairs, she insisted for some strange reason on pushing her way down an aisle of vacant chairs until she came to mine, i.e. the one in front of me, and sat down. The other healers' chairs soon filled up with the people filing in.

The second I placed my hands on Tayja's head I felt a bolt of energy. There was a frequency in my body—a motion that came from elsewhere. I was aware of a holy presence engulfing my own body. It was, I knew, coming from God, the Holy Spirit, through the instrumentality of my spiritual guide and teacher, Swami Sivananda.

I placed my hands over Tayja's eyes. I found my breathing becoming perfectly synchronized with hers, as if we were one, even in heartbeat. Then I went into a trance, which I am told lasted 10 to 12 minutes.

John told me later that he could hear Sivananda speaking through me, although I was unconscious of it at the time, and telling Tayja that she would be able to see. Finally, he asked Tayja through me to affirm aloud that she could indeed now see.

Suddenly I could hear Tayja yelling, "I can see! God is real! I can see the light! The lights! I can see you!" She was standing up in front of the chair, looking around, laughing and crying at the same time. As she looked at me I noticed that her eyes—which before had been closed slits with only a white edge showing—were now like the clear new eyes of a healthy, wide-eyed child.

By this time the commotion of Tayja's enthusiasm—and mine— had literally stopped the service. When the people became aware of what had happened, there was tremendous applause and rejoicing in the Spirit throughout the congregation. Tayja asked if she could be taken outside to see the grass and the trees, and the beauty of nature which for many years she had missed seeing in her world of darkness.

One of the first things Tayja asked was to see Daisy. At first I was quite shocked, because "Daisy" is the name of a little Indian child in spirit who died over 200 years ago who has been a constant companion and joy guide of mine since earliest childhood. But in this case, I learned that Daisy—by some Jungian variety of synchronicity—was the name of Tayja's Seeing Eye dog . . . whom Tayja had never seen before with her blind eyes but could now behold as well as touch!

Perhaps one of the most astounding things about this event was the mystery it revealed to me about human reactions to the mighty works of God.

While 98% of those present rejoiced, gave thanks . . . and some even wept with joy . . . there was one man—himself a liberal Christian minister and a supposed believer in healing—who became inexplicably enraged. He seemed actually to be enraged that so much outspoken emotion had broken up the calm of the service!

Before he bothered to determine the facts, on the following morning this man attacked me verbally for God knows what, and even seemed to hold Tayja responsible for being healed in such a disreputable, low class manner! Here on the Carleton College campus, before departing for Montreal, I watched a Christian minister attack me for doing what Jesus had spent his ministry doing! I wept. But just then a beautiful soul, a young Jewish rabbi, a Hassid, came up to me from the group. He embraced me in an attempt to comfort me and said: "There is an old Jewish parable: If the king sends his messenger with a message that the people don't want to hear, they will kill the messenger."

My husband, a priest but a truly universal soul, was asked to preach the sermon at the Spiritual Science Fellowship service in Montreal that evening after we had returned home. He preached on the text of St. John's Gospel 9:1-41, which is the story of religious teachers, the Scribes and the Pharisees, who attacked Jesus for healing a man born blind. In the story, Jesus' attackers first tried to say that the man hadn't really been blind. And when this wouldn't hold up, they retreated to saying that the "form" of the healing had been wrong anyway, i.e. that Jesus had disrupted the Sabbath by healing on that day and was therefore a sinner.

In the contemporary story of the healing of Tayja Wiger by that same Eternal Christ, in me and in her, all of the same elements of dark human reaction to the Light were still present. The cast of actors has changed, but the facts remain.

Tayja had been given a medical examination in a Minnesota hospital as late as February 1985. She had been declared legally blind for the purposes of a state pension and a Seeing Eye dog. A clinical professor of medicine confirmed the mysterious disapparance of Tayja Wiger's blindness. He had examined her a few months before. "The patient is legally blind," he wrote at the time. "She cannot distinguish light from dark." She was tested at a hospital clinic. He again examined Tayja after the healing service later in June, 1985 and reported that she had regained all her sight with the aid of a spiritual healer.

Is this a "psychosomatic" healing? The answer depends upon what one means by psychosomatic. Surely there was a physical healing as well as a mental and emotional one. But was it Tayja's own subconscious mind which caused the physical retinas to repair, the psychological and neurological synapses governing sight—and epilepsy and dyslexia—to repair? If so, the subconscious mind has tremendous powers that conventional Western medicine needs to understand much better.

Perhaps another way to look at this event is through the eyes of a shaman . . . which Tayja herself is.

We should note that in the shamanistic world view, "initiatory illnesses" are not merely psychosomatic, or psychologically caused; they are said to be caused by the encounter of the same creative and destructive forces of the cosmos that have produced the material world—and our physical bodies—in their present mix: partly glorious and yet partly defective.

In Tayja's case, this would mean that, in the shamanistic perspective, she was physically blind and afflicted with neurological impairment known as epilepsy as a result of a lengthy encounter in her psyche, or soul, between conflicting creative forces of the cosmos. Upon the reconciliation of these conflicting forces, the gradually materialized physical effects of this long-standing inner conflict within her "soul body" could be instantaneously dissolved and re-created. In shamanistic lore, the soul body is the mold around which the physical body is formed.

Only in the philosophical traditions of ancient Egypt, Persia, Greece, and in the Ayurvedic medicine of India or the folk medicine of China and Asia do we find similar conceptions of an astral body, or soul body which serves as the invisible mold, or three dimensional blueprint, for the formation, dissolution, and re-creation of the physical body.

Modern Western medicine does not yet have adequate models comparable to these by which instantaneous physiological healings, or "remissions" can be understood. But anecdotal materials stemming from reported experiences of Modern Spiritualists, Theosophists, Mesmerists, Occultists, New Thought advocates, and UFO'logists— as well as the great Marian shrines of the Catholic Church and the healings of Pentecostalists alike—abound with testimonies of such miraculous physical healings.

In conclusion, I realize that in professional terms this healing cannot be explained. But for my part, I know in terms of my own spiritualist faith—that God, the One Universal Creator, acting through the Eternal Christ in whom we all live and move and have our being, healed Tayja Wiger. He did this through the Holy Spirit in the instrumentality of the particular spirit and intelligence of the deceased saint Swami Sivananda who was working through my physical and astral bodies . . . upon the mind, and the astral and physical bodies of Tayja. But all of this was possible, I believe, only because Tayja Wiger was ready to be healed, ready to emerge from her "initiatory sickness" and become whole again.

She is now an initiated shaman who must spend her life in helping others to "see," to walk an authentic Spiritual Path to the Cosmic Mountain of the Great White Spirit, the God who has healed her.

The Step
Forward

Basically, very basically, the shaman uses altered states of consciousness to communicate with and influence the forces of nature and the universe for the benefit of society. In order to do this, the shaman everywhere practices the accumulation of inner power. These are the three most distinguishing features of the shaman, then: the use of altered states; influencing events for social benefit; and the accumulation of inner power. [1]

—*Serge King*
The Way of the Adventurer

When I first met Tayja, her power was certainly not obvious, and I did not pay much attention to her on the busy evening of our first public meeting of Blind Awareness Project of Minnesota. On that April evening I was probably introduced to Tayja, but the contact made no personal impact on me. I noticed her as an isolated part of the crowd, a heavy woman condensed into her own small world. Her head was bowed, her unseeing eyes squinted to the floor as she felt her way with a white cane. Her wooden face was expressionless, and her voice a deep, dull monotone. Her gait was stiff as she clumsily propelled her legs which had been afflicted from birth by cerebral palsy. I learned later that she was still recovering from surgery on both legs. On that initial evening she did not seem important in my life. Yet it was the first step in a miraculous association.

Tayja and I were drawn to this crucial meeting on October 23rd, 1981. The event was an introductory talk on Project Blind Awareness by its founder, Carol Ann Liaros, at Unity Unitarian Church in St. Paul, Minnesota. Our flier for this meeting described it as follows:

1

Mrs. Liaros will give us all a glimpse of our hidden potential through the experiences of blind students she has trained while director of Project Blind Awareness, Buffalo, New York. She is a psychic-sensitive who teaches parapsychology and ESP throughout the U.S. and Canada. Her innovative work with the blind has received international recognition and has been described in many books including *Superlearning* by Ostrander and Schroeder.

Program

We will discover how blind students learn to "see" by utilizing senses they don't know they have, to perceive energy fields they don't know exist. We will see new ways to meet a new age with a new consciousness where ESP and modern science join hands in an exciting human drama. The work of blind students will be illustrated through lecture, slides, and a video tape showing achievements by the blind as featured on "That's Incredible," ABC-TV, April, 1980.

The young woman that Carol Ann's audience met on the video of "That's Incredible" during that important spring evening had surely mastered a level of consciousness not usually recognized in our society. What we saw was a fifteen-minute video of a fourteen-year old blind girl lying on a couch in what might be termed a state of self-hypnosis. We saw and heard her as she accurately described the livng room of a house in California which neither she nor her questioner, Carol Ann, had seen. As we watched the girl describe the house in a dreamy tone, we were puzzled, as Carol Ann appeared to be, concerning the form the blind girl was "seeing" in the window of the California house. She could not find words for the shape and moved her hands in the form of a crescent. We understood when the camera moved from New York where the filming was taking place to the living-room window in California. Hanging in the uncurtained window was a crescent moon formed by a neon outline. Given only the address, how did this girl's consciousness travel to California? More important, what does her traveling perception do to our skull-trapped view of consciousness?

Most of us have learned to doubt our ability to perceive beyond the reach of our senses. We see with our limiting eyes. I later learned that Tayja "sees" with an undiscriminating belief in a strange world beyond her physical senses.

Mastering consciousness, as Carol Ann's video student and many like her have done, is the first step in developing inner power. Using that power for personal and social transformation is, as Dr. King defines it, the mark of the shaman.

Although Tayja was unable to see Carol Ann's pictured demonstration, she, perhaps more than anyone in the audience, had the capacity to venture into the depths of her own consciousness—perhaps not because her capacity was greater than yours or mine, but because her beliefs permitted it. She grew up in the chaos of an unpredictable and dangerous world, one in which she saw no consensual reality. As the beliefs she was taught as a child could not protect her against the wounds of her life, her open belief system provided an inner path to eventual healing.

Tayja's first Indian name was "Ysaza" meaning "deadly." Her name is now Tayja Tushi Wiger; Tayja meaning "white dove," Tushi, "freedom," and Wiger, the name of her therapeutic family. In her name as in her life is the medicine our civilization needs: guidance from the deadly violence of our times to freedom from fear on the wings of the dove of peace, the Christian symbol in Tayja's unique shamanic faith.

Chaos in individual lives contributes to chaos on our planet; as "we are the world," we change our world as we change ourselves. Now, as our Earth is entering a time of fear, violence and fragmentation, we, the human race, are in need of a decision for peace and wholeness. We can bring this cosmic quest to a microcosmic focus by looking at Tayja's life, a dramatic example of hope for all people. She untangles the strands of violence, fear, pain, anger and guilt to find a way out: "If you don't like what you have done, change it, don't judge it." This Tayja speaks, not in words only, but in the living of her life on this planetary Medicine Wheel, the Sioux wheel of learning that makes all life its lesson. As Tayja's life may seem fragmented, so may the different belief-frameworks discussed in this book. We ask you to keep in mind that, around the wheel of life, there are many paths to the same center. Although unity may be lost along the way, it will be found in the end. Tayja traveled many paths as she progressed from blindness to psychospiritual vision, seeing first with her mind, then with her eyes. Now firmly walking the path of the shaman, Tayja has returned her leader dog and become a leader of people. This story urges all people to do the same, each in his or her own way.

The function of the Shaman as described by Serge King, a modern shaman who was trained from an early age as a Kahuna shaman, may not satisfy all traditions. However, his explanation agrees with Tayja's and mine.

"Shaman" is a Siberian word. Through accepted usage, it has come to refer generally to the sprital leaders of natural-world peoples of many tribes and races. Because shamans are individualized, each one unique, no general definition is all inclusive. Shamans do, however, tend to follow one of two paths. Serge King identifies them:

> The most widely known and practiced is the Way of the Warrior, characterized by an emphasis on danger, the development of hyper-alertness, an ascetic and harsh self-discipline, the destruction of enemies and cultivation of allies, the practice of survival/fighting skills, and an ethic of conquer or be conquered. This is the Way followed by the majority of American Indian shamans, for instance, and it is a good way because its intent is good.

On the other hand, the Way of the Adventurer emphasizes:
> the development of hyper-awareness and a goal-oriented self-discipline, the cultivation of friendship and unity, the practice of survival/exploring skills, and an ethic of love and be loved. It is not a 'better' way, since both paths of shamanism have healing in broad terms as their social purpose, and both can lead to the same realms of high personal development. But it is a different way, and the differences may have profound social and personal effects. The typical ideal for the warrior shaman is to act impeccably, that is, without error, and there is a great emphasis on developing and maintaining the strength to protect oneself and others from enemies . . . On the other hand, the typical ideal for the Adventurer shaman is to act appropriately, or in such a way as to get the best results in a given situation, and the emphasis is on enjoyment and creating peace.[2]

Although Tayja has known danger and fear on the Warrior path, today she has moved beyond it to a position of love and healing, and it is the way of the Adventurer that Tayja and I see as the most practical way for the modern shaman.

Shamanism is very much alive today where it exists in the traditions of the natural-world peoples of five continents. Not only does it flourish in ancient civilizations; it is enjoying a renaissance among technological civilizations as consciousness-changing techniques are adopted by university students, doctors and business men in modern cities as well as thatchers in Asia, medicine people in Canada, "witch doctors" in Africa and trappers in Siberia and Greenland. More and more people are discovering that their minds follow their wills so that they can make their own truths by accepting limitation or, conversely, by extending their worlds toward infinity. *Birth of a Modern Shaman* is a leap beyond our cultural confines in which the powers of the ancients join with the power of the modern age. As the shamans affirm, we do indeed influence outer events through the action of our minds.

"Go beyond existence," Tayja says, "beyond the world to be born into a new universe."

Not until Tayja and I completed *Birth of a Modern Shaman* did I realize the power in Tayja's life-blood which flowed behind the words I was writing. Not until I reached the final chapter did I realize the *personal power*—the birthright of all people—which was to be born in my own life through working close to a modern shaman in the preparation of this book. This story of a new birth is first Tayja's experience, then my own, and most important, the experience of you, the reader. The story can lead to the self-healing and the power for peace which is in us all.

This power echoes through the ages:

> I could hear the thunder beings coming in the earth, and I could hear them saying, "It is time to do the work of your 'Grandfathers.'"
>
> I think I have told you, but if I have not, you must have understood, that a man who has a vision is not able to use the power of it until after he has performed the vision on earth for the people to see.
>
> *Black Elk Speaks*[3]

Today the thunder beings have indeed entered the Earth and are loud in their protestations of anger against the people who destroy, not only their four legged, winged and finned brothers and sisters, but each other and themselves as well. It is this pervasive global turmoil that the modern shaman is born to heal, each one in his or her own unique way. The path, for each One, is latent within the Self. The purpose of the modern shaman is to know that indwelling power, then to use it for peaceful harmony, first in Self, then in the world. In this sense, each of us is pregnant with an embryo shaman waiting for birth.

After I saw Tayja "born into a new universe," I had a vision of bringing that birth to Earth "for the people to see." This book is the vision reenacted.

Tayja is a Native American who, within her being, struggles against the warring fragments of herself and a violent world to find wholeness. Tayja's has been a life of cleansing and healing—first herself, then others. "Unity is my main task," she states.

Now it is time for all of us to cleanse our lives, then turn ourselves inside out for all to share. How much longer will the world wait for its children to know their spiritual Grandfathers and love their Earth Mother?

The world of inspired visions and the world of physical action on this Earth held many layers of confusion for Tayja, as I am sure they do for all the peoples and nations of this planet.

"We have been here since the beginning," the native American traditionalist will tell you, "and we will be here until the end." The Buddhist, speaking from the same shamanic roots in eternity will dissolve time and space saying, "All is Buddha." The shaman has been a bridge between matter and spirit, between life and death, between Earth and sky, since the "two leggeds" first walked our planet. A shaman is destined to conquer the forces of darkness and obtain vision beyond the five senses, to master the change called "death" and bring healing, first to self, then to others. The shaman can control the levels of knowing and move at will from physical consciousness to a spiritual state which includes consciousness of discarnate beings who may be people who have died recently or eons ago. The discarnate beings come in many guises depending on the spiritual situation and psychic development of the shaman perceiving them. The shaman's body is prepared to channel strong energies which modern science is just now beginning to understand with the help of Kirlian photography, biofeedback and other contemporary techniques. Each shaman conquers his or her particular darkness and obtains a specific vision, lives a unique mission. Yet all are technicians of the human mind, able to change the form of their consciousness as the heat of the Sun can change ice to water. Each shaman develops his or her psyche with a control most of us in the Western world deny to ourselves and attribute to machines, expecting control to come from without rather than within. Society accepts the x-ray, but denies that human vision can pierce beneath the skin; it accepts the telegraph, but denies word perception beyond the range of the human ear; we achieve travel to the Moon, but deny the ability of the mind to travel outside the confines of the body; our surgeons achieve miracles with the scalpel, yet deny miracles achieved by human beings channeling healing energy. Although the sophistication of modern technology surpasses that of "natural world peoples," their sophistication of the mind surpasses our society's limited concepts of mind power, for these wonders I have enumerated, shamans have accomplished.

Tayja is an urban shaman who grew up without the cultural support of shamanic tradition. Her teachers are within. "I have good guides, and they tell me what I need to know. All of them are Indian." Without physical teachers, her way was hard. Yet her trials and initiation were woven into the fabric of her life, and she lived through them often without society's understanding or support.

As the elements of shamanism move slowly into our society, so they moved slowly into Tayja's realization. Her spiritual incubation is surrounded by events which often hide her light, but even in darkness it is there. Tayja's darkness in living was mine in writing, and at times I found it difficult to believe in the miraculous light so completely hidden in many of the dark pages of Tayja's journal. The abuses revealed read like a catalog of the ills of our society: chemical dependency, physical and sexual abuse, prostitution, multiple personalities, suspected mental retardation, reform schools, psychiatric institutions and hospitals. Yet, as the darkness in her life became mine—just as the darkness of my society is mine—so did the light.

About two years ago, I had spent a dim winter day reading through the "darkened streets" of Tayja's journal. That evening I had a vision which I didn't understand at the time: I saw a light shining through the window of a dingy building on a dark street,—just one lighted window. Although I didn't see her, I sensed the presence of Tayja, and I came out of the meditation with a feeling of intense isolation and loneliness which I couldn't seem to shake. The next day when I told her of this, Tayja said, "I think I know what your vision means. I spent a lot of my adolescent years in institutions. It was hard, and I kept trying to stay with the light in my dreams and visions." Through the pages of this book, at times the light may seem to flicker and go out, yet in Tayja's life as in the turmoil of our world, the potential for new birth remains.

None of us moves into spiritual consciousness alone, and Tayja took many with her, as many had prepared her way. For me, she provided an ancient link with the knowledge I had of psychic and spiritual movements of the 1980's, and I gained awareness of the new birth of shamanism hand in hand with modern technologies.

One winter morning I was meditating in a friend's electric sauna in the basement of her condominium surrounded by the warm glow and scent of cedar and the light energies of my friends, much like the cleansing sweat lodges Tayja knows. A vision was shown me: an old shaman lay dying. His lower belly was distended as though pregnant. It was not a sad sight, for out of the old I felt the birthing of the new. Man and woman alike are pregnant with the New Age, the Red and Blue Days which are dawning.

Shamans from many nations have prophesied a time of darkness followed by a time when the Sun would turn red and the Moon blue: a time of great hardship for individuals as for the whole planet, followed by the healing of our mother, the Earth. Many of today's scientists have unknowingly joined with the ancient predictions as they anticipate extreme pollution of the atmosphere which dims the Sun. Changes in planetary movements resulting in eclipses may also play their part in darkness as in cosmic energy changes. Atmospheric pollution can certainly darken the sky, then filter the colors of the Sun and Moon as the cleansing light returns. As Black Elk has spoken, "The world is happier after the terror of the storm."

Tayja's is a life born into a dark cloud of pollution. Yet it is important to remember that, although it may be hidden for a time, the light of our creating source is never dimmed. In the extremes of physical, emotional, mental and spiritual anguish which Tayja suffered, that light was always present. Society has called her blind, crippled, retarded, insane, delinquent. She is now sighted, physically sound, intelligent, sane, and working as a shaman: healer, ordained minister, counselor and laughing friend of the Light.

The healing energies so long recognized in ancient civilizations: Ki to the Japanese, Chi to the Chinese, Prana to the Hindus, Bioplasmic energy to Russian researchers, Light to Christ, Mana to Kahunas, bio-energy or vital force in English, are here for technological people too. I have experienced, as Tayja has, that with those energies we can remove the darkness from our lives and from the planet, if we so choose, for it is possible for humans to direct their personal evolution just as they have directed their technological evolution. Using only the receptive powers of his own mind, a native American shaman predicted far beyond his Stone Age to see that "an eagle would fly to the Moon." Just as he envisioned, the farseeing "Eagle" carried the first men to the Moon, so performing the vision for earth people to see.

Tayja's life is an individualized step in the "giant leap for mankind," the spiritual leap into the inner potentials of our Space Age.

Chapter One
My Medicine Lake

"The Medicine Wheel, my children," said the Chief, "is the Mirroring of the Great Spirit, the Universe, among men. We are all the Medicine River. And the Universe is the Medicine River that man is Mirrored upon, my children. And we in our turn see the Medicines of men Mirrored in the Universe."
—Hyemeyohsts Storm
Seven Arrows

I am grateful to Tayja for freely sharing her life. To her story, I must mirror my vision as each of you will mirror yours, for we cannot travel without ourselves as we cannot travel without each other. My trust is that her story of growth beyond expected limitation will give to all who share it, windows to a wider vision beyond sensual limitation to touch the world of wholeness.

The sophisticated spirituality of Tayja's Sioux ancestors is simple in its wholeness and complex in the fitting of all life's pieces into that wholeness, a medicine wheel of life which includes all learning. According to the ancient way (the nation's hoop), this physical world is seen as symbolic of the spiritual reality that exists beyond all things and gives to them their form.

According to the modern way, we follow the investigative tools of science as it explores the spiraling construction of the universe from the minute atom to the giant macrocosm of the solar system. The spiral growth forms within our smallest atom reach to the stars for their pattern, and modern quantum-relativistic physics tells us that our time and space are relative, and matter and energy are not separate and distinct but different manifestations of a similar substance

11

as are ice, water and steam. As the "matter" of thought powers growth, so Tayja's spiritual consciousness powers her life through the pages of this book. It is the medicine of wholeness; it is progress to purpose and a mission. In terms of modern systems theory, it is a holographic paradigm.

I will tell you of my "medicine," the learning which has prepared me for this book. As all of us start our lives in water, we all swim in a symbolic "medicine lake," a mirror to the learning by which we are surrounded. For over fifty years I have gone swimming in the same physical lake. We know each other, and it speaks to me. It is my friend, the mirror of my life. As a child, I traveled it in a canoe with my father. Together we went turtle hunting, catching painted turtles, then letting them go free. I didn't know then that the shell-protected turtle is symbolic of eternal life. When I was older, hunting turtles by myself, I dared to catch a snapping turtle in my hands. The action of reaching into the dark water came without fear because somehow I knew that I would not be hurt by a creature from that lake, womb of my earth mother.

Again in that same lake, I met a teacher in a boat. As I was swimming on my back watching the clouds and the swooping of a purple martin, she touched me on the arm just as I was about to bang my head against her boat. We talked as I treaded water. Before she rowed away, she said, "Come to school, or I may never see you again." So I went to The School for Social Development, and I taught communicaton once a week in her class room of physically and mentally disabled adults. For eight years I was given stories by people with feelings and ideas trapped in bodies with lips and tongues which would not obey their minds. I listened many hours to joys and pains that were pushed out of spastic mouths. The sunken treasures of their inner lakes made me rich indeed.

I came together with Tayja and the concept of this book with a feeling of inevitability which had its roots ten years back when I experienced my first psychic reading from Rev. Ralph Jordan, an internationally known psychic and spiritual counselor. He quickly established his authenticity for me by describing a vision I had had the night before and repeating verbatim the words which had been spoken to me. As I had not told anyone of this experience, I knew it could come only from a spiritual paradigm beyond the physical one which had limited my thinking before this meeting. Ralph continued speaking quickly and accurately of my past life, then predicting my future for nearly an hour. I listened in awe as I experienced for the first time the deep level on which we are all joined. As he saw my past accurately, could it be that he was seeing my future with the same clear vision? Among the things I would do, he told of a book I would write "bringing together the intellectual and the psychic, the psychological and the spiritual." He specifically mentioned Transactional Analysis, schizophrenia, and physical disabilities including blindness. Since I knew nothing of these things at the time, I dismissed them from my consciousness, yet they seemed to direct my life as I worked for my master's degree studying altered states of consciousness and *The Possible Human* with Jean Houston, new directions in psychic studies with the Wrekin Trust in England, the collaboration of modern psychology and trance mediumship with the psychic, Ross Peterson and the psychologist, Frank Farrelly, and reincarnation with Helen Wambach.

I shared my graduate advisor's counseling sessions with a client who was working out the integration of a multiple personality and coming to terms with a childhood of physical and sexual abuse. Shortly afterward I learned of another environment Tayja experienced when I interned in a chemical dependency treatment hospital.

Another method of growth significant to Tayja is reparenting, a specialized extension of Transactional Analysis. I learned about this system as applied to schizophrenics with the originator of the procedure, Jacqui Schiff.

After completing my master's degree, I worked for a short time in Tayja's reparenting home assisting in the newly established day school for reparenting schizophrenics and other psychotic clients. (This process will be described in more detail in Chapter 5.) Although Tayja was there at the time, I did not meet her then; but I did learn of an emotionally demanding structure in which she spent much of her life between 1977 and 1981. The curriculum included Transactional Analysis theory, "baby time" in which the "kids" were given a safe environment in which to complete unfinished developmental tasks, and group therapy sessions. My job was to act as a surrogate caretaker and hold the adult "babies," sometimes giving them bottles. While sitting in the circle with my "baby," I watched and heard the extraordinary release of anger by a young woman diagnosed as hebephrenic (a violent form of schizophrenia). On the surface, she seemed adaptive, even smilingly winsome. She stood up when it came her turn to work. The surrogate "father" and two of the "big boys" stood up with her. In the moments before release, I watched her eyes narrow, the tension of rage completely transforming her face. The physical release followed. She kicked, screamed and swore, punching at pillows which the men held to protect themselves. All the while she knew she would not be allowed to hurt herself or anyone else. Finally, when her violence was spent, she was caressed and told she was loved, a beautiful baby to be nurtured and cared for.

Throughout this turmoil, my baby passively sucked on the water bottle I held for her. Although taller than I, her body, curled in a fetal position, was that of an infant only a few months old. It surprised me at first, yet I found it was not so hard to recapture for at least part of the time, the maternal feelings I had had with my own babies. But this was not a healthy infant I held. She was sucking mechanically, apparently unaware of anything going on around her including any stroking or words I spoke to her. I began to feel as though I were attached to an energy vacuum sucking me dry of vitality. (I subsequently learned that this behavior should have been confronted so that unhealthy infantile experiences would not be reinforced.)

Adding to the violence, pain and apathy of the emotional atmosphere was the oppressiveness of the damp room, its gray stone walls holding the moisture. Although it was a warm and humid June day, we spent the whole time inside with doors and windows closed in a futile attempt to keep out the moisture. The acrid smell of schizophrenia pervaded the air, the brightly colored pillows, even the stone walls enclosing us. I did not at that time have experience in coping with violence or the healing skills to recharge my energy. Within four days, I found the work too enervating to continue, although I respected the knowledge and dedication of the young woman in charge of the school. I learned later that she was one of Tayja's supportive sisters during Tayja's last two years in the reparenting home.

This and much more led me on the path to writing *Birth of a Modern Shaman* with Tayja. As I read her journals written at the time of her reparenting experience, I often recalled my experience, thinking of how confusing it would be for an adult to regress to life as a baby. In a dream, I saw Tayja as a tiny infant who appeared old, a Siamese twin in the arms of a confused mother attempting to treat her divided child as one, while half the baby attacks her as the other half reaches out for nurturing. I see these same conflicting forces working throughout our country, throughout our world.

After my experience in the reparenting home, I became a Reiki and MariEL healer, studying with the master, Ethel Lombardi, as did Tayja. In my work with healing, I have shared intense experiences with incest victims and realized the power of transformation, paired as it always is with forgiveness.

Tayja and I both became acquainted with the teachings of shamanism by Tsonakwa, an Abenaki Indian. I have studied trance mediumship with Marilyn Rossner who played a leading role in Tayja's miraculous healing; and perhaps most important, I learned of teaching blind students physical and mental orientation through PSI techniques. It was there, as Blind Awareness instructors, that Tayja and I met. After that meeting we were often together, and I was standing beside her in the chapel at Carleton College at the time she regained her vision. It was the same chapel where, so many years before, I had received my undergraduate degree in English, expecting to be a writer.

I was ordained as a minister, as was Tayja, by a free-thinking spiritualist who had given up psychic readings and seances in favor of teaching her students to make their own contacts with their spirit guides and higher selves. I studied with her, not seeking ordination at the time. "You will need it," she told me, forseeing my present occupation as a psychospiritual teacher and healer using her philosophy of teaching students to make their own spiritual contacts. I mention it here because I know that all who read this book have "honorary ordinations" from life, and it is for us to accept its gifts and responsibilities.

These are a few of the things reflected in my medicine lake. Each of you has your own, yet they are One just as each separate raindrop when it falls into the ocean becomes the ocean. So must the ocean of my world be one, no longer separate warring droplets, for in Unity, each of us becomes far greater than we believe we are, at the same time both self and other. I believe the size and power of the ocean depend on the separate drops that join it.

Most important: As you read of the twisted path of Tayja's life, see the pains and fears as signposts to light and laughter, remembering that healing is joy.

Chapter Two
Rainbow Bridge

I looked ahead and saw the mountains there with rocks and forests on them, and from the mountains flashed all colors upward to the heavens. Then I was standing on the highest mountain of them all, and round about beneath me was the whole hoop of the world. And while I stood there I saw more than I can tell, and I understood more than I saw; for I was seeing in a sacred manner the shapes of all things in the spirit, and the shape of all shapes as they must live together like one being.

—Black Elk Speaks[1]

Using the crystal is like bringing the other reflection—the spirit world—into manifestation . . . [That world] has mastery over all other realms—it is called rainbow world.

—Agnes Whistling Elk
As quoted in *Flight of the Seventh Moon.*[2]

From our center which can be any place we are, a rainbow bridge leads through the spectrum and ends in blazing light linking Earth and sky, our mother and our father. Before the coming of the rainbow, there may be a gentle cleansing rain, but in Tayja's life, as in the lives of most shamans, the light came only after a long and violent storm, a struggle with death out of which the shaman is born. In the beginning of this life, storm clouds over Tayja's eyes turned the rainbow gray, the guarded hue of a prison wall. It took her thirty years to learn that in her own mind was the power to dissolve that wall.

As is true for many shamans, each in a unique way, Tayja's was a special birth. Her life began with death when she entered the world beside a dead twin. Her early life is the story of attacks. Fear and pain had entered her tiny body even before its premature birth from a chemically dependent and physically abused Sioux mother. Her first challenge was a physical one, to keep her soul in the damaged body she thought of as herself. It was hard work. Her white father battered her physically and mentally, expressing violent contempt for Indians. "The only good Indian is a dead Indian," is an expression the sensitive child heard from birth, while physical blows pounded in its meaning.

Tayja's life is also the story of defense against the cruelties which surrounded her early years. The personality, like a crystal meant for receiving light, is a fragile thing. Harsh blows split hers into warring fragments, a civil war within her, making Tayja's life all but unlivable. In defense against the cruelties she experienced, she developed buffer zones—a kind of no-man's-land—between the injured shards of her shattered personality, so that parts of herself became strangers to one another. The extremes of a battered body and an open psychic awareness without spiritual direction strained the ties between the left and right hemispheres of her brain so that the bridge between the two, the corpus callosum, did not function, resulting in massive perceptual disorder. Her physical and psychic growth proceeded without a spiritual awareness which could bring them to ordered unity.

Tayja survived infancy without adequate nurturing from her physical parents, and escaped from a violent home to search elsewhere to fill the void. She struggled to find light in the depressing dark of institutional life, allowed herself to be regressed to infancy and took a second chance to grow out of fear and pain and rage. With knowledge gained from Transactional Analysis, she struggled to find her whole self among the immature fragments she had developed. She also gained insights from a reading of her past lives and heard her destiny from an astrologer who interpreted her natal chart. Still she searched for sense in her life.

The cruelties she suffered seemed literally to fracture her mind, as her body was often fractured, permitting her to escape into a consciousness beyond her damaged senses. Then, with support and training, she realized what she already had—vision without sight. Tayja's is the story of spirits entering the rift carved by the blows of life and teaching her their gentle ways. Finally, she learned the way of the shaman, the way to her life's mission.

An Abenaki Indian and "Warrior of the Rainbow," (a spiritual leader) Tsonakwa was one of Tayja's teachers as she made her final preparations for the birth of her new vision. He speaks of spirit contact:

> We live to please the spirits too, for they intrude upon our world, and we intrude upon theirs, and we need not be amazed at all. We can invoke them through the doorways that are open in the tops of our heads and in the channels of our hearts, and it's in these soft places that even the Great Spirit knows to take his moccasins off and walk in silence.[3]

In traditional Indian culture, protective methods against harmful entry would be taught. But that "open doorway" in the top of Tayja's head was one she did not know how to close, so it was violated, not with the sensitivity of spirits' bare feet or even moccasins, but by hobnailed boots. She was raped spiritually as she was raped physically.

The rainbow bridge between the forces of light and darkness speaks its language of color on many levels. As it arches from Earth to sky and back again, it bridges from the womb of Earth-Mother to Sky-Father where the lights of the Grandfathers dwell beside the Great Spirit and guide the affairs of earth peoples, including those we call "animals." In the rainbow, water from the womb of Earth-Mother supplies the prisms which divide the breath of spirit, separating air to show Earth's people colors of the light. The rainbow may be seen as one last radiant display of colors before our perception bridges the borderland to One Unified Center of Light where the body's senses are not necessary. With almost no earth in her astrological chart, Tayja, child of air and water, can naturally find her place in the rainbow of life.

Through the eyes of earth people, the lights of the rainbow draw meaning from the colors of this world and speak on a personal level, a cultural level and a universal or archetypal level. Red, as the color of blood and of fire, holds great energy which can be for life or death, good or evil, depending on its use. In her journal, during one of the most painful parts of her life, Tayja writes, "The fire is like the wizards of the hell inside the ape inside us." Then, speaking from inner pain, ". . . . the smell of death that comes over me, blood that comes from the inner self . . . " So, even without color vision, Tayja's ideas tapped a concept of color. Blue, the color of sky and of water is calm and passive, something which man does not influence, but must accept as the dome of sky above us and the water of our lakes. Yet sky and water can be harsh and we can see them gray. Tayja writes, "The clouds come from me, the rains come from the eyes of the body, and the rains put out the flame, and the sun seems to run." Yes, sadness and depression hide clear thought and bright vision: the yellow of the Sun. Each of these hues can take on infinite variations depending on individual interpretations and the cultures they represent. Each of us paints our own rainbow, and our inner weather brightens colors for eyes that accept new visions of an ancient way. A change in world view can change the world viewed, for physical and mental events merge and influence each other.

The visionary exieriences of shamans round the world and from pole to pole show the living roots of an ancient spiritualism. The birth of a modern shaman is but one more green leaf budding on our ancestral tree, for the birth of shamans has never ceased since it first began, and still there are shamans on six continents practicing the ancient ways. One new leaf is nothing special, yet it is an extraordinary happening just as all leaves are extraordinary happenings.

As plans for this book were budding, Tayja lent me her copy of *Shamanic Voices* by the anthropologist, Dr. Joan Halifax. Tayja had marked the following passage told by the modern shaman, Brooke Medicine Eagle:

> In the philosophy of the true Indian people, Indian is an attitude, a state of mind; Indian is a state of being, the place of the heart. To allow the heart to be the distributor of energy on this planet . . . to pull that energy from the earth, from the sky; to pull it down and distribute it from your heart, the very center of your being—that is our purpose.[4]

Tayja was coming to the end of her trials and near to seeing her life in love when she met the Abenaki artist from Quebec, Tsonakwa, an Abenaki name which means "Wild Man Waiting At The North" and is given to those who prove themselves as teachers. His hand extended to her as she crossed the Rainbow Bridge and for the first time, understood her life from the perspective of a shaman.

Tayja was a student in Tsonakwa's class, "Touch the Earth," which he taught at Carleton College in June of 1984. With no hesitation, she selected Tsonakwa's class from the Spiritual Frontiers Fellowship Retreat brochure, a class I had taken the previous year. Among his white students, Tsonakwa may have been surprised to see the high cheekbones and wide features of an Indian woman. Tayja appears to be taller than her five feet six inches, is heavily built and distinctively Indian. Her heavy dark hair, lit with a hint of brown, grows from low over her eyebrows. Then, her eyes were only slits with lids clenched protectively over them, but her thin-lipped mouth supplied the animation her eyes lacked, always ready for a gentle smile or a boisterous laugh, deep and rich. Perhaps Tsonakwa did not yet know how truly he spoke to Tayja when he said, "The Human Spirit Is Like A Great Light Beamed Into The Sky."

He had a deeply involved listener when he spoke in tones that gently blend a French Canadian accent with shades of the Abenaki dialect of his childhood: Tayja listened from deep within the experience of her life as Tsonakwa told of the crossing from the world of matter to the world of spirit, a journey which Tayja recognized as her own.

> . . . I'll talk a little bit about Shamanism, spiritualism. The first thing in my definition of spiritualism is that it is the background of all religion. When I speak of spiritualism, I am not necessarily speaking of a church or an organized religion . . .
>
> A shaman is hard to define. There are no two alike . . . What happens, a shaman goes through a catastrophe or a string of catastrophes that enhance certain abilities within him . . . Most often the shaman has to go through a severe trauma, severe illness or severe psychosis and recover from it before he learns the recovery process that he can use. He might fall into the depths of depression or insanity, for instance, and be literally crossed off by his society and then, somehow, through the strength of his spiritual life and through the strength of his intellectual life and his emotional life, somehow he heals himself, and this has happened in psychiatry, in some cases psychiatrists take credit for it and in other cases are mystified by it.[5]

All this and much more that Tsonakwa told described the trials Tayja had passed through. For the first time, in Tayja's words, "My life from beginning to now" began to make sense.

Tsonakwa saw the goal of bringing understanding and peace to all people of all races and feels an American Indian Renaissance moving among us. "My father knew no difference between people, and he taught me none," Tsonakwa spoke.

Yet in our culture, there is a polarity of positive and negative ideas about Indians. From her white father, Tayja learned the negative one we saw so much of in old Western movies. It is still alive in our cultural consciousness. This view was demonstrated to me in a dream told by a woman in my evening trance-development class. She was a child of abuse; and at the time of her dream, she feared for her daughter as she saw the girl being threatened by a group of Indians coming into her home bearing bows and arrows. While her daughter walked fearlessly toward them, the mother cried out in fear. She woke with no resolution, but since that time her attitudes have changed completely, and as she released the violence in her personal past, she has released the cultural images of violence.

During meditation, another participant in the same class received the mystical vision of a circle of chanting shamans who stayed with him the whole time of the meditation. On coming out of his trance, he spoke of his experience, his gentle voice resonating the awe he felt. This vision shows another level of the American Indian Renaissance Tsonakwa tells of: "Our prayers can be sung in front of all people, and we need not be ashamed, but proud that this is part of our world view—that our prayers spread round the world and benefit all of mankind."[6]

This joining of rainbow hands speaks to Tayja and me. Our union in our friendship and in this book does not come from this physical world. If we looked in a mirror and saw our physical faces, we would be very different. Her face is strong and blunt in its features as though carved of rock, my features made from smaller bones, more delicate. I am twice her age. She is dark of hair and complexion, I am lighter, my hair gray. Our physical lives are just as distinct from each other. Her background was poor, mine affluent. Her early life was harsh, mine gentle. She lived in many places, I have known of six generations of my family in one valley. My health has always been good, she has suffered many illnesses. She had difficulty getting her general education degree, I have taught in a state university. I love and feel at home in the natural world, she is a city woman. She enjoys the stimulation of people around her, I like solitude and peace much of the time. She is a single woman, I have a husband of 40 years, three children and six grandchildren. I know of violence and of psychological illnesses from others, she from her own experience. Yet with all

Tayja Wiger

Cynthia Bend

our differences, Tayja and I often seem to be in the hands of the same puppeteer, and in significant ways, our strings are pulled in unison. So for this book, our shared experiences take hands with our differences and we look in that distant mirror and see, not our different faces, but our spirits joined. Both of us wish, in Tsonakwa's words, to "fight evil by planting good in its face." But first we must recognize the good in our own.

Then, after the cleansing rain, on the far side of the rainbow, will come the good red and blue days, often called the "Rainbow Days."

Chapter Three
Survival

*We are lost in mists of shifting dreams and fearful thoughts,
our eyes shut tight against the light.*
                                    The Course in Miracles[1]

Like all babies, Tayja came to this world a stranger trapped in a defenseless body; unlike most babies, her trap did not release. She did not dare reach far with eyes, legs or voice from the dubious protection of her damaged body and her frightened mind. (Although she was born with some sight, her vision became progressively worse as she grew older.) Tayja tells her story, the bare bones of physical survival:

All my life I've had to do a lot of hard work to survive, both emotionally and physically. There are many paths I was on, some in the dark, some in the light—like a body torn in many directions.

I was born in Minnesota to an Indian mother. My father was white. He wasn't born in this country, but he moved to Seattle when he was a young child. My mother lived on a reservation in North Dakota. She didn't say where, only that she had to leave. I don't know why. Three weeks after leaving she met my father, and they got married and lived in St. Paul. They moved a lot, and the different houses get mixed up in my mind. At first my parents couldn't talk because my mother spoke only Sioux, and he didn't understand. He didn't talk much except when he was angry he'd blow up.

I remember my mother fairly well. She wore an Indian dress with a star of beads on the front. She was a thin woman, oh, about five feet five inches I think. Even now I can hear her voice sometimes, clear in my head.

She had five children. She gave birth to my oldest brother, White

25

Feather, in 1952 and the second boy, Pony, in 1953, then third which was me in 1954. My Indian name was Ysaza, I guess meaning deadly. I had a twin brother who was born dead, and I was blamed. I almost died too. We had white names, but I never liked my white name. My sister was born a year later in '55, named Silver Wings, because of her silver hair. The fifth child, my youngest sister, came in 1958. The new baby's name was Wild Feet, I guess because she, too, almost died. Two boys and three girls, and out of five children, only two were born okay. My mother had trouble with the delivery of three: myself, Wild Feet and Pony, the brother fourteen months older than me. My brother, Pony, was born partly blind and with pneumonia; me premature, two pounds six ounces and partially blind too, and with cerebral palsy in my legs. Because of my birth problems, I wasn't able to walk until I was seven years old. Then my mind pushed me into walking.

My youngest sister, Wild Feet, was premature, only three pounds, and with eye problems so severe she saw only shadows. She also had lung problems, so she stayed in bed for three years with a tube down her throat. When she was born, I was four. I knew something was wrong, knew she was born really strange. How I wanted to understand why! From my bed, I prayed for her. I could sense the signs of death. But why? I didn't understand. I heard my mother cry a lot. My father hit the wall over and over yelling, "Why did we have these kids?" Anger and even more anger filled the house.

Finally he stopped yelling, and I came out of my room crawling since I couldn't walk yet. I remember hearing them say, "She's too small," and my mother speaking some Indian words to the new baby. I think she was saying a blessing, the same words she'd say when my father would come to my room at night to hurt me, sometimes by beating, sometimes by cutting me, and often sex. I felt so mixed up and scared and angry. God, I prayed that I too would live! My pain was hard, but I knew even at four years old that I needed to live for my mother. I know my mother loved us, but she didn't know how to show it. She drank a lot, like quarts a day. I was born addicted. My father drank too, until he had to quit when I was four or five because of his heart. He fed me brandy to keep me quiet. I loved my mother, but I feared my father and that's all. I feared him my whole life. The things that would happen, I didn't understand but knew they must be wrong. My father hurt everyone in the family, everyone. With Pony and me it was sexual, but the others got mostly beatings. Why he had five children I really don't know. He didn't make enough money to support them, and he hated everyone in the family. I didn't really understand his angry self. I got beatings for any reason or no reason. I thought why, what did I do? What?

When Wild Feet was born, we lived at the edge of the city in a broken down house with a dirt floor. There was no grass in front of it. I was too little to remember much about this house, but I was told later by an aunt on my father's side. There was no one near, no neighbors to help us because the closest one was about half a mile away. I remember all five of us kids in one room. Our parents had a room to themselves. I don't think there were any pictures on the walls, but my sight wasn't very good then either.

My father was a very hurt and angry man. From what he said, and I believe him, he was very abused by his father. He was an atheist. I remember hearing him say, "If I ever went to church, my father would wake up out of his grave." I was scared most of the time. Since I was four I remember having spirit friends, but I didn't dare tell my father. I wasn't allowed to be outside. I got closed off in my bedroom for one thing or another, but I never really understood what I had done. Or was this how all children were kept? The first time I remember going out was at age seven. All I saw of outside was from my window, but my eyes couldn't see that well, so I couldn't understand by them. My spirit friends used to tell me what was out there.

In my despair I learned how to escape through inner sight and to survive in a world I didn't know much about. I learned to keep safe by sensing things that happened from where I was in my room. I could watch my father leave work, see where he waited for his bus, watch him riding and get out and walk toward the house. I remember feelings so deep inside that I couldn't explain them even to me, the feeling like my stomach was going to fall out. I could watch him come inside; then the fear would rise in my heart. Sometimes I tried not to see, but the visions were just there. I didn't understand this, because with my eyes I only saw blurred images, but when I saw in my mind, the images were very clear. Sometimes I heard words. I could hear people say things before they talked, and I would answer them before they talked or while they were asking the question. But I didn't understand the pictures or the words.

I prayed many nights for help, "Either help me die or help me live." Often I could feel my friends were there, but danger was also there, and I felt that too. The pain in my mind and in my body was so great. It was often hard to keep wanting to live.

One day I saw a beautiful white glow in my room. I remember very clearly; the light came over to me and spoke. I wasn't frightened at all. I just knew it must be from God because where else could it come from? I talked back. "You're here to help me."

The spirit said, "Yes, we are here to protect you from this problem in this house." Sometimes they spoke in thoughts I understood, not just words. So they taught me how to go inside and push off the pain that kept being inflicted on my body and my mind. They said to listen to them, and they would show me how to live. So I listened no matter what anyone said, but I didn't tell about it. I pushed away society's rules and lived by theirs. They told me to pray hard for what I needed, and it would be given to me. Many spirits visited me and protected me and helped me become strong.

Sometimes angry spirits came. When I was little, I didn't know how to protect myself from them, and anyway it just felt natural. If my father gets angry and my mother, why not some of my spirit friends? When I got a little older I felt some spirits weren't for me, and I learned how to send them to the light I could see in my head. Some spirits I felt sorry for and let them come often before I knew they weren't so good and sent them away. My mother helped by teaching me to meditate and say Indian chants and prayers. When my father heard her talking Sioux, he would beat her for that. I was never sure if I should learn the Indian ways she taught, but I learned them anyway. So my mother and my spirit friends helped me through the first part of my journey, through the first seven years of hell.

The second seven years of my life were also hell. There was a long amount of incest and more beatings, and I couldn't get away. I didn't know why I couldn't walk like the others. I heard someone say my mother was very ill and she might not make it for long. Who will help me understand what's happening to me? Who will hold me and touch me and say prayers for me? God I was afraid. I wished I could get away like my older brother, White Feather. He was small in words and stayed with friends a lot.

My brother, Pony, and I seemed to be my father's big target. Pony and I helped each other. Before I was six and learned to walk, he went out to the trash heap near our house and got me things to eat as well as my pillow and book, even though I couldn't read it, but I kept it under my pillow. When I was eleven or twelve, Pony and I decided we would join in and play baseball with the other kids in spite of our poor vision. I was pitcher and Pony was up to bat. I thought I was back far enough and pitched the ball, but he didn't hit the ball when he swung his bat; I was so close he hit me right in the face. Not long after that Pony started to change and get mean. He was hurting himself, once by stabbing himself with a kitchen knife and often by beating on the walls until he broke his knuckles. He also stopped eating for days at a time. At night he was screaming in his dreams and visions. I think he was possessed. I think the whole family was; my father for sure.

So all kinds of things were going on inside and around me, but I couldn't understand them or see them clearly. It wasn't just that I had to be close to see. I had eye problems I couldn't understand. Everything was turned around and upside down, so learning was a problem. Later I learned it is called "dyslexia." My father, I learned later, couldn't read or write much either. But I don't know if it was dyslexia.

A good thing when I was young was healing. Sometimes it was friends I played with, more often my brother and sister. When Pony was eleven years old, he was climbing a tree when he fell and broke his wrist. He came in the house crying, and I could feel the bone coming through the skin, and as I put my hand on it, I felt a great amount of heat coming through my hand. Then in a very few minutes the bone was healed with not even a scar. Another healing happened after my sister had stepped on a rusty nail sticking out of a piece of wood. She came to me, and I could feel the blood running into my hand, and then all of a sudden the hole in her foot was gone, and she also was healed. My father broke my arm many times, also cut my arms, and I healed them very fast.

But I couldn't heal my mother. She became very ill. She was drinking a lot and very sick. She would not eat anything, and I thought she was going to die. She held me and told me to take care of the younger ones. So, yes, she was going to die. When I was nine she did die, and another woman came into our house three months after. I remember the woman saying she was our mother, but I said, "No! My mother died." I never believed she was my mother at all. I prayed to my friends that my mother would come back. I took care of the youngers the best I could, but at nine years I felt very lost. I loved my mother and felt sorry for her, also angry that she left me in this crazy house.

My father was working two jobs. I was glad. The less he was home, the more I felt better. The woman drank, and there were nothing but fights when my father was around, the woman and him. Then I was blamed for their fights. Why? Why? Why? I kept praying to my friends for help and "please bring my mother home." They did what they could do, but that couldn't happen.

I was not even baptized until I was ten years old when my stepmother came to my house. She was a non-practicing Baptist, but she was pressured by her sister who was Lutheran to get us baptized Lutheran. So she did. I was made to get up early Sundays along with brothers and sisters to go to Sunday school which I hated. I didn't really believe what they were saying about sin. "What's sin?" I asked the minister.

His answer I remember very clearly. "When you do something against God, you have sinned." That didn't make sense to me because I didn't think I did anything to God.

I told the minister about my spirit friends, and he told me it was just my imagination. "Anyone who has or can see spirits is sinning against God." He told me my visions were "foolish nonsense," so I should stop talking about it. So I didn't tell anyone after that. But it was hard. The thoughts came through. "Is this bad or is this good?" I couldn't ask my mother. She was gone, I thought for good. When I got older, she came back to me in spirit and helped me.

We moved about that time, and I started getting myself into many more problems. I kinda stopped listening to my spirit friends, maybe because my fears got in the way, and more of the spirits frightened me. I would feel very angry and upset to the point of wondering if there was anything that was going to help or even if I would become a better person (one without problems). I was eleven when we moved into a new housing project in a neighborhood that was mostly black. I remember green screens between the units and lots of kids. There were many problems in school and with the boys in the block. I started being forced into having sex by the older boys in our block. God, I felt frightened! If I said, "No," the boys beat me, so I gave in. What is happening to me? Who can tell me!? Then I met a priest by my house, and we talked, but he didn't help me either. He just confused me more. I didn't understand the word, "sin," or I wouldn't accept the word. I really didn't know which. I felt very strong on my own feelings, so I went with them, knowing never to say anything else to anyone. I often cried at night to get help, but I kept getting into trouble. Still, deep down inside I knew I was capable of loving.

As I grew up, I started to help others who had trouble like mine with beatings and incest. Some lived long enough to work through their problems, others, like my best friend, died because of them. But in spite of the bad things I did, I knew I helped other children by caring about them and understanding when no one else did. Also, when I could sense that I hurt someone, I would feel deep remorse, but I couldn't express it. When people would say things to me like, "I don't like you" or "you're insane," I felt strong hurt in the pit of my stomach. Am I really insane—the things I do? The thing I remember praying for the most was, "Don't let me be like my father, Please! Please! Please!" I didn't want to be cruel or hurtful.

At twelve and a half or thirteen, I got pregnant and went to North Virginia and stayed with my father's brother. He was a test pilot for airplanes, and his insurance paid for my baby. After I had the baby, I came back to Minnesota. The baby was a lot of trouble. He had a heart condition, also he was mongoloid, and that hurt me a lot. The baby stayed with the father. His mother helped, so we didn't have to place the baby in an institution.

I wanted to go back and stay with uncle Ed. My father and the woman didn't know why, but they agreed it might help. I stayed there one year. After that I moved around a lot but didn't live at home again. These years between thirteen and eighteen when I went into drug treatment were confused. I went to every state in the U.S., even Alaska, also Mexico. I went by myself by bus or hitching. When I was traveling, I lived in different types of communities: Italian, Jewish, black, city Indian and New Mexico border towns. I hitched with truck drivers a lot, and they gave me bennies and other stuff. I don't remember all that very well. I didn't have much time for details.

School was very difficult for me because I wasn't able to read well. Also I was shifted from school to school because they didn't know what to do with me. Since the schools didn't suit my physical needs—the dyslexia, blindness and seizures, many teachers said, "The only thing wrong with you is you don't want to learn." Others said it was just behavior, so they came down on me too hard. My report cards were mostly C- and D-, and teachers always wrote "bad conduct." Confusion was so strong. What could I do? So I acted like they thought I was. I kept getting into trouble and wondering if I would ever discover why I do things I knew were wrong, but it was like I couldn't control my urges to be angry and to lash out at others.

The kids I hung around with were drug people. They sold and took. Adults helped by buying us liquor. All we had to do was hang out by liquor stores, and some adult would get it for us. By the age of 14 I was a drug addicted person, already chronic, and I had been with many pimps. During my teenage years I was arrested 42 times and sent to correctional institutions sixteen times: Woodview and many others I don't remember. Most of the arrests were for disturbing the peace, stealing in order to survive, fighting or drinking. By fifteen I completely left my family, running for whatever safety I could find.

My baby only lived until it was two years old, then died from pneumonia and heart complications. So we buried that baby, and soon I was pregnant again at fifteen years old. That baby was born dead. The pain and fear was so deep! I would go into a hospital and be so scared, "Am I going to die?" Each time I felt myself getting more worried about keeping my own heart for me. I had this belief that my heart was going to be taken from me. The feeling of love I didn't understand, but I knew that it literally hurt at times. I would pray to keep my heart.

Then I found a pimp named Michael who was a real great person. He didn't beat me like the others had attempted. He was great to me, kind and tender—not the way they all portray pimps. He made me a hostess of his house a lot of the time, so I didn't have to have sex with the Johns. He treated me very good, like a brother to me, the kind of brother I never had in my real family. He bought me nice things, listened to my problems and held me when I was afraid. There was no sex between us because he was gay. We were close friends and loved each other as that. I guess he was much good for me. I spent about fifteen years with Michael off and on. To this day I keep his picture, and I feel some respect for the man even though I don't approve of his business anymore.

At sixteen I split my time between having children and being a bouncer at a bar. The owner was an ex-cop I knew. I was a good fighter, and he knew that, also that I had a lot of friends in the bar. Then I started doing weight-lifting because I needed my arms stronger to do my job and get money. What I would do is break up fights, and I probably created many too. But what I remember is the strength and quick thinking I had, which I needed because my legs weren't so good.

My pimp knew me as many different people, but I was confused and thought they were my spirit friends I was changing into. Maybe I was right. I didn't know about or understand my multiple personalities then, but now I think that sometimes Jim came out. He was the personality that was very violent. Sometimes I came home with black eyes or split lips from being hit, but you should have seen the other guy. The people in the bar knew me as "Debbie," the personality that needed excitement. She was very persuasive and very sexual. When she asked, "Why don't you buy me a drink?" someone usually did. At this age I was what some said was a wildcat. Fast cars, drugs, beer and sex describes this time of my life. People called me a rebel without a cause.

At sixteen I became pregnant for the third time. I knew I just had to have a baby and get it to live. That baby lived only three months and died in what they call crib syndrome. I thought, "I can't have my children."

Finally, at seventeen, I met a man I married and got pregnant in 1972. I thought it was love for him, but it was really love for my baby. My husband had come from a very large family of ten childen, he being the oldest. They were tired of him, and I was too before long. He was 23 years old and a wreck. He wasn't working much because he was a kleptomaniac and lost jobs. He also liked to drink and play nasty games. He would do things like set off firecrackers in the house when I was in the bathtub so I couldn't hide or find out who it was. He would also hide things, like when I bought a box of potato chips, he would divide them in half and hide his half, then eat mine. He did that with all the stuff I bought, then he'd be mad at me when my potato chips or cigarettes were gone. His were still hidden, but he'd ask me, "How can you eat so much? or "How come you smoked all the cigarettes? Then I had to split myself to function with Michael and my husband—very confusing.

The birth of that baby was my hardest. I was a wreck mentally and physically. I almost lost the baby and my own life through a problem with a kidney. [According to a 1974 medical report, Tayja had nephritis, perhaps caused by her chemical dependency.] The doctors also discovered I had ecchymosis [the escape of blood from ruptured blood vessels which could be caused by a serious blood disease or by bruising]. The illness was very strong, my husband very little support, my own family no support at all. I was the outcast. So with the drugs I was on and all the illnesses, I felt like I wanted to just not wake up. But

I prayed to get through it, and I did. My fourth child, James, was finally born June 14, 1973. My husband wasn't even there. I guess he went fishing with his cousin. The baby was only twelve inches long and weighed three pounds, but he was in pretty good health.

Me, I had both physical and emotional problems, many seizures and much trouble with my kidneys and high blood pressure. I had nine major surgeries after James' birth: one kidney removed, tumors on the ovaries, a hysterectomy for cancer seven months after Jim was born, surgery for tumors on the inside of the throat, surgery on my feet, surgery for bleeding ulcers, surgery on my eyes for blood clots, surgery on different cancer areas after that, all by the age of eighteen and a half. Then I had chemotherapy. [Tayja had insufficient money for medical bills at this time so went to doctors under assumed names, changing doctors as she was pressured for money.] Nine surgeries in one year. So my son was often placed in foster homes and with friends. My husband and I split up after nine months. He and I were just not making it together with all the physical handicaps I had to battle.

Finally, at the end of my eighteenth year, I was told by my therapist that I either went into drug treatment or she would take my son permanently. Jimmy was two or three then. So in 1974 I went into long-term treatment in Minneapolis for one year, and my son visited me there.

A 1974 medical history taken when Tayja was in the University Hospital for drug treatment itemizes "two exploratory laparotomies one of which included a hysterectomy last year. She has been diagnosed as having nephritis and has some pains in her left knee. She denies any other serious medical illnesses or injuries." Although the two surgical sections of the abdominal wall are accounted for, these procedures are not explained as there is no mention in the report of either ulcers or cancer. Under "Mental Status" the report states: "She was not psychotic. I did not feel the risk of suicide was increased. She showed no conceptual disorganization, denied hallucinations and her thought content was not unusual. She related in an appropriate fashion. She showed no suspiciousness nor grandiosity. She described mild depressive moods. She described moderate anxiety. She did appear tense in that she rocked back and forth in the chair and wiggled her leg throughout much of the interview. There were no unusual mannerisms. She was co-operative and not hostile."

It is important to note that Tayja's multiple personality and/or possession had not been diagnosed at this time, and her behavior could change drastically when other personalities took over. The doctor's impressions and recommendations follow:

1. Chemical dependency—drugs and alcohol.
2. Personality disorder—probably passive-aggressive type.
3. Psychophysiological genitourinary reaction—frigidity.

He recommended that she "complete the alcoholic treatment program" and then "be transferred to 3A for some exploratory psychotherapy," beginning in the hospital, then continuing in the office.

The cancer was still strong, but at least I had a chance to fight it then. I fought to gain my 19th year of life when my cancer became a part of my plans for death. I couldn't think what I was going to do with my son. I didn't even know who I was, let alone who my son was going to be. Finally, my ex-husband filed to adopt him and took him away from me because I was a junky and mentally ill. I had no one to help fight it. It was me on one side of the court room all alone and my husband and his whole family on the other. I was feeling so sick and also getting blinder, so I gave up. The verbal agreement was I was going to be able to see him, but they pulled that from me too. He has been with them since, and they told him I was no longer living, but I know some day we'll see each other again.

After treatment in the hospital they accepted me in the halfway house because they could see through the hard tough act. I thanked God that they helped me find the path. Then things turned around for me. I finally felt more together than I had ever felt. I saw people care about each other. I saw people hold and touch one another, something I hadn't seen before. I still didn't understand, but I knew it was something that I could kind of believe. Finally I could let others see me cry, and the tears came out. I knew I couldn't tell them everything about me, so I kept my feeling of the path of the spirit to myself. They didn't try to change my spirituality. Then I could believe there really was a Higher Power, and I tried to be that. The spirits kept coming more and more. It was harder to keep to myself, especially when they said it was an honest program. But still I kept seeing without sight. I hung on to the Higher Power, still getting into some problems with other belief systems. I prayed hard. I wanted to live.

I was still working with Michael as much as possible, still keeping a part of the old and the new. I was opening up in other levels of my life. I was determined to stay sober, and to this day, I've been sober and off drugs. Thank God.

So for five years I was totally devoted to A.A. I was afraid I'd start drinking again, so I went to groups every day and sometimes two a day or more. In those five years I was told over and over, "Indians can't stay sober," which is basically a lie. I started my G.E.D. (General Education Degree) to complete my last year of high school while still in treatment. I had to take that test over and over fifteen times. I wanted to complete something in my life. The judge said anyone as persistent as I was deserved the chance even though I wasn't supposed to try the test so many times. I passed with one extra point.

At 20 years the cancer had slowed down, and I felt better physically, but emotionally I was a wreck. I was still going to A.A. and helping others but couldn't help me. I had been in many treatment centers in the Twin Cities prior to the U. of M., also in California. I was in the Synanon program when it first started, but they kicked me out. But I survived the U. of M.

The hospital released me on much medication and said I shouldn't have the problems as long as I stayed on the meds. So finally I took myself off. Then, when I went to see my doctor, she was angry that I had gone off meds, and she put me back in the hospital by tricking me onto the ward. She put me on 72 hour hold and wouldn't let me go, so I got very angry and felt I was betrayed. [A doctor comments: "They cannot keep anyone beyond 72 hours unless it's established in court that they are a danger to themselves or others. She may have been tricked onto the ward but a) I'm sure the doctor (who must have known her well by then) felt it was definitely in Tayja's best interests, and b) she couldn't have stayed there over 72 hours unless others agree."] I proceeded to sit in the hospital doing nothing. At least I had protection. That was really what I needed. My friends said it was the right thing for me. I was on one drug that was really strong. I hated it, but by this time I needed rest anyway. I remember asking for guidance because I didn't know what was going to become of me. Would it never end? The answer came, "Just wait; you'll get your answer."

Then I went to Hewitt House, a halfway house in St. Paul for adults with emotional problems. I was accepted there because they didn't know what else to do with me. I knew that I really didn't belong there, but I needed more time to figure out where I was going next. I stayed there six months, not telling about my spiritual part. I knew from my heart I still needed more. What would I do afterwards? I wanted to try school, so I signed up for the community college and it was terrible. I think I flunked the first three weeks. So I started crying in the lunchroom and a girl came over to me and said she thought I needed the program she was in that would give me new parents. So I called them and went out there, and they talked to me. Then I started groups there. I was on medication, but out there I went off. The groups were strange to me, but I kept going from 1977 to 1981.

I still had a long way to go to get to Unity.

Chapter Four
A Light in a Dark Building

We Sioux believe that there is something within us that
controls us, something like a second person almost. We call
it "nagi," what other people might call soul, spirit or essence.
One can't see it, feel it or taste it.

—*Lame Deer*
Seeker of Visions.[1]

Tayja did not understand her "second person." Its light was hidden, its ways a mystery. "Nagi, Nagi, Nagi," hummed in her mind, and she wrote it in her journal, yet she may never have known that it is the Sioux word for spirit.

"What is happening to me? Who can tell me?" she asks. "I fought for what people called "being normal," but I still didn't know what that was. I would feel very angry and upset to the point where I wasn't sure that there really was anything that was going to help, or even that I would become a better person. I kept getting into trouble. I wondered if I would ever discover why I do things I know are wrong, but it was like I couldn't contain my urges to be angry and lash out at others. When I hurt people I would feel deep remorse and deep scare, scared of some part of me that was like my father, scared of a hell inside of me."

Tayja had embarked on a crisis journey embracing the sky or home of the Great Spirit, the Earth or Mother, and the underworld or "hell" as many Christians would call it. As the shaman learns to make transitions between these three levels, he or she must die in one level to be born into the next. The shaman becomes a human bridge between the three realms. As the developing shaman learns to cross these thresholds by changing levels of consciousness, both spiritual and earthly guidance is useful. Direction from both sides is called for because the shaman needs both spiritual power and the knowledge to use the power wisely here on Earth. Without a supportive culture, the new territory is strange and frightening. Terrors are experienced with no destination in sight, no understanding of purpose to the pain and suffering experienced. "Will it never end? Why? Why? Why?" was the drumbeat of Tayja's mind.

Shamans from other cultures have asked the same questions, have had the same fears. Manuel Cordova-Rios, a South American Amahuaca, said of his initiation:

> At times during all this, which went on for months, I became nervous, high strung and afraid of going insane. The chief and the old women noticed this. They took pains to explain and reassure me that as long as I followed the diet and instructions everything would come out well.[2]

Unlike Cordova-Rios, Tayja had no chief or old women to teach her. Her life was stretched between two medicines, ancient and modern, spiritual and material. We usually think of "medicine" as a substance used in treating disease. Within that material philosophy, reality is seen as physical; as such, it can be touched, heard, seen, smelled and tasted. The body is the mechanism for doing these things and can be manipulated according to the physical and chemical laws of medicine. Like a complex machine, it can be, within its biological limits, restructured and repaired by a specialist. This philosophy, when carried into the psychological, results in a treatment which, physically and chemically, manipulates the body and its surroundings with the aim of changing behavior. Of course, not all Western psychology ignores the spiritual. (A.A. with its "higher power as you understand it," makes spiritual commitment a strong part of its program, and for Tayja, it proved to be a healing experience. Programs which ignored her personal faith, or "medicine," failed.)

Medicine to the Plains Indians includes everything on Earth and in the heavens. All is seen as a mirror for the people in which to see the spirit of their lives reflected to them. For them, the physical reality has symbolic meaning. Black Elk says it well as he speaks of his cousin:

Crazy Horse dreamed and went into a world where there is
nothing but the spirits of all things. That is the real world that
is behind this one, and everything we see here is something
like a shadow from that world.[3]

These shadows around us, then, are symbols of the reality beyond, and they speak of spirit in many ways. It is a total gift, this
medicine wheel of life.

But for Tayja, the ancient ways died with her mother when she
was nine years old, before she had the judgement to separate the wisdom from the hurt. She was as confused by her doctor's expectations
as she was by her often-defiled Indian heritage. Her doctors asked
her to be healthy. She says, "but what is 'healthy'? I didn't know. I'd
never seen it. I couldn't understand it. We do what we see."

The initiation of a shaman transcends the confines of any culture, and especially it transcends a technological culture. Paradoxically, pain continued to be Tayja's healing medicine, for she had to
learn to heal herself before she would have the ability to heal others.
This was the time her light was hidden beyond the reach of those who
tried to know her, and from herself as well.

Tayja's adolescent years were indeed dark, and she does not like
to relive them. In telling her story, she has taken just one sentence to
say that she was "arrested 42 times and sent to correctional institutions about 16 times: Woodview and many others I don't remember.

Her medical reports have more to say about it:

Between the ages of 15 and 24, when she entered
Wiger Woods, [her reparenting home] she required hospital
or institutional treatment at least once yearly. She had three
psychiatric hospitalizations in California, the first one, at age
15, in a locked unit for six months; two in Iowa, and two in
Minnesota. She presented a mixed and flagrant psy-
chopathology [defined as inability to deal with everyday
reality constructively] with episodes of withdrawal, regressive
rocking movements, [rhythmic rocking movements are typical of people in trance or altered states of consciousness]
refusal to eat, periods of depression with suicidal attempts
(cutting wrists), violent behavior, hallucinations and paranoid
delusions. She spent six months, in 1977, in the psychiatric
rehabilitation program Hewitt House, St. Paul, and was still
overtly psychotic at that time with delusional thinking [not in

touch with consensual reality], suicidal and assaultive behavior, and insomnia. She still required antipsychotic and anti-depressive medication (Loxitane and Elavil). In addition, she needed several medical hospitalizations. (2/27/80)

Tayja can't count the schools she has attended or the counselors and doctors who have examined her. These were years of confused drifting or violent confrontation in a society with which she felt no bonds of understanding. "My main task was to keep myself separate, but I didn't know how." Not only did she not know how, but she didn't know why.

Yet within, unknown to herself as to others, her destiny as a sha-man was forming, shielded by her cocoon of defenses. As she writes in her journal, "I began to feel angry in my head, saying 'I am me alone. You can't help me, no one can. I'll take care of me'." To emerge as a strong-winged butterfly, the winged one must force open its own door in the cocoon it has formed for its protection during its natural metamorphosis. To have its shelter opened by an outside source will weaken the butterfly by depriving it of the strengthening effort of breaking out, and it will die. This, over-eager scientists have dis-covered. Rollo May translates this biological experience to human terms: "Many of society's most valuable people have come from the most calamitous childhoods. A smooth and successful childhood can have very negative effects."[4] It was to be a long, hard fight before Tayja would learn to fly on her own wings.

Although there are many societies in which shamanism plays a part, it is the Plains Indians with whom Tayja relates most strongly, and it is their view of the person which best fits her.

Each person is a unique Living Medicine Wheel, pow-erful beyond imagination, that has been limited and placed upon this earth, to Touch, Experience and Learn. The Six Grandfathers, [each grandfather represents one of the four directions and up and down] taught me that each man, woman, and child at one time was a Living Power that exist-ed somewhere in time and space. These Powers were with-out form, but they were aware. They were alive.[5]

This view expressed by Hyemeyohsts Storm is not so different in substance from the transpersonal therapist Emily Susann's:

I've come to view the human being as a multi-faceted crystal reflecting the light of the Universal Mind. Since each human crystal is like a holograph of the Universal Mind, not only are we all linked, but each of us has limitless access to illumination.[6]

A potent reason for the American Indian Renaissance today (along with Eastern thought systems) is this readmission of spiritual values into practical life through wholistic concepts.

In Sioux villages, teepees were arranged in circular patterns (or were until the white man destroyed the "nation's hoop," pushing the people to live in gray wooden boxes). This form was the physical pattern of their spirituality, balanced to include all directions. The dances of the Plains Indians are enacted with physical and spiritual meanings united. Each direction of the medicine wheel, South, West, North and East, has their totem animal and symbolic color which may differ from tribe to tribe. Each person has a beginning place and comes into the world symbolically linked to a totem animal, the meaning of which may be thought of as a spiritual reality reflected by that animal's behavior on Earth. This wheel of the universe links the individual to plants and colors as well as animals, and is a large enough system to allow for each individual to occupy a unique place. The spiritual concept of the medicine wheel is realized  physically in a dance around a symbolic wheel drawn on the ground. Each individual has his or her natural starting point, then progresses around the wheel learning each position in turn. It is a pattern of unity, and the fully developed individual knows the giving, caring wisdom of the northern buffalo who gave totally of its substance to feed, clothe and house the people, the far vision of the eastern eagle, the touching sensitivity and detailed perception of the southern mouse and the inner vision of the western bear.

The multiplicity of doctors from various disciplines who examined Tayja were not only unaware of her spiritual heritage and its physical manifestations, but they were unaware of her multiple personalities or possessing spirits who gave them conflicting messages. Within this confusion, they did the best they could. On April 18, 1977, a report signed by two physicians begins:

This is the first University of Minnesota Hospitals ad-mission for this 23-year-old ambidextrous right female from an ambidextrous family who presents with multiple com-plaints—left sided weakness, numbness, palpitations, Ray-naud's phenomenon [Raynaud's phenomenon is a spasm of blood vessels in the fingers when exposed to cold, result-ing in white numb fingers, then purple painful fingers when rewarmed. It can be unrelated to other disease, with no known cause, or it can be associated with a variety of rheumatoid arthritis-like diseases; potentially serious.], tun-nel vision, and so on.

With no unifying concept identified, the doctors used their brief examination times to catalog ailments and make cautious and often conflicting diagnostic statements. The complex person who was Tayja was labeled by each doctor with the most appropriate term he knew, then referred to the next doctor, counselor or teacher. No one had the opportunity to work with Tayja long enough to know her. "They wanted me to be what they wanted, not what I was," she said.

Institutions did not make Tayja "well," but they did give her time to develop the strength she would need to take her individual path separate from society's throughway. When she "graduated" from her unique school of experience, she had learned the ways of an uncount-able variety of unusual individuals, knowledge which was to help her in future healing work. Experience combined with psychic insights now permit her to see to the core of human problems which would be puzzling to many therapists. She also learned a diversity of thera-peutic approaches. In this she was helped along by her ability to parrot the new vocabularies and fit into the changing system to which she was exposed. She never stayed in a single system long enough to become bound by it. As the examining psychiatrist associated with Tayja's reparenting home put it, "I would describe her insight as very good; she has learned well to be psychologically minded."

Perceiving visions (or the reality beyond the shadows of this world), is another mark of the shaman. While Tayja was in her teens, spirits were both her greatest friends and worst enemies because she had formed no world view which included them in a functional way. The question of what was a split fragment from her own personality and what was an intruding spirit had not been asked, much less answered. Unlike shamans living in compatible societies, Tayja was exposed to no one who affirmed her visions and spirit contacts as a normal part of a child's psychic experience. Instead, she was called "crazy." As a result, the most sacred part of her nature was driven underground and permitted to mature without human intervention. Dr. Smythies affirms that a child's world is "quasi-hallucinatory," with visions a normal part of the child's psychic experience.[7] Certainly visions were a normal part of Tayja's world. As a small child, she had little control over the comings and goings of spirits, and this continued into adolescence. She did not wish to give up her spirits. Since no distinction had been made between positive spiritual guidance and negative spirit entities, she experienced them as a unit and did not want to risk losing them *all*.

A January 21, 1977 University of Minnesota Hospitals Psychiatric Report stated that Tayja "reported acute episodes of distress and suicidal ideation which occurred when she experienced an auditory hallucination instructing her to kill herself because she was worthless." I ask, how could she eliminate these hurtful messages without also eliminating the positive ones she received from her Grandfathers? She indeed had "more work to do" before she would gain the Buffalo Wisdom of the North or the Eagle Vision of the East, as she was not in contact with anyone who could help her put her spirits and visions into a useful perspective. Although her doctors were ready to accept her dark visions as illness, what about the light visions? Would her doctors accept them in the light? Tayja didn't care to risk it, and there were no mentions of benevolent spirits in Tayja's medical reports until 1980 when she was living in her reparenting home.

In a transfer summary from the University of Minnesota Hospitals, April 18, 1977, Tayja's "visual and auditory hallucinations" are described as follows: "The patient states that she hears voices stating 'you are stupid' and sees mice, bears, and people who she knows aren't really there." Could these ancient Sioux symbols hold a meaning which escaped the examining doctor? In his book, *Seven Arrows*, Hyemeyohsts Storm writes, "As we learn, we always change, and so does our perceiving. This changed perception then becomes a new Teacher inside of us."[8] How might Tayja's images of mice and bears have taught her? Could her "crazy symptoms" be part of an inner drove toward wholeness?

The fiery territory within the Earth and the spirit space above it are not physical, so the means of communicating from those realms must change from our normal way of thinking and expressing. The spiritual guides use language and images symbolically, and the symbols they use depend on ideas which each individual tunes into. For example, a Christian may see a vision of Christ, a Jew see Moses, a Hindu may see Krishna, a Native American may see one of the Grandfathers, or any one of the above may see an animal, and the meaning of that animal will depend in part on the nature of the animal (the archetypal meaning), in part on the culture of the individual seeing it, and in part on personal associations.

In her "hallucinations," Tayja saw bears and mice. It is significant that these two animals were the only ones specifically mentioned in Tayja's medical reports. These animals have an important place as two of the four main animals on the Sioux wheel, and their symbolic meaning remained true without Tayja's conscious understanding. Her first sign is the bear, as she now knows. It symbolizes the looks-within place, and Tayja knew of hibernating in her bed or other protected place. Also, she was the power and strength of the bear. But she did not have the wisdom of the buffalo, giver of all gifts needed for life, to live life wholly. She didn't know then what it was she needed, so her vision ran inside her life, going over and over its pieces repeating the question, "Why?" She had also been wounded, so the power and strength of the bear were ready to attack, yet they didn't know who to attack.

Another sign Tayja knew was the mouse. She was surrounded by the stems of grass obstructing the far vision of the eagle, hiding enemies she could hear but not see. Not seeing the whole of her life, she could only touch its pieces, one by one.

It is unlikely that Tayja's doctors were familiar with *Seven Arrows*:

> Mice live all their lives next to the ground, building their nests and gathering their food among the roots of the tall grass and bushes of the prairie. Because of this, Mice never see things at a distance. Everything they can see is right in front of them, where they can sniff at it with their noses and Touch it with their whiskers. Their lives are spent in Touching things in this way, and in gathering seeds and berries to eat. [Here we might ask whether a person with Tayja's limited vision would perceive in this near-sighted way, or was her perception the cause of her limited vision?] A Mouse Person would be . . . a gatherer of things. He might gather

facts, information, material objects, or even ideas. But because he could not see far enough to connect his world with
that of the great prairie of the world around him, he would
never be able to use or understand all that he saw and
gathered.[9]

—Or, did the doctor see the mouse as a dirty gray thing struggling in a trap or perhaps poisoned and vomiting blood? As Tayja
says of her psychologists, "They don't look beyond the image they're
getting to the spiritual meaning beyond it." Child abuse and schizophrenia were part of the prairie the doctors knew; shamanism was
not.

Then, what of the bear of Tayja's visions? "In the West is the Sign
of the Bear. The West is the Looks-Within Place, which speaks of the
Introspective nature of man. The Color of this Place is Black . . . "[10]
Institutional living was often black for Tayja, and especially at night
she often experienced what she later learned to call "autism." In her
journal she writes, "I feel like I want to crawl into a pit and hide."

A man or woman who perceives only from the West will go over
the same thought again and again in their mind, and will always be
undecided. "I am buried in the wall of hell," Tayja writes and often
repeats feelings of "being in a pit."

What of the "people who she knows aren't really there?" Most
people see spirits in some form or another, although they may call
them, "dreams, twilight images," or some other term. For many very
sane individuals it is ordinary to see images of people both living and
dead. For me, such perception is not amazing at all, but merely
another mystery, perhaps less explained scientifically than this word
processor I'm now using. Not being a scientist, I'm used to utilizing
techniques I can not understand.

When dealing with a patient who experiences and believes in
spirit communication, it might be useful for doctors and counselors to
check out counseling techniques which accept such communication.
(Check Appendix II for suggestions helpful for working with an
individual's inner wisdom.) The following quote from Tayja's Discharge Summary from the University of Minnesota Hospitals, February 3, 1977, while observant and stated in an appropriately
objective manner, illustrates a doctor's tendency to overlook possibilities outside his paradigm:

She spoke slowly in a low voice, and her speech was interrupted by many inexplicable silences, and she appeared to
look at someone when no one was there during the initial
interview. She was preoccupied with the content of her
hallucinations . . .

Most of us who have received messages from other consciousness levels or listened to psychic readings have heard the medium
hesitate as he or she gains information from "the other side," then
relates the message, then pauses again for clarification or new
information.

The fear and hatred which frequently built up within Tayja could
be expected to attract a spiritual counterpart of violence, and that is
what happened. An examining doctor reported:

She stated that she became very friendly with one
young male in an hallucination and that she used to have
long discussions with this young man. She cut her wrists with
a razor blade six years ago and again nine months prior to
admission respectively following the orders of this young
man in the hallucination. She stated that she had been told
. . . to cut her wrists or to kill others and it became gradually
more difficult for her to resist his orders . . . she stated that
there was no hope in her life. (2/3/77)

It would be some years before Tayja would learn that there is a
choice of roads in the spiritual realms just as surely as there is a choice
in the physical and then find a balance for utilizing her spirit helpers
while excluding destructive elements. Love will attract itself in the
spiritual world just as fear and hate will attract fearful and hateful
spirits. Tayja needed to *know* her power, then use positive control
over her thoughts and feelings.

Although shamanic destiny may, to some extent, control the
power of attraction and the strength of visions held by an individual, it
does not control the will of the shaman, who is free to choose his or
her spiritual direction. Shamans are human. Their emotions are
human ones, their minds fallible. The greatest of them learn that what
they give returns to them, and they choose the way of the heart. In
shamanic tradition, it was not always so. Some shamans were
warriors too, and they used powers for war as well as for healing.
Always there is choice working hand in hand with destiny, and power
exists independently of how it is used.

Tayja's choices vacillated between outward compliance and violent antagonism toward authorities. Her medical records refer to "lack of comfort with authority," or, more strongly, she "showed considerable conflict with authorities." One can regard this as an asset when one considers her first authoritative figure, her father. "Difficulty in developing emotional closeness and interpersonal sharing and cooperation" is also easily explained by the experiences which taught her. Although Tayja's rejection of authority often resulted in violent and hurtful actions, her strength not only saved her life with parents and peers who threatened her, but, paradoxically, protected the sensitive embryo of the shaman growing in a space of its own within the whirlwind of her life.

Tayja's doctors also questioned her mental acuity:

> She responded to the Raven progressive matrices in a rapid and possibly random fashion. [This is a test of intellectual functioning given to check for brain damage.] She showed little effort and very little concentration. Her total score of 19 represents a percentile score of less than 5 . . . Some of her avoidance and denial may mask more severe thought disturbances and cognitive slippage. Intellectual assessment is recommended . . . (2/21/77)

Further confusions were reported in a February 21, 1977 University of Minnesota medical report: Her MMPI (Minnesota Multiphasic Personality Inventory) was "technically invalid, and this appeared to be because of her reported reading difficulties." On her discharge from this admission, March 16, 1977, it was stated that, "Neuropsychological testing revealed borderline mental deficiency probably secondary to moderate diffuse organic cerebral dysfunction." ["Diffuse organic cerebral dysfunction" refers to a brain that doesn't work well because of a number of possible reasons: birth damage (cerebral palsy or others) drugs, alcohol, disease, stroke, etc.] The report continues: "It was noticed that she did not appear to put much effort into tests during the neuropsychological testing, and a retest was recommended when her functional [emotional and psychological] problems abate." For whatever reason, this result puts another veil of confusion over Tayja's inner growth.

Her eyesight, too, may be considered from the standpoint of Tayja's shamanic destiny. Her test results were often confused because of "poor visual acuity" (inability to read a normal eyechart well). Whatever the reasons for Tayja's visual problems, they did contribute to keeping her isolated from mainstream social thinking. A quote from the physical examination on discharge from the University of Minnesota Hospitals states, "Visual field examination revealed bilateral constricted vision and a pinprick and vibration were decreased on the left side. These findings were compatible with hysterical sensory findings." (2/3/77)

Visual field is that part of the scene in front of the patient that she can see. Tunnel vision refers to the constriction of the visual field. "Pinprick and vibration" tests check for increased skin sensation. Certain patterns are seen in "real" (organic) disease due to distribution of the skin nerves. If an abnormal pattern is not seen, it is most likely that the patient is imagining the numbness.

Tayja's blindness, whether physical, psychological, or a combination, kept her "in the dark" until she was mature enough to withstand the temptation to gather society's approval by seeing as they saw. Shamanic causes are first spiritual, and physical results are considered secondary to the spirit and to the mind. Christianity espouses a similar idea which is clearly expressed in the story of Saul's blindness. Saul, "breathing threats and murder against the disciples of the Lord" went on a journey when "suddenly a light from heaven flashed about him. And he fell to the ground." At this point in his life, Saul was ill prepared for such glory, and when he rose in response to Jesus' command, "his eyes were opened, but he could see nothing." Following many prayers, the Lord called on him saying, "he is a chosen instrument of mine . . . " He was duly healed by Ananias who said, "Brother Saul, the Lord Jesus who appeared to you on the road by which you came, has sent me that you may regain your sight and be filled with the Holy Spirit.' And immediately something like scales fell from his eyes and he regained his sight."

In any event, the scales of Tayja's blindness served to protect her spiritual seed. For the spirit to take control, the mind must become subservient to the spirit. Once it has taken its rightful place, the mind—as servant to spirit—may expand to greater power with benefit to the shaman.

But first, the roller coaster of Tayja's life was to take her on another ride, this time into a psychological system that explored her childhood by leading her to enter it a second time.

Chapter Five
Reparenting,
A Healing Bridge

*Not caring for one another has always caused sickness
among a People. It is one of the means of the Medicine to
each man to care for his brothers.*

—Hyemeyohsts Storm
Seven Arrows[1]

The medicine of sickness was a powerful means for teaching Tayja, as well as the brothers and sisters who helped her along the way. The sickness that was Tayja's, born as it was of violence and non-caring, can be perceived as the microscopic reflection of the sickness of this planet where fear and anger or apathy often govern behavior, not only between nations but within nations, within families and within individuals. Even the Earth seems to respond to the violence on its surface as it trembles and quakes, boils with fire, pours acid tears from its clouds and blows buildings upon its people. It seems as though the Earth itself needs caring parents.

Surely Tayja needed such parents when, in desperation, she cried out in the lunchroom of the community college. Tayja was not completely surprised when ears were there to hear and a solution for the immediate problem was at hand. It was not the first time Tayja had felt that her guides were steering her life in some way beyond her own understanding; so it was in 1977 when the young woman in the cafeteria told Tayja she needed the program of reparenting which she herself was involved in. Tayja, anorexic at the time, responded by mustering what strength remained and calling a stranger, then going out to the Wigers' home for an interview with the woman who was to become her new mother.

Jeanne Wiger was well-qualified for her profession. She was psycho-education director for Wiger Woods (now The Creative Learning Center) and a clinical teaching member of the International Transactional Analysis Association. She had fifteen years experience in working with severely psychotic individuals and living with them as members of her family. The treatment she used involved a process of regressing the adult client to the time when the personality was damaged (usually babyhood), then assisting him or her to grow up again, this time in a healthy manner.

Not all at once, but gradually, wise caring spread its power, winning through a harsh test of love which often needed to be tough, waking to life the spiritual center that is the power of life. Tayja's reparenting mother came to recognize her new child's strong thrust toward health.

> When spirituality is thwarted [her new mother explained], its misdirected energy creates an increasing problem. I believe that a person is a spirit which, in my concept, started long before birth and will continue long after death. If a person is battered or eroded or damaged or whatever word you want to use with a father's hatred, by abuse of chemicals, or even by a genetic component so that normal evolution is distorted, then in some way that person will rebel. It will defend itself in an attempt to survive. So when the intensity of the spiritual drive is unusually great, it can be even more destructive. To use electricity as an example, you get more of a shock when you're running 220 volts through than when you're running 110.

Like any natural mother, Tayja's reparenting mother enjoyed recalling the promise Tayja showed in her "second childhood," and she laughed warmly as she described:

> When Tayja was little but old enough to be exploratory and up through four and five years old, I remember she'd crawl around the group room with a toy on a string, and she'd swing it around, and she'd say "Hang on, Jesus, you're going for a ride!" It was almost a trademark.

The Christ spirit would have to wait a while before Tayja learned to "swing it" through herself. As she wrote, "I prayed and prayed about being healed, asking the Grandfathers when it would be time. But not yet. I keep hearing, 'More work to be done.' "

Tayja's new mother explained the process:

> If you're going to bring mind, emotions, body and spirit into balance so that the person is free to use their talents productively, you need to break unsatisfactory patterns in order to permit change. I like to use the metaphor of a broken bone. If you put a broken and dislocated arm in a cast without setting it, the bone heals crippled. Then that bone may have to be rebroken so it can mend in a healthy way.

The same process is described in Halifax's *Shamanic Voices:*

> Shamanic initiation demands a rending of the individual from all that constitutes his or her past.[2] [Even the metaphor of bone is repeated in shamanic annals.]
>
> Bone, like seed, represents the very source of life. To divest oneself of flesh and be reduced to a skeleton is a process of reentering the womb of primordial life in order to be born anew into a mystical condition. Furthermore, bone, like a quartz crystal or seed, is the enduring source from which light and life spring anew. Shamans, like other religious ascetics, divest themselves of flesh, reduce their bodies to that mysterious yet durable matter . . . [3]

What Tayja's new mother saw was not a fledgling shaman, but a young woman plagued by anorexia, bulimia, and probably schizophrenia. It was clear to her that Tayja had missed out on healthy parenting the first time around, but it was not clear that Tayja's new mother was about to embark on the training of a shaman. Although her aims were more modest, they made room for growth without imposing limits. Jeanne explained:

> The goal of this is to facilitate the human ability to function in the world in such a way that the person can effectively use and share those talents which best make up their personalities. In order to do that, four areas of life: mind, emotions, body and spirit, have to be addressed and brought into harmony in a unified way. [Tayja's mother explained

this process, not with categorical labels, but as an organic process of growth.] This restructuring is especially necessary for people who have grown up in atypical homes, isolated, battered, whatever it might be that sets the groundwork for problems.

Before Tayja could find shamanic balance, her new mother would need to support her as she constructed the physical foundation. Although her mother knew something of that foundation, she did not know the structure that would be built upon it:

> The shaman is a healed healer who has retrieved the broken pieces of his or her body and psyche and, through a personal rite of transformation, has integrated many planes of life experience: the body and the spirit, the ordinary and the nonordinary, the individual and the community, nature and supernature, the mythic and the historical, the past, the present and the future. The threshold place of the initiatory experience is the two-light world.[4]

The first light Tayja's mother addressed was that of mind. Jeanne explains:

> Because of environmental deprivations or faulty train ing and example, there are unsatisfactory ways to come to conclusions, unsatisfactory ways to solve life's problems. Often such people get on until they leave home, then have problems because the world won't accept the ways of functioning which may have been acceptable in their family structure. So ways of thinking and reasoning are the first aspects of life that need addressing.
>
> The second is the emotions. Where there is a great deal of emotional and mental confusion, it is not enough to change the reasoning process. When thinking, feeling and actions are in harmony, the person is free to pursue an integrated life pattern, but when they clash, the individual is in trouble.
>
> We have all said, "I knew better, but I did it anyway." Re-educating the mind, although necessary, is not sufficient. Emotions have to be addressd also.
>
> The third aspect is the body which certainly impacts on

the therapy I find important to do. Every cell really is a hologram, and more and more we're aware of that. We are microcosms of the whole cosmic universe. You can't expect long-lasting, meaningful change to take place if you don't involve the body in it. As I understand it, the difference between counseling which is mental and concentrates on talk, and therapy which I understand as wholistic, is this body involvement. You literally go in and create opportunity for people to make basic root changes within the body where emotional life experiences are stored.

Finally, the spirit has to be involved—Not some kind of religion, but that quality that makes humans aspire beyond what we think of as physical reality.

Without reservation, Tayja believes in the ability of the spirit to change the mental, emotional and physical bodies, a shamanic view in harmony with the psychological views of her reparenting family which was to prove important to her recovery.

Some of the warping of Tayja's spiritual thrust may be seen in her relationship with her brother, Pony, with whom she had a powerful psychic communication. Pony showed her both care and violence. Although nearly blind himself, he made his way to the garbage dump near their home and brought his sister discarded food and a few "treasures." Yet he also threatened and frightened her—as well as himself.

Perhaps most important, her biological mother supported Tayja's spiritual life and recognized her visions as communications from a God-directed spiritual world guiding Tayja's life. Yet she, alcoholic and battered herself, neglected her child's basic needs for care. Spirituality in Tayja's experience was clouded by fear, pain, and abandonment. She had seen death and violence at a young age, and predictably, her fears and rages brought nightmares and horrifying thoughts and visions which, more often than not, crowded out the gentle voice of comfort she occasionally knew. Yet those small voices never totally left her, and she continued to contact her "friends." (Now she calls them her "spirit guides.")

Jeanne outlines conditions for change:

To permit constructive change in the mind, emotions, body and spirit of the individual, three conditions need to be met: First, the mind needs to be made aware of the process; second, a safe environment in which to work out new patterns needs to be provided; third, developmental gaps need to be filled in.

Tayja's mother explains these conditions and the methods of addressing them which are used in the reparenting home:

First we deal with that thinking process so each individual has the understanding to participate in his or her evolvement. It's not a one-up one-down proposition. If there is a false reasoning process, the missing pieces have to be supplied so the person has the tools with which to think and solve problems. Otherwise the person is like someone who has a computer, but nobody has shown her now to turn it on or how to use it.

The second thing is, there has to be a safe place in which a person can move back through a catharsis around the pain that they experienced, whether that pain is birth trauma or incest or child abuse or abandonment or anything that interrupted the individual's mind/body/spirit's development.

Tayja refers to this in her journal:

"I have figured out the reason all the violence has started coming out at this point is because two years ago it wouldn't of been safe. [Tayja entered Wiger Woods in the fall of 1977.] The protections needed to be clear and straight. 1. rope, 2. cuffs, 3. treatment. Needed to know the investment of Mama and Daddy, if the going got rough if they would leave me. *And they haven't.*" (The safety measures Tayja refers to will be explained later.)

Jeanne continued,

The life pattern, like the badly healed arm, needs to be broken, then reset. This time the person is shown how to move back through the experience with enough support so that the outcome can be different. Every person is on the horns of a dilemma; first, a thrust toward growth, toward change; second, terror of the unknown. So there is a pulling to make the present be like the past and an attempt to reestablish the status quo. The greater the trauma, the greater the dilemma.

In corroboration Tayja journals, "I feel confused and the grief of giving up the crazy." Jeanne continues:

> During this process, support is essential so that the outcome of the reexperiencing is really different than it was the first time.

In the Wiger home, safety was not achieved easily. Tayja's new brothers and sisters might suddenly attempt to attack each other or her. They could retreat into autistic silence, jabber meaninglessly, or be stricken by paranoid fears. For their safety, they might be restrained in their beds at night or "put on the rope" in the day time. This involved tying a rope around the disturbed person's waist, then putting a caring brother or sister in charge by tying the other end around his or her waist. On January 3, 1980, Tayja journals, "Today I feel very violent . . . I feel like killing me or someone . . . Mom asked me if I wanted to go on the rope, and I said, 'Yes, for my own protection.' "

The necessity to restrain the kids was difficult for all concerned. On June 9, 1980, Tayja writes:

"I woke up pulling frantically at the handcuffs. What I had in my mind was to get out no matter what. I started to pull and pull. I was feeling very strange in my body. There was a cold sweat and the adrenaline. It felt like my skin was racing. Then I finally cathected my adult and felt okay again . . . [Tayja had been taught how to invest her Adult ego state with libidinal energy; how to become conscious of and use her adult thought processes.] "Mama took all my razor blades and Aspirin so that I couldn't take them and hurt myself. I feel really frightened and feel like it's going to be really scarey keeping myself safe. Mama is glad I gave her the razor blades. She gave me a hug and said, 'Thanks.'

August 4, 1980. I hope Mama not sick because of the problems I've had all week . . . I picked up that it's hard for her when I have to go into handcuffs at night."

Occasionally Jeanne would read her kids' journals, but not without their permission. She wrote Tayja a note, answering her concern:

Dear Tayja,

You're right. It is hard for me to see my kids in handcuffs, still I know it is a good way for you to have protection, and that is by far the most important. Your safety needs to come first . . . It is important you stay close to me and the rest of the family while you are going through this.

Love, Mama

Jeanne continues to explain conditions for growth which reparenting techniques address:

Finally, the third aspect: Since there are specific developmental tasks that need to be performed at each stage of growth, whenever any of those tasks are missed, it leaves a hole, a blank spot that continues to show up regardless of how good the life or parenting may be the rest of the way. As it's not possible for any human being to be a perfect parent, there are missing pieces for all of us. Most of us can function without too much trouble with the small gaps we have; however, if there has been a serious developmental gap that is reinforced along the way, then the interruption in the adult life can reach such a magnitude that it can be destructive.

Although Piaget's research regarding developmental stages was based in a linear time framework so that the stages, once passed, were passed forever, later research has shown that experience can, indeed, be relived. Tayja's reparenting mother says:

What is exciting to me is that you can reopen that little window in time. Chronological time has nothing to do with it, so there really is that opportunity to correct the flow, given the proper setting and the willingness of the individual to do the hard work involved. She can go back and reclaim the things that were missing. That's why the regression work is so important. It isn't just play acting, not merely a gestalt; it is literally going back through that little window in time and reliving formative experiences in her early childhood, redoing what was missed the first time. Then she doesn't have to go through life empty-handed.

Tayja got in touch with that empty-handed feeling during regression work and wrote on June 23, 1980:

" . . . The image was an infant age about one or two, and the bars on the crib were awful . . . I play the tape of 'Brahms Lullaby.' It sounded really special to me. I cried and felt very sad and unhappy. I kept hearing the message, 'Look what I have missed.' My small Child was hurting."

Jeanne summed up her explanation:

That's how I experience it: four areas dealt with in three ways, three ways which have to be carefully separated to keep them from becoming muddled. For example, if a person goes back to a two-year-old experience, that has to be dealt with as regards the emotional trauma stored in the body, also the learning experience of the two-year-old so the healthy and the unhealthy don't become enmeshed. Then those processes have to be clear in the mind.

A prime condition for implementing these aims is a framework of understanding and communication. Toward this end, a working knowledge of transactional analysis was taught to all participants in the reparenting program within the first few sessions. This system of explaining the personality provided an important tool for clarifying mental/emotional patterns and communicating within a mutually understood linguistic system.

In Transactional Analysis theory, the human ego is perceived as being divided into three parts which, in the standard T.A. diagram, are depicted in three circles stacked up like a snowman: the Parent on top, the Adult in the middle and the Child on the bottom. The Parent ego state, primarily programmed by the child's parents, gives healthy or unhealthy messages about life and by so doing presents the personality with a "script" by which to make sense (or non-sense) of self, others and the world at large.

This concept of subtle programming somewhere below the level of a child's consciousness is by no means new. One hundred years ago J. M. Barrie, the visionary who wrote *Peter Pan* describes a mother:

When the children are in bed she likes to sit beside them tidying up their minds as if they were drawers. If they could keep awake, they might see her repacking . . . many articles of the mind that have strayed during the day . . . When they wake in the morning the naughtinesses with which they went to bed are not, alas, blown away, but they are placed at the bottom of the drawer; and at the top, beautifully aired, are their prettier thoughts ready for the new day.

Tayja's thoughts were not so conventionally programmed. She did not consider her spirituality "acceptably pretty," and other messages were scrambled in the drawer of her mind in unusual ways. Near the end of her reparenting experience in the spring of 1982, she gave the script her Child ego state received from her parents as follows:

3. Infants are not fed enough food
4. Infants don't cry
5. Infants take care of themselves
6. Infants are in pain
7. Infants go away a lot—away from mothers
8. Infants are no good

Tayja's reparenting mother adds, "Infants are not safe; the world is not a safe place."

To clarify the script messages she wished to change, Tayja then reversed the above, stating her aims for restructuring her Child ego state in reparenting. Tayja's corrections of 6 and 8 are:

6. Infants don't need pain to know they're alive.
8. Infants are fun people—boys or girls, good and healthy, smart, special.

The Adult ego state is the rational part of the personality which handles problem solving, memory and thinking. The Adult ego state may be contaminated by judgements from the Parent ego state which has been incorporated into the personality (not to be confused with the actual parents who give the messages). Young children may garble the adult ideas, and by so doing incorporate programming different from the messages intended by the adults. The Adult may also be contaminated by emotions from the Child ego state. The Child harbors feelings, needs, and adaptive behaviors employed to get needs met so as to feel loved and nurtured. The Child needs "stroking," the T.A. term for both physical and verbal nurturing, to feel loved and worthwhile.

According to T.A. reparenting theory, health for the psychotic person can be achieved by removing, "decathecting" (or removing energy from) the unhealthy parent messages which have registered in the person's Parent ego state and replacing them with healthy messages. Some of the Parent messages Tayja has listed are, "I think it's funny to hurt, funny to be sad, to suffer. What else can you do? No one loves you. Who cares? Life isn't for you, cut up, fool them all, fuck up." Reversing harmful messages is accomplished by assisting the client to regress to babyhood, a state easily arrived at by most schizophrenics, for on some level they seem to know they need a second chance to grow up. This is also an easy accomplishment for many extremely psychic people, as is Tayja. So for her, reparenting (including rebirthing which will be explained later) was an extremely important part of self-integration.

Once the vulnerable baby is exposed, the explosive store of emotions can be released and in the calm after the storm, the new Child is ready to be reprogrammed with loving, nurturing messages. The adult "baby" then learns that anger will not bring rejection, and violence may be appropriately released in a controlled manner which will not result in harm to self or others. With many difficulties and setbacks, the door to love and trust begins to open.

Although her Indian mother stayed in Tayja's heart as the blood connection to her people, the neglect she suffered as an infant marked her personality with painful thoughts and feelings she needed to leave behind her in order to grow.

"Mom says the reason I have so much anger has to do with that's all my parents showed was anger. Mom says I need to cut off family ties altogether, so I am going to do that. It makes me too upset to talk to them . . . I am really scared too . . . I need to bury old Mom, and I want to do it Indian style like she would have wanted. She always said she wanted to be with her people. I can't really blame her. Nagi Nagi Nagi, Yka Yka Yka, Yua Yua mo Yua mo." (12/5/78)

Now Tayja looks at the Indian words in her journal and asks, "Whatever that means?"

She had gained a new mother. On August 26, 1980, Tayja wrote:

"Mama gave me bottle and held me, exactly what I wanted, that kind of closeness from her. I feel so little when Mama holds me. I would love to crawl inside and feel the warmth of her body, also feel the sides of her stomach touching me ever so gently. [Here it is interesting to see that the "I" Tayja forms is a womblike circle. The bonding becomes extremely close.] It was okay. Mom says she loves me, and I know I love her. I think this is the only family that I have or ever had . . . "

According to the medicine wheel of the Plains Indians, the place of trust is with the mouse in the warm grass of the south:

To Touch and Feel is to Experience. Many people live out their entire lives without ever really Touching or being Touched by anything. These people live within a world of mind and imagination that may move them sometimes to joy, tears, happiness or sorrow. But these people never really Touch. They do not live and become one with life.[5]

The emphasis on touching was part of the reparenting program. Tayja, seemingly like the clients in the reparenting home, had not learned to accept the loving words and gentle stroking which must be part of a normal child's development. Lacking this, Tayja had learned autism. With child logic, she formed the idea that a cry which brings abuse must be stifled on pain of death. The rage goes underground where it resides in the unconscious, waiting to erupt, often without notice either to the one experiencing the explosion or the one receiving the violent treatment. In this way the child gives what he or she was given, thus perpetuating the violent family pattern.

As might be expected, many in the psychiatric profession are skeptical of the reparenting of adults. Physical intimacy with patients is generally regarded as unprofessional, hence it is avoided either because of belief in regression as a pathological symptom or out of fear of censure. However, before accepting a negative view of the process, it is important to consider the alternatives. Many severely psychotic young people, especially those with no family support, are locked in the back wards of institutions, often drugged, often kept from hurting themselves or others by physical restraints. Tayja, who had been on the streets endeavoring to support herself since she was fourteen, had few alternatives, yet she continued to seek for a way to survive. A letter 'To Whom It May Concern" from the Minnesota Department of Economic Security, Division of Vocational Rehabilitation has this to say concerning Tayja's condition:

The psychologist's opinion stated that the client was

introverted, emotionally labile and lacked personal insight and foresight. An unusual problem was that she could read at an eighth grade level only if the material were presented upside down. She had great difficulty reading right side up at even the first grade level.

The hospital material indicated a severely disturbed family history and a long history of severe mental disturbances with a variety of both functional and psychotic diagnoses including somatic muscle weakness. [This refers to muscle weakness but doesn't specify whether it is due to emotional or "organic"—i.e. disease related problems. "Somatic symptoms" *usually* refer to emotionally induced bodily symptoms.] The list continues: Chemical dependency, personality disorder, frigidity, depressive neurosis, dependent personality and atypical psychosis. In addition, the client has had a number of surgical interventions and physical diseases and has irreversible damage to her kidneys and a chronic nephritis for which she may need periodic treatment for the remainder of her life.

It is my opinion that without intensive individual and group treatment this person's life span will be drastically shortened by her combination of functional and psychotic disorders which will either lead her to possible suicide or severe physically debilitating functional disorders. On a cost-benefit basis I believe that the client's current choice of therapy has a better chance of succeeding than more traditional therapy approaches. (3/14/78)

On that thin note of hope, Tayja entered her reparenting home in the fall of 1977 to remain until the spring of 1982. It was time to steer a new course to health and wholeness. She writes of the beginning of her stay in her new home:

"We spent time just attempting to be able to ride in the car with me because I couldn't see things. Suddenly buildings or other cars would just be there, real close, and I was scared we'd be hit and grabbed at the dashboard or the steering wheel. My mother said she had a hard time with me, and long trips were hard."

What was right side up and what was upside down? Out of her visual mist, Tayja reached for a wheel to steer her own life to safety, sometimes attempting to grab it from the hands of her reparenting mother.

"The groups were strange to me. I had problems just eating enough to stay alive. I got much confrontation. I went out there on Halloween night, my first real encounter with the treatment. Everyone was dressed in masks, and I felt very scared because I didn't know anyone. I started to meet the family one by one. They were roasting a pig, and God, that was terrible! All I could think of was that poor pig. In my growing up, animals had been my friends and also got the same abuse I did. The woman and the man looked so big to me! The woman of the program was six feet tall, and the man was six feet two or so. The two biological sons were also what I saw as giant size.

"I went to nine groups a week and had two private appointments. There were seven people in the groups at that time. Besides the treatment things, I got involved making suppers and cleaning to keep myself busy. The house was big and full of antiques, and they also had a library that I didn't like. The home had a pool and lots of ground to walk around. I found a place to make as my ground to just sit and ask my friends (guides) for help. The Grandfathers would come, and the wind people, and I even had a squirrel or two come and sit for a long time while I talked to the Grandfathers."

One of the disciplines employed as part of the treatment was journaling. Every day the "kids" were expected to enter their experiences of the day, especially the issues confronted and feelings aroused in group work. Tayja kept her journals faithfully in ten spiral notebooks, over 200 pages from 1977 to 1982. Brief mentions of feelings and hurts are often repeated. Equally abbreviated are dramatic stories of her childhood. All are given with minimal visual detail. Tayja had five or six distinctly different handwritings, only some of which were dyslexic. Most of them were clearly legible, and written or printed on the lines of the paper. Whatever authorships they may have, they express Tayja's intimate feelings about this strange new experience, one that was to make her wise in the ways of pathological behavior.

Tayja had, according to medical records, "given much effort to organizing, rationalizing, and reliving her past, and this may make her a good candidate for reconstructive varieties of psychotherapy." (2/21/77)

Facilitating growth from an unhealthy to a healthy state necessitates a view of health: the ability to see the essential goodness and potential for growth in every human soul. Tayja could not see her own. She was mirror to confusions, externally and internally, emotionally and behaviorally: What age was she? What was expected of her? What did she feel? Where was safety? Then perhaps most important, who was she? Through her journals, Tayja tries to sort it out:

"Dec. 1, 1977. Mom spent time with me in morn. She fed me a bottle. I feel really strange with that. I feel really exposed and vulnerable . . . There was a man in group I felt really uncomfortable with . He looked like he was lying on the woman he came with which scared the hell out of me . . . Fear of violence . . . *No sleep.*

" . . . worked on some sadness in group but I have it so blocked I couldn't really get into it . . . My feelings sometimes get mixed up. What is anger and what is sadness and what is fear? [In an atmosphere of violence, the immobilizing effect of fear can, paradoxically, be experienced as too fearful an emotion to tolerate and may be replaced with anger, so masking passivity which could be felt as life-threatening.]

"Next group was really different. I needed to work on sadness and hurt because my chest felt like there was fifty pounds on it. [. . . as though Frightened Mouse was being crushed by Wounded Bear.] So I laid on the mat, and they laid across my chest, and two people held my arms. God what pain! I started motions of throwing up, but I just couldn't . . . Just tight scared! And sick. Mom worked with me and helped me. I feel good about that . . . Sleep really poor, two hours.

"Dec. 4, '77. Well, today I asked C. to give me a bottle, and she did, but I felt really uncomfortable with it. I like to be talked to or sung to. I had to ask for that. My head hurts a whole lot. I am feeling sick to my stomach, and I am feeling for the first time, depressed. It must be the feelings of sadness and hurt. I am fighting from feeling them. I resist a lot. I'm going to sit for C.'s kids, and I'm just exhausted. I feel so rotten . . .

"Dec. 5, '77. Didn't eat all day.

"Dec. 7, '77. Well, counseled with Mom and got some good information in my adult. Mom wants me to be able to pick up information first. I felt close to Mom. I sense like I am starting to cling to her, and I don't know if I can let myself start doing that. The fear of her leaving me scares me a lot.

"Dec. 10, '77. Worked in group on anger and got into becoming so little that I didn't do anything for myself for at least two and a half hours. Mom gave me a bottle and held me. I was so afraid . . . Have been really fearful at night a lot again. But too afraid to tell Mom.

"Dec. 11, '77. Today was a strange day. Mom made me sit and try to eat something, but I couldn't. She says I have to work on it. She's not going to allow me not to eat. She says it's schizophrenia behavior."

Tayja was ready to work. Her choice is made clear in the following poem which she wrote later in December:

"I feel the need to write a poem or something, what that is I don't know. I've never written before. Well, I'm going to drink my bottle and go to sleep.

God, please take care of me
Guide me through the night
Let me be able to wake up and
Get what I need, do what I need
I love thee so much, I know you won't let me down
You love people who love themselves enough to Change
So please, I pray that you'll help me
Go over the hump to Freedom of Life.
Thanks, God, for listening to me.

Finally cried self to sleep . . . tears began to flow really heavy . . . God took care of me."

Chapter Six
Shamanic Illness

The encounter with dying and death and the subsequent experience of rebirth and illumination are the authentic initiation for the shaman. Although this process frequently takes the form of an inner experience, the symbolism and feelings have many unusual parallels in the experience of actual biological birth. Furthermore, it provides a very different perspective on so-called psychopathological states, whether they be "culture-bound reactive syndromes" such as "Arctic hysteria" or "acute schizophrenia" in the West.

—Halifax
Shamanic Voices[1]

From the threshold between life and death, Tayja cries for help, for release to one side or the other:

> 5/4/77   HELP KILL ME
> HELP KILL ME
> HELP KILL ME

Who could understand the shamanic voices in the womb of her being—the voices she herself did not understand? Few in Western culture had heard them in the conscious mind.

Those who have nearly died, through an accident or severe illness, or who have suffered a psychological or spiritual trauma of such proportions that they are catapulted into the territory of death will come to know the inner workings of crisis.[2]

Tayja had drugged herself, starved herself and mutilated herself until body and soul seemed strangers to each other. Yet wholeness is a fact of being which Tayja fought to realize. On March 27, 1978 after she had been in reparenting for one year, Tayja writes:

"I am going to get well in spite of what else happens, no matter what is put in the way. God is testing me again.
Alone. Don't leave me alone!!
God help me!!"

Crisis in the exploding atom, crisis in the individual psyche, and crisis on our planet are more closely related than our categorically isolated thinking has led us to believe. From sources as ancient as the Bible and as modern as holonomic theory of the eighties, it is affirmed that healing the part is tantamount to healing the whole. As the mystic poet George Russell writes, "There are corridors in the House of our being, leading into the hearts of others, and windows which open into eternity, and we hardly can tell where our own Being ends and another begins, or if there is any end to our Being."

Likewise, holonomic theory holds that all exists in each of us, and we exist in all. In the words of the physicist Werner Heisenberg, one of the founders of quantum theory: "The world thus appears as a complicated tissue of events, in which connections of different kinds alternate or overlap or combine and thereby determine the texture of the whole."[3]

In the case of mental illness, this normally changing "tissue of events" may be blocked in a clutch of fear and stored in the body. The shaman must break clear of these entrapments, melt the blocks of fear, changing them to a stream of experience. Doing this will bring the unconscious realms of the dark and the transpersonal lights of the spiritual realms to a unity—the balance of the middle way or "red road" as the native American shaman would term it. In the shamanic disciplines of Asia, it is the still place between pairs of opposites, the place of divine balance. So long as exclusive definitions such as sick or well, dark or light, male or female, good or evil, past or present, life or death, pull people away from the red road, we can look at one side while closing our eyes to the other. But the shaman must change the or's to and's and look at opposites from a two-light threshold. Here opposing forces are not obliterated, but transformed. This is accomplished through an alteration of consciousness.

As Korean shamanism perceives it, the shaman's personality must become fractured to permit guiding spirits to enter. Through this fracture, hurtful spirits or energies may also enter, and it is the presence of these dark energies that is known the world over as shamanic illness. Only through dedicated work can the shaman complete the initiation and gain control of these energies. Then he or she is ready to fulfill life's mission.

According to traditional shamanic religion, Tayja would be thought to be afflicted by malign spirits who had entered and claimed her mind. The shamanic treatment objective would be to expel the evil spirits from her mind and body. This task was thought to be most effectively accomplished by one who had succeeded in expelling evil entities from his or her own being: a healed healer.

Tayja was not born in a tepee and welcomed as a shaman into the unified hoop of the Sioux nation. Instead, her modern urban society called her mentally ill, a schizophrenic.

A modern psychiatrist stated, and many share his view that: "Schizophrenia is a brain disorder just as multiple sclerosis is a brain disorder, and it is chemical in causation. It is not caused by problems in childhood." Research on laboratory animals and treatment of human subjects have, in part, supported the doctor's thesis. He would probably not dispute that there is more to say, but he would stop far short of carrying the sources of schizophrenia into realms of the soul's choice and spiritual destiny.

Tayja's reparenting mother sees a fine line between the psychic and the psychotic. The transpersonal psychiatrist Stanislav Grof describes this relationship:

> In a large group of transpersonal experiences, the extension of consciousness seems to go beyond both the phenomenal world and the time-space continuum as we perceive it in our everyday life. Common examples are the experiences of encounters with spirits of deceased human beings or suprahuman spiritual entities . . . This expanded cartography of the unconscious is of critical importance for any serious approach to such phenomena as psychedelic states, shamanism, religion, mysticism, rites of passage, mythology, parapsychology, and schizophrenia . . . It has deep and revolutionary implications for the understanding of psychopathology and offers new therapeutic possibilities undreamed of by traditional psychiatry.[4]

This view of consciousness goes a long way toward bridging the no man's land between ancient spiritualism, or shamanism, and modern psychology. Tayja had much work to do before she could walk that bridge. When she began therapy in her reparenting home, she received a complete medical and psychiatric examination. She was given consistent monthly examinations thereafter by the same psychiatrist. An excerpt from Tayja's psychiatrist's first report follows:

> It is my professional opinion that a change in diagnosis is indicated. Tayja's previous diagnosis was "Dependent Personality Disorder" which describes, "an individual who subordinates one's own need to a dominant other person to avoid responsibility and decision making." In contrast to his type, she has avoided close relationships. She is dependent only in a functional sense, due to her general mental impairment, but not in a psychological sense.

> Another of Tayja's previous diagnosis was "Borderline Personality Disorder." This also was ruled out.

> The new diagnostic category for "borderline" is Schizotypal Personality Disorder which describes essentially the same features as "borderline": social isolation, oddities of thinking, perception, and behavior, dysphoric mood, suspiciousness, and proneness to eccentric convictions. Both diagnoses describe personality disorders and are invalidated when psychotic manifestations are present. [Psychiatry contends with frequent changes concerning precise categorical definitions for mental illness.] Her past and current mental condition meets, unfortunately, the criteria for Schizophrenia Hebephrenic Type. Her mental illness is chronic. (2/27/80)

Perhaps the popular term for schizophrenia, "split personality," opening the door to imprecision, describes Tayja's mental/emotional/ spiritual state more inclusively.

The inclusion of opposing states of mind without integration shows up in Tayja's journals:

> "December 7, 1977. I feel like I just want to follow Mom around and be under her feet all the time . . . [Then in the same journal entry] Oh, watch yourself, she can get you that way. [As well as vacillating between trust and suspicion, Tayja vacillated between adult and child

comprehension] Mom came back to work with me, and I told her that I was feeling really scared and like I didn't understand what people were saying to me sometimes. Or I will repeat myself without understanding what I really was saying. She says that's from getting little."

Tayja's reparenting sister, Jane (not her real name), has an explanation of hebrephenia which comes closer to the shamanic model. Her story begins with their meeting: "When I met Tayja, I was just a baby myself. It seems so long ago." The young woman in her thirties had been a baby just six years ago. Now she has earned her M.A. and is working as a reparenting therapist at The Creative Learning Center helping others as she was helped.

When I asked for her first impression of Tayja, she described the dark pole to Tayja's personality:

> The first time I saw her, she was down on the mat with five people holding her. She wanted to murder every person in the room. The amount of hatred, violence, and venom she was pouring into everybody was pretty overwhelming. Then I saw her get extremely little and extremely like a baby. At that time she was going to nine or ten groups a week and even doing work outside of those groups. So I thought, "This person is very disturbed."

I asked Jane to tell me her concept of hebephrenia. She had just returned from a workshop in California and was eager to share her information.

> When someone gets the label, "hebephrenic," that person is considered by many professionals as state-hospital back-wards material, and automatically professionals give up. It is the most difficult kind of schizophrenia to treat. A hebephrenic schizophrenic can be very dangerous. They can be out to kill everybody. If you know that the person who is sitting across from you has a fantasy of taking a knife and cutting your heart out and eating it and is enjoying the fantasy, you get kind of an idea of what thoughts might go through that person's mind and what some are, in fact, capable of doing.

Tayja, however, never hurt anyone at any time during her years of reparenting. Jane continues:

To put this diagnosis into perspective, only about seventeen per cent of the hebephrenics treated by reparenting therapists get well. It is very primitive, meaning that it starts very early in life. The problem often begins prenatally. The earlier your problems originate, the more primitive the disorders and the less the chances are for cure.

Usually people who are hebephrenic have been diagnosed childhood schizophrenic first. [Tayja was not. Her reparenting mother believes that, had she not been Native American, she would probably have been diagnosed earlier.] Symptoms will show up almost as soon as the person starts to mature and develop. There is some disruption in primitive physiological responses. When a baby is born, it is a natural response for the baby to feel hunger and cry, and then as a response to crying either get a bottle or breast. That's an early, primitive cycle. For people who are hebephrenic, that cycle doesn't get connected. Sometimes hebephrenic babies are premature, were tube fed, then, since feeding was automatic, never learned to recognize the hunger stimulus, then connect it with an external environment which could provide them with nurturing.

These were the conditions of Tayja's premature birth. Because of this, she could not suck through a straw.

Whatever the reason in the external environment, what ends up happening is that the baby over-adapts to the mother or caretaker to the pathological degree that they don't allow themselves to feel hunger, and they don't make demands. Then what happens is that hebephrenic babies generally do not cry and will lie there and wait for their caretakers to feed them. So they don't have any sense of power. A person builds power in the world by learning that when they make demands, some response is forthcoming from a caretaker or some other person. A hebephrenic baby doesn't feel hunger, doesn't cry, doesn't learn she or he can have an impact on the world, and is passive. Then, not feeling the pain of hunger generalizes to not feeling physical pain, period. They discount their body because they don't feel it. So there is a mix-up between pleasure and pain.

Tayja gives her side of this situation journaling on August 12, 1980: "This A.M. I was not physically feeling anything, total shut down—Questions, where did I go? How did I get hurt and not know it?"

Jane continues:

> In order for the baby not to feel physical sensations, a neurological pattern forms in the brain so the person does not have a [functioning] bridge, the corpus callosum, between the right and left halves of the brain.

The great bridge between the hemispheres is made up of a band of nerve fibers which make it possible for nerve impulses to travel between the right and left hemispheres of the brain, thereby coordinating thought and action. In people with hebephrenia there is massive perceptual disorder with neurological signs similar to those resulting when the corpus callosum has been severed between the two hemispheres of the brain, thinking is not generalized and quite literally, the right hand does not know what the left is doing. This sets up the mechanism for denial which is, as Jane explains:

> a major part of the way they deal with all of reality, including themselves and other people.
> This includes denial of stimuli, denial of information, even denial of their own being. The number one problem for somebody who is hebephrenic is that of *existence*. They simply don't know that they are alive in a body on earth. That's because existence for each of us is connected to those physical sensations of hunger, pain and pleasure. A person who is hebephrenic does not have those connections, and they don't know that they are alive.
> Yet a part of them is obsessed with evidence that shows life, and that's why blood is often an obsession for people who are hebephrenic, because if you bleed or if they bleed, then they cannot deny that they are alive. So hebephrenics, without exception and even as children, exhibit behaviors where they self-mutilate. They'll make themselves bleed, they'll cut themselves, they'll burn themselves. The blood is some kind of indication to them that they must be alive, yet they don't really believe it when they see it, so they have to do it all over again.

The other thing that goes wrong for people who are hebephrenics is something happens when they are babies that prohibits them from doing normal everyday exploratory work. It could be that they were kept in a playpen way too much and were never allowed to crawl around. [Tayja spent most of the first six years of her life in a crib.] It could be some problem where they had casts on their legs like Tayja did, or something else stopped them from walking around on the floor and putting things in their mouth and exploring like healthy babies do.

These babies miss the oral work as well as the exploratory experience, leaving serious developmental gaps. Without a way of acquiring sensual experience of the world, they have no real sense of what the world is. They don't explore, so they don't know boundaries. Jane continues:

The baby needs to make an attachment to a mother, but in order to do that, the baby has to know it's alive, and hebephrenics don't know that. Since they don't form an attachment to a mother, they don't form attachments to other people either. So they are like formless beings that aren't anchored to the body or to the earth, and they use denial of how much pain and hunger they experience as their basis for functioning.

This absence of a link to physical existence is an important structure to consider in the bridge between physical and transpersonal consciousness. If one doesn't realize existence in a body, the barrier to allowing the consciousness to leave it is removed. Thus Tayja's use of extrasensory abilities may have a base in the denial of a restraining physical body.

Tayja's sister describes hebephrenia in terms of the chakras, observing, "It is a crown chakra disorder."

The seven major chakras of the body are energy concentrations which may be seen as spirals of light by some people and felt as heat by nearly everyone who has experience in psychic or spiritual healing. These centers are located at the crown of the head, between and slightly above the eyes, at the throat, the heart, the solar plexus, about three inches below the navel and at the base of the spine. The energy of these spirals alternates so that each moves in the opposite direction from the one directly above and below it, so forming an orderly series of figure eights evenly balancing the energy.

Knowledge of these energy centers is shared by American shamans:

> All during the life of the person, the soul lives in the head. It is the soft spot, the crown of the head. It is the same thing, the crown and the life . . . That life force, it is as though it were connected to one by a fine thread. It is like spider's silk, this thread . . . When one is asleep, the life can leave the body.[5]

Most people are unaware of their chakras. Shamans, however, learn to control these doors in order to release their mind from its usual limits within the body. People afflicted with hebephrenia have an unusual problem. Tayja's reparenting sister explains:

> I've noticed the crown chakra is not connected to the other chakras. So you see, people with hebephrenia don't feel their root, their physical existence. When you see the energy field of a person with that problem, usually it feels like they are walking around with their crown chakra open all the time, and they're not grounded at all. Or they don't have a way to be grounded, and then they can fall prey to whatever energies on the etheric level want to connect with them at that point. It's because they are not grounded to the earth. I don't mean they are possessed in terms of demon possession. Rather it's a psychospiritual problem that allows their crown chakra to grow open leaving them unconnected to the lower chakras in such a way that they don't know that they're here. Then when other energies enter them, they don't know that they are not a part of the intruding energies. They don't feel separation or boundaries from those other energies.
>
> So the only way I've seen a hebephrenic person get control of their reality outside of therapy is by being violent. The violence really comes from their own being, the angry, hungry, needy part. When they walk around being that

sweet, silly part of them,—that's denying everything. They're very open prey for whatever etheric spirits are going to jump in and say, "Let's make a connection." When a hebephrenic person gets into the violence, that is their claim on their body and their claim on existence. They're very angry about the whole idea that they don't exist. I think that pretty much explains why a person with hebephrenia who hasn't resolved that question of existence becomes violent sooner or later.

Since the genesis of Tayja's denial of her existence began before birth, that was the point at which healing was necessary. "Mom took me on a fantasy of my birth," Tayja writes. To those of us who have difficulty remembering the events of our childhood, this reliving of infant states and even embryonic states, seems implausible. However, in the remarkable computer of our brain/mind, these memories lie dormant, waiting to be accessed. This faculty of consciousness has been extensively researched by Stanislav Grof and others. As Dr. Grof explains:

> Clinical observations from LSD psychotherapy suggest that the human unconscious contains repositories or matrices, the activation of which leads to the reliving of biological birth and a profound confrontation with death. The resulting process of death and rebirth is typically associated with an opening of intrinsic spiritual areas in the human mind that are independent of the individual's racial, cultural, and educational background . . .
>
> In this perinatal experience, LSD subjects can relive elements of their biological birth in all its complexity, and sometimes with astonishing objectively verifiable details.[6]

Although LSD was employed in Dr. Grof's consciousness research, he acknowledges that the same results have been achieved by others using nondrug psychotherapies, various kinds of body work, and meditation techniques.

As her reparenting mother remembers:

> With Tayja, the going back and dealing with the abuse— the chemical abuse, the battering by her father—was important because these abuses were already established in utero. Not only was she abused by her father, but her mother was abused by the medical profession. Because of being Native

American, because of the prejudices people have, Tayja's mother was shuffled from pillar to post. Then there were additional problems with the twin's death. I remember the guilt that Tayja lived with because she lived, and the other twin died. Guilt about this had been foisted on her, and she had been made to feel guilty, feel like a murderess because she survived while her brother died. This was considered her fault, so any abuse, any kind of mistreatment could be perpetrated against her because she had committed this awful crime. So it was important for her to go back and go through that whole experience claiming her own wholeness, her separateness and her health. This was necessary so she could see a purpose for coming into this life and choosing that particular vehicle, time and place and way in which to come into the world.

The extremes to which this abuse was carried appear in Tayja's journals:

"November 19, 1979. The Crazy beliefs, the crazy understandings, I had from my parents. What they did to my brother Pony and I. I went through the whole thing [in a group therapy session] how they tied us together for days at a time. I think I was two and he was three and a half. He screaming and I screaming."

Jeanne Wiger continues:

> I think that our approach to rebirthing is perhaps a little different than a lot of other approaches because we do think that a lot of things happen in utero for children. This has been validated by research.

For Tayja, her time in the womb was spent under the influence of alcohol from her mother's addiction and the effects of her father's physical abuse which undoubtedly caused a chemical stress reaction which reached the twin embryos directly through the umbilical cords. Of the time before birth Tayja writes, "I felt real little, just floating, upset though."

The dangerous trip through the birth canal is described by Dr. Grof:

> It is characterized by an excessive generation of various instinctual impulses with a simultaneous blockage of

external motor expression of any kind in the context of an extremely brutal, life-threatening, and painful situation. This appears to be the natural basis for the deepest roots of the Freudian superego, which is cruel, savage, and primitive. Its connection to pain, masochism, self-mutilation, violence, and suicide (ego death) is easily comprehensible and constitutes no puzzle or mystery if seen as an introjection of the merciless impact of the birth canal.[7]

In her journal, Tayja tells her side of the rebirthing experience:

"Mom had me get into a fetal position and started me going back and back to being in the womb and seeing my twin brother who was next to me. And we're sending messages back and forth about his not going to make it. The feelings I was having were terrible. Mom said, 'Start getting bigger in the womb, getting ready to be born.'

"I was born and already decided that I had to die. But my brother was the one that chose to die. I felt really sad and got teary eyed. After, I asked Mother to hold me, and she did, and we talked more. She says there are more good-byes to the twin brother and lots of tears and sadness to get over." (12/30/77)

The next day, Tayja continued her work. "I counseled with Mom, dealt with early birth, withdrawal problems during birth. Mom and I talked about going through it again during group and going through the scare. My biggest fear was to stop breathing. I asked Mom to hold me so I could get little and go through some tears. Infant tears is really hard for me to get in touch with."

Tayja goes on to tell of the life-threatening anoxia in her premature delivery:

"I worked on becoming small and going through the fear and the breathing thing. They pressed on my stomach and then they helped me clean my lungs by allowing me to spit up the junk in the lungs. I felt pretty good afterwards."

Completing the work around her traumatic birth was a long process. On July 31, 1980, two and a half years after her first rebirthing experience, Tayja chronicled in a childish scrawl, the suffering of a hero's journey:

"I not ready. Problems when I arrived, the cord being

cut. Where am I? I can't breath okay. God, what's happen to me? Mama, save me, don't push me away. Love me, take care of me. I can't live out here. I want to go back where I came from!!"

The personal triumph of birth, so long delayed, was now being recognized by Tayja's reparenting mother. "She needed to go through it in a way that was healthy and protected and nurturing, repeat the birth in a way she really could be the center of the universe and be nurtured and cared for."

Tayja writes, "Evening group back into it. I cried and felt my body jerk and also the neck was very hard to move. Went rigid, and Mom had a hard time. I cried, I screamed, it hurt, it hurt! I felt something happen in my head, but I really don't know what it is. My body was next to seizures. I felt so scared and pain, pain, pain. Something is happening, and more is to come—links, I hunch, are the right and left brain . . . Mom did Reiki on my head, and it came out that I was able to connect the right and left brain . . . "

The desperate emotion Tayja expressed on emerging from the tunnel of birth is understandable when one considers what Dr. Grof explains:

a certainty about the supply of life-giving oxygen is necessary before one can feel hunger or cold, notice whether the
mother is present or absent, or distinguish the nuances of
the nurturing experience.

Birth and death are events of fundamental relevance
that occupy a metaposition in relation to all the other experiences of life. They are the alpha and the omega of
human existence; a psychological system that does not
incorporate them is bound to remain superficial, incomplete, and of limited relevance.[8]

Was Tayja in this world, or had she left it with the consciousness of her dead twin? They had been so close. This identity confusion was to mark the next thirty years of her life. In the words of Tayja's sister, Jane, this struggle for identity becomes so desperate that:

You have a raving homicidal maniac who feels so violent
and so hungry that she could decide that she wants to kill
every person who she comes in contact with, but particularly

anybody who has been kind or anybody who has nurtured her. [Here it bears repeating that, although she did have the opportunity, Tayja never hurt anyone in her reparenting home.] That's why you have people with hebephrenic histories turning on their parents, so most hebephrenics end up being in prison if they're not hospitalized or dead.

Although Tayja never hurt anyone in her reparenting home, she was fearful of doing so:

"June 9, 1980. I told Dad that I felt worried about him because of my hebephrenic stuff, that he would be the one I would go after . . . To be careful. The homicidal Parent [Tayja's parent ego state] is getting more and more out front . . .

"June 22, 1980. Well, I've been in a very icky place . . . The dreams I've been having around killing Mom is awful. I am really scared . . . Mom confronted me about what's been happening. I didn't want to tell her, but I did, and she told me to clean it up."

Jane continues:

Because of the extreme denial system, they shift from violence to denial, then when they're in denial, they don't know how violent they've been. So often they won't remember that they attacked somebody. When the person is in denial, they are often very, very sweet and very, very adaptive, much like the passive baby who never made demands. They will mold themselves to do whatever the caretaker or person they perceive to be in authority wants them to do. Since they don't really know they exist, they are always looking at the external environment for cues of what they should be acting like, and their sweetness is a very shallow cover for denial of all sensations and feelings.

The discounting and denial of reality reaches almost unbelievable proportions in this disorder.

Tayja's sister hesitated.

We generally don't talk about these things because most people wouldn't believe it. But it is, nevertheless, true. I remember one time after group, everyone was sitting around the fireplace.—This wasn't Tayja—this was another woman who was diagnosed hebephrenic, who slipped out of the

sweet-and-silly into the homicidal. We had an open fireplace at that time, and she picked up a burning coal and
went after my mother with it. She was promptly restrained,
and one person got burned in trying to restrain her. But her
hands and body weren't burned at all from picking up the
burning coal.

Thus, the shifting of pain can mean a shift of reality for the body
as well as the mind. This is a powerful example of the power of our
minds to alter the physical body, and a conformation of the Eastern
theory of mind having supremacy over the body. The ability of Asian
shamans to walk on coals and even through fire has now been accepted
by many modern scientists, although they have no explanation for it.
A recent educational television program on the human brain showed
a segment of a Hindu shaman walking through fire and emerging
without burns. But one does not have to be a Hindu to accomplish
this. The Institute of Noetic Sciences reports:

> Times have changed. Over the past several years thou-
> sands of people have experienced firewalking themselves,
> and numerous articles have appeared on firewalking seminars
> being carried out regularly in North America and Europe.[9]

This same skill has a more practical application. Tayja's sister
continues:

> People who are hebephrenic can heal themselves and
> heal their physical bodies simply by thinking about it. If they
> happen to fall down and break a bone, they probably need
> to have people around them point out that it is broken. They
> may not be aware of it because they don't feel the pain. Then
> if it is x-rayed and a cast put on it, they will usually have the
> bone healed within 24 hours. This has to do with the denial
> of the physical body, "I'm not going to feel hunger; I'm not
> going to feel pain,"—to rearrange—that's what we get into
> when we talk about hebephrenia.
>
> When you are treating a person who's hebephrenic,
> getting them to think and solve problems is most difficult, so
> usually you spend the first two years of treatment getting
> them to think. You tell them about their diagnosis, and you
> work at getting them to stop the discounting and denial sys-
> tem. They need to relate to being whole people. You're not
> somebody who is going to kill them, or you're not somebody

who they have the right to kill. You make them real by teaching that life basically isn't that dramatic.

Because there is so much denial around their existence, they have to create a lot of drama around themselves in order to penetrate their denial system. Even ordinary things get charged with drama.

Jane reached for the ketchup bottle on our restaurant table as she was talking.

For instance, they can see a bottle of ketchup and think it's a bottle of blood and then imagine that the waitress probably slit her wrist and it dripped in there drop by drop before she brought it to the table.

Jane described the mental processes that push a hebephrenic person into homicidal behavior:

If somebody makes a mistake, then getting rid of them, maybe by sending them away or maybe by killing, is the logical thing to do according to that disorder. They don't know it's not okay. Basically they don't know there's a consensual reality because they don't think they exist. They don't know that other people agree on reality, so that gives them the right to change the rules.

They have a way of being very competitive around parents. If a parent, meaning somebody in authority who defines situations and sets limits, tries to tell a hebephrenic person how it should be, she'll hassle you unmercifully about why it should't be that way and think up all kinds of exceptions. Then, if you don't go along with their exception, they'll use that as a basis for why they should kill you or why they should be violent. They feel it's a life-threatening situation for them if they accept your version of reality. If they see things the way you say they are, then they have to relate to the fact that they're hungry and have bodies that feel—little things like that. They enjoy the drama of turning things around that you would call true and showing how they're not true in some dramatic way. It is typical for them to make up some kind of energy-charged fantasy and make everybody else relate to that reality. Mundane reality is outside their experience, that you get up, eat breakfast, go to work.

You know you have to relate to that, but they'd much rather keep things on a life-and-death level because on that level they begin to sense that they're alive.

Tayja demonstrated this kind of behavior in the course of her reparenting. Over a period of time she received a series of violent letters signed by her stepmother (her biological father's second wife). Among other things, they told Tayja of the death of her father. For a time her reparenting family believed the letters actually were from her stepmother. However, nearly a year later, the death of her father was reported in the obituary column of the newspaper. Jeanne Wiger then packaged the letters together with samples of Tayja's writing and mailed them to Mary Rowan, a graphologist. Her analysis established that the letters were, indeed, all written by Tayja in spite of drastic changes in the writing.

Jane continues:

So there are a lot of fantasies about lies and rejection, and because they're so dangerous as people and so malicious, rejecting them is sometimes a good option. It's the only type of schizophrenic disorder where this works. You say, "unless you stop acting like this, you can't live with us." You have to be firm and cold, and they absolutely hate that. They really do, because that means they have to relate to you and your reality. The only chance you have of winning in the competition is saying, "This is how I want you to relate to me, and if you don't relate to me this way, I'm not going to deal with you." When they hassle about reality, it really is for them a life and death struggle.

(Tayja says her reparenting family never threatened to reject her.)

They don't relate to a system of values which says, I'm important and you're important, it's okay for you to solve problems and have feelings and know you're alive; it's okay for you to be of service and loving to other people around you." So instead of changing what they do in response to a system of values, people with that disorder change what they do or who they are in response to whether they're bored or not. They want the kind of excitement they can find in a life-and-death situation.

There is a problem with hebephrenic people as they start to get well. What ends up happening is that, instead of being violent toward other people and deciding to kill others, what they do is get into all kinds of physical problems. That is, essentially, the violence turning itself inward, and it happens because they are still denying the grief about not having attachments.

The problem in Tayja's case was to change her thinking, then change her actions by non-acceptance of hurtful behavior, then she would "have freedom of life," as she put it, and be able to love. Once the joy of love relationships was felt, she had, far more than most people, the ability to heal herself and others.—Or do we all have it in equal measure? Can we all make our own reality? Is it our faith rather than our ability that is lacking? How strong are our minds? If Tayja can learn, then spread loving kindness, can't we all?

To complete the circle and attempt a bridge between physical and spiritual definitions of schizophrenia, it is helpful to look at consciousness as layers of awareness leading from the body to a spiritual awareness transcending it. As mentioned earlier, schizophrenia has been recognized as a chemical brain disease and has been successfully treated with drugs; however, the precise manner in which the chemistry becomes unbalanced is unknown. Since the brain functions as the most prolific gland in the human body producing 34 different secretions, both singly and in combination, the possibilities for malfunction are many and complex. Little wonder that it is difficult to find the perfect balance of medications for its correction!

When evaluating a non-chemical approach such as reparenting, it is the triggering of natural "medication" from that drugstore in the brain which should be considered. The brain can be described as spiritually tuned, and it will respond chemically to stimulation by positive mental/emotional experiences, and conversely it will respond hurtfully to negative stimulation. Many doctors have experienced patients taking a turn for the worse after a diagnosis of cancer. Important research by the medical researcher, clinician, philosopher and author Dr. Walter Cannon bears out the power of thought. In a paper on voodoo death, Dr. Cannon reports on his study of witch doctors. He found that their hexes do work; they have caused death. However, on examining the victims, Dr. Cannon found that they had actually caused their own deaths, literally scaring themselves to death through power over their own thought processes. Considering the power of emotions to influence brain chemistry, psychological approaches to the treatment of the roots of the chemical imbalance may well show a syndrome of causes which include both psychological and physical origins.

From a shamanic world view, the red road was missing from Tayja's map at that stage of her development. But even though she did not know her path, looking from a new time and space, it would seem that her shamanic path knew her. She would have to wait until June of 1984 to hear Tsonakwa say:

> A shaman, for the most part, falls into shamanism against his will. What happens, a shaman goes through a catastrophe or a string of catastrophes that enhance certain abilities within him and pull out unnecessary things to that purpose . . . He might fall into the depths of depression or insanity, for instance, and be literally crossed off by his society and then somehow through the strength of his spiritual life and through the strength of his intellectual life and his emotional life, somehow he heals himself, and this has happened in psychiatry, and in some cases psychiatrists take credit for it and in other cases are mystified by it.

The shamanic illness is usually not ended in a single stroke.

> He will have relapses time and time again either from an illness or psychosis or whatever, but each time he brings himself out of it, and each time he learns a little bit more about his process for himself, and it's a process that he cannot know or explain to anyone. There's something so deep and so spiritual and subconscious that he doesn't even fully understand what it is. It's more of a feel than think thing.

Tsonakwa did not feel that his best was an adequate explanation, but, "it's the only way I can describe it."[10]

Tayja's reparenting family began their joint work by peeling away the levels of Tayja's consciousness on the way to discover a treasure no one knew was buried there. On November 29th, 1977 at 9:30 A.M. Tayja made her first journal entry:

"I've already been in reparenting about nine weeks. Just now decided to write a little on how I feel and what I am going through.

Each day I'll write something for this book, feelings and violence or whatever comes up. I'll start from last night working in group. Nov. 28, last night I worked on feelings of not wanting to explode when I was on the mat. I felt like everyone was going to hurt me. But then I felt, no they're helping me. I started to visualize my father running after me with a knife and wonder why? Then I started going farther, then the screams came. The head-banging came then. My body was quivering and my blood seem to stop running for awhile. Now I can hardly breathe, and I am gasping for air. The violence has hit me. The screams got louder and louder, then my jaw closed tight. My foster mother pulled it down. The fear was great. Everyone held me down. Dad on my legs. Mom on my head. J. on my arm and L. on my leg. Then it was quiet. Mom and the rest massaged my body and then Mom fed me a bottle. My feelings when I am small are really overwhelming. I am really scared and really afraid. My body starts involuntary muscle spasms (seizures). My nerves in back of neck twitch. I can stay into my infancy kinda long, but still feels hard to ask for what I want. Bottle is good. Crying hasn't come easy for me yet. As a baby I cry little. My fear of being hit has a lot to do with it. I feel really helpless and very vulnerable. I feel really bad that I am not well. I feel it should just come natural, not forcing it out.

For Tayja this was only the beginning, and Tsonakwa's hopeful words of a future of strength between two worlds was years away.

> Shamanic initiation demands a rending of the individual from all that constitutes his or her past. Among the Siberian Yakut, the shaman is an observer of his or her own dismemberment. In that state of awareness, he or she learns the territory of death . . . spiritual forces that will guide as they consume.[11]

Just what is this force that shamans deal with? Tsonakwa's explanation depicts a shaman on the earth level. From that point he must reach from the dark cave of the underworld to the realm of the Grandfathers in the starry heights. He is helped to do this by the governing power of innua:

> Innua being the spirit that is given by the creator to each and every thing . . . Some people call it a "soul." Scientists may call it "chemical energy," and I call it "spirit." I was taught that there's no difference in a blade of grass in its life

and me in mine and that I was of no greater value than it. We are all integral parts of the sacred web of life, each responsible for a very weak strand. If one is plucked, the whole web will vibrate; if one is cut, the whole web is weakened.

Inside of the earth is the spirit of the earth. It's a living thing, our mother, and so the earth lives and will go on forever, and the grass grows in the spring, and the grass passes on the spirit of grass to its child, and the deer comes and eats the grass and takes the spirit of the grass into its life, and the deer gives birth to its child in spring, and they pass on the spirit and life of the deer so the deer will go on forever, and then mankind comes with his mighty bow, and he kills the deer, and he takes the spirit of the deer into his life, and we have our children, and we pass on our spirit, and we will go on forever too. So the earth feeds the grass, and the grass feeds the deer, and the deer feeds man, and if we reach down through that, we can touch the earth.

In opposition to this eternal life, there is "tonghak." As Tsonakwa describes it:

Tonghak is an anti-us. We don't see it normally, but it manifests itself in illness and trauma and psychosis in our lives. Tonghak is dangerous, it's malevolent. It's capricious. It can sweep down on an individual or a whole nation. It can come out of nowhere. It could be anything from small pox to war. Tonghak is an entity with which the shaman has learned to deal.[12]

Tayja was learning:

" . . . worked on my issues with my [old] father cutting my vagina up, castrating me. I was hitting myself, and Mom and Dad held me and told me to push the energy out, and Dad kept telling me he loved me, and he wasn't going to hurt me as old Dad did. Got in touch with power that I have. I forgot that I have power. Got lots of strokes."

Although Tayja had not yet heard the word, "tonghak," she knew: "Even in times when I stopped moving forward emotionally, I never gave up hope and faith. I knew exactly what was happening to me deep inside my spiritual mind."

Chapter Seven
Multiple Personalities;
Spirit Possession?

You and I are the problem, and not the world, because the world is the projection of ourselves and to understand the world we must understand ourselves. The world is not separate from us ... To be is to be related.

—*J. Krishnamurti*
The First and Last Freedom

The extreme separations fracturing our world today all seem to be reflected within Tayja. From the beginning she did not know who she was: "I drew two fetuses. I don't know which one is me or if either one is me ... I don't know what's a lie from the truth ... How did I get hurt and not know it?"

The developing shaman is traditionally a mystery to both self and others. Shamanic behavior seems bizarre to those within other cultural "realities" and nearly always frightens the uninitiated. Society's fear drives out the nurturing love which a shaman's developing human side needs in order to become congruent with Spirit. That spiritual light—the truth, the wisdom, the love within all life—propels the shaman latent within *all* people, to realize in physical behavior the spiritual pattern within the soul.

As has been shown, Tayja was physically isolated from consensual reality. Her crown chakra was open to the full spectrum: love/hate, wisdom/foolishness, truth/falsehood. Like a pendulum, her mind swung from one end of the spectrum to the other.

What was the resulting condition of Tayja's physical mind/body?

Many of her symptoms fit with a description of "Multiple Personality Disorder."

Many of her symptoms fit with the shamanic concept of "Spirit Possession."

This chapter will not give a diagnosis, but it will bring light to the two possibilities and show the thrust toward uniting the two. Tayja herself believed in both. Many shamans believe in mental illness, Tsonakwa among them. Some psychiatrists believe in the possibility of spirit possession, Dr. Ralph Allison is one of them.[1] Dr. Adam Crabtree, author of *Multiple Man: Explorations in Possession & Multiple Personality*, is another. His book with its insightful and nonjudgmental treatment of both psychological and spiritual approaches is important reading for those interested in this subject.

Who was Tayja, this changing woman, this woman who lived so intimately with death?

From the womb of her beginning Tayja's existence was unsure. She—perhaps all of us—had left the spiritual womb of creation. To replace that home, she had found no physical or mental unity within herself or separation from others. From a point of confusion with her twin brother as they exchanged messages in the womb, she moved to a point of confusion with her brother, Pony. As she had been tied to her twin in the womb, she had been physically tied to Pony, then tied to him mentally, her undeveloped sensory boundaries giving her no protection from intrusion of consciousness from beyond her body. Although it may be an asset to be without boundaries separating us from our creator, it is certainly not an asset to be without boundaries in this physical world. In her journal, Tayja recounts the exploitative use of an open consciousness.

"January 25, 1978. Well, met with Mom today, and she and I talked about the accidents I've been having. I told Mom that I have lots of feelings, but I don't know how to express them. So she told me to lie down on the couch.

I went back somewhere, and I could see my brother there, and I felt what was going to happen before it happened. My brother and I had a transference in minds. I took his mind, and at that time I felt his body [as mine]. He would tie me to a bed and start telling me he was going to enter my body, that I should close my eyes because it might hurt. So I would do that. He kept doing that 'till I wasn't sure anymore whose body was whose. I started seeing a cock when I would look in the mirror. He would be like a girl, I think. God, I was so scared of him! He was crazy. His aim was to make me hurt and rape women. He

would punish me in his own way. [I would do crazy things] since I took on his body. The body was not mine. It took lots of energy to fight him. I finally got free. Mom got me to let him go out of my body, but I don't feel he is really gone. My body is feeling really good now that I am free. I can finally feel my body. Mom says she didn't want me going to group because of being weak and needing the change. She doesn't want me to get hurt anymore. I had broken my toes on Tuesday, so they were still sore. But my foot doesn't hurt so much now." (Tayja had dropped a large package of frozen meat on her foot.)

Tayja's reparenting mother recalls another instance of the life/death relationship Tayja had with her brother, Pony:

Tayja said that, as children, she and her brother had made a pact that if one of them died, the other one would go to the grave and allow the spirit of the dead one to come into her body. Then, while she was with us, she got word that her brother had died violently. At that point she was determined to go to the grave and she, I really think, expected that she would die in that process. We did everything we could. I remember calling Jaqui [the originator of the reparenting technique used by the Wigers]. She made suggestions, and we followed that direction and did what we needed to do so that Tayja wouldn't be allowed to leave the house and do something that would be destructive to her. I remember we worked with her all through one night and into the next day. Jeanne laughed as she told me, "I remember her shouting, "You cows get off of me! I'm going to go *now*." There were five or six people holding her down, maybe more than that.

It is evident that Tayja did not have a clear concept of a female identity—one more confusion! On December 15, 1978, another of her sleepless nights, Tayja journals:

"Second group I worked on feelings of being a woman, and it went better than I thought. I got really angry when he told me I had a vagina and breasts. It really seemed impossible. For years all I heard from old Dad was that if you became a woman, he'd kill me, but my decision has to be I am a woman, and that's a fact . . . Mom says I am holding on to old Dad by hanging on to old messages. Mom gave me a bottle . . . I allowed myself to cry."

Sexual identity is one of the pairs of opposites for which the sha-man needs to find a balance. As Halifax describes it:

> The dissolution of the contraries—life and death, light and dark, male and female—and reconstitution of the frac-tured forms is one of the most consistent impulses in the initiation and transformation process as experienced by the shaman . . . It's manifestations in the realms of sacred be-havior are manifold.[2]

Krishnamurti's concept of a related world as quoted at the beginning of this chapter spins a many-hued web of relationships. The traditional Sioux join this concept of a related world, proclaiming that there is only one power, and it is the mirror for the universe reflecting its meaning to each individual. We can learn to connect in fear; we can learn to connect in love. We can change.

Modern science, as it spirals to wider and wider understanding with more and more interconnections, is now at the point of joining with the spiritual roots of most religions. Although it may still stop short of postulating a single source of all power, it does recognize an increasing number of connecting links, and there are an ever increas-ing number of holistic systems being postulated to hold the rapid growth of knowledge now exploding among us. Yet even as these joining forces draw together, people are defending against each other on both an individual and on a collective level.

In the face of these conflicting unifying/divisive developments, it is interesting that cases of Multiple Personality Disorder, once con-sidered extremely rare, are now mushrooming. Dr. Martin Orne, reporting in the *International Journal of Clinical and Experimental Hypnosis*, estimated that, "at least two to three times as many cases . . . have been reported in the last 10-15 years than in the entire 100-150 years prior to 1970."[3]

As we see our spiritual reflection, we gain the power to change our human behaviors which conflict with it. The individual multiple can be conceived as a metaphor of our fragmented world. Many of us wring our hands, assuming that because people are so conflicted, they can never come together. Perhaps the story of Multiple Per-sonality Disorder as the struggle of the human race reduced to the story of one individual can give hope even as it depicts a condition of inner war. Multiple Personality Disorder has been defined as "an extraordinary syndrome in which two or more integrated alter selves co-exist simultaneously in a single body. It appears to have roots in severe child abuse." Ninety seven percent of multiples report a history of childhood trauma.[4]

Tayja, in the biological and environmental experiences of her life, clearly demonstrates the four factors operative in the development of multiplicity as listed by Dr. Richard Kluft:

> 1. A biological capacity for dissociation. 2. A history of trauma or abuse. 3. Specific psychological structures or contents that can be used in the creation of alternate personalities. 4. A lack of adequate nurturing or opportunities to recover from abuse. [Although Kluft places the ability to dissociate first, the triggering factor for using this ability is abuse,] some set of traumatic experiences that overwhelm the individual's capacity to cope with them by any means other than dissociation. A growing and terrible body of evidence now shows that this is usually severe physical, sexual or psychological abuse by a parent or significant other in the child's life.[5]

Unbearable pain drives pieces of the whole into the unconscious mind where intense fear and the anger and hate each fragment harbors, may be kept—for a time—from destroying the person's ability to function or even to live at all. Shattering of the personality is a survival technique in response to extraordinary circumstances. As Tayja journals, "I feel like a ball of flesh waiting to explode." The pressure of emotion, like lava in an active volcano, may erupt at any time. With it comes one of the personalities which may or may not be known to the host or core personality. However, since the personality has split, each immature and separated bit, unaware of its fragmented state, attempts to direct the person as a whole. Dr. Kluft's first factor, the ability to isolate feelings and memories from conscious awareness, is evident in Tayja's quick-silver consciousness. Boundaries, in her life experience, had been unpredictable, fearful and often dangerous restraints. Imprisoned in a crib, unable to walk, Tayja had but one way to escape them: flights of consciousness. It was as if the glue which binds most people's experiences into some kind of totality was missing in Tayja. This opening in the structure of consciousness is considered a vital factor in the developing shaman as it is in the developing multiple. Korean shamanic religion holds that:

Spirits in search of human beings to possess and use as mediums tend to gravitate toward those individuals whose "heart" or "soul" has already been "fractured" and made vulnerable by some psychological distresses. They also believe that all potential shamans experience "possession sickness" of varying duration, during which time they may behave in ways that can cause them to be mislabeled as insane. Moreover, they believe that recruits can become permanently crazy if shamans officiating at their initiation rite . . . fail to guide properly the entry into and possession of their bodies by their possessing spirits.[6]

Note the importance of the "officiating shaman" in aiding the fledgling to claim his or her destiny. Shamanic sensitivity—the ease with which potential shamans are infiltrated because of the fluid state of their consciousness, makes them prone to all manner of influences. Tayja's sister discussed the disconnected state of the chakras (energy centers) making it all but impossible for hebephrenic people and perhaps multiples as well, to "ground" or attach to the Earth on which they live.

Dr. Eugene Bliss of the University of Utah explains how dissociation and hypnotic amnesia apply to multiples, nearly all of whom are highly hypnotizable. It is as though shamanism, in order to develop, needed a door through which to enter. Dr. Bliss explains it psychologically:

If hypnosis can allow the individual to forget experiences, feelings, or even native language, why should he or she not be able to forget himself or herself? There is a rapid switch and the individual forgets herself, or to describe it in a slightly different form, the individual goes into hypnosis, disappears, and then is hidden in hypnosis like a personality, while the alter personality emerges into the real world, no longer in hypnosis.[7]

Dr. Kluft's observations are confirmed by Dr. Eugene Bliss who has noted that the same mental mechanisms which produce trance are also core mechanisms of Multiple Personality Disorder:

All of these patients clinically are excellent hypnotic subjects, while some are hypnotic virtuosos; most will enter deep trances rapidly when formally hypnotized for the first time; many report a multitude of spontaneous "trance" experiences in the past.[8]

Jeanne Wiger is a trained hypnotist, and she frequently used hypnosis techniques with Tayja. "I worked with Mom on hypnosis," Tayja journals, "and I didn't remember any of what really happened until later started putting the puzzle together." In that session on January 2, 1979, Tayja got in touch with Tommy, "an infant personality of mine." Hypnosis is an effective tool for recovering experiences which were separated from consciousness early in life.

Dr. Kluft's third factor in the development of multiplicity refers to "all the psychological structures, ego contents and other unique shaping influences that a multiple can enlist in the creation of alter personalities."[9] The distorted ego development resulting from splitting early in life involves polarizations of emotional identification so that the child fails to integrate experiences of "good" and "bad." In line with this, Tayja's personalities, typically, split off pairs of personalities which seemed to be emotional opposites. Patterns derived from her mother and from her father were split off into separate and opposite personalities.

Kluft's fourth factor, a lack of restorative opportunity, is abundantly evident in Tayja's history which showed sparse incidents of nurturing. In this atmosphere, her defenses were supported, and she continued to isolate fragments of herself behind unconscious barriers of oblivion. Only when she reached her reparenting home did conditions of safety permit the gradual wholing of her personality.

When they first enter treatment, most people with Multiple Personality Disorder are not aware of the existence of other personalities. It is also difficult for the medical profession to diagnose, and there is a difference of opinion concerning what does or doesn't constitute it. Eighty-nine percent of those with Multiple Personality Disorder have been mis-diagnosed at least once. "Frequent alternate or mis-diagnoses include depression, borderline personality disorder, sociopathic personality disorder, epilepsy, manic-depressive illness and schizophrenia."[10] At one time or another, Tayja's diagnoses included all of them. Her reparenting mother confirms:

In diagnostic work the multiple personality didn't show up. I was introduced to it when Tayja told me of different aspects of her that were not acquainted with other parts. Each seemed to have his or her own lifestyle and his or her own voice. We made a tape, and a variety of different attitudes and voices showed up in that process.

Of this process, Tayja writes in her journal:

"I made a tape that has all the voices on it. I taped with the other personalities knowing, and the tape came through. So I might let Mom hear the tape. I haven't decided yet."

Tayja recounts that because of the severity of the violence expressed, the tape was destroyed on the recommendation of her reparenting mother.

The cues indicating a personality change are not only verbal. The researcher, Thomas J. Hurley III, and others who have come to know multiples observe that:

> What gradually impresses one meeting a true multiple is less the obvious differences between personalities and more the nonverbal, intangible dimensions of personality that are rich, subtle and difficult to fake. These qualities of being tend to be subconscious and are usually perceived subconsciously; it is the discrepancy between them from one personality to another in a multiple that eventually shakes one's sense of what is real and what is not.[11]

Tayja's reparenting mother notes these differences:

> You could tell, for instance, by the style of clothing she chose to wear and different words and attitudes of the different personas. You knew she was moving into a persona that was destructive when she'd start wearing hats. A lot of potentially dangerous stuff was likely to happen then.

To make the multiple inhabitants of her psyche easier to distinguish, Tayja summarized the characters who shared her body. She did so with an acceptance of Multiple Personality Disorder as the explanation for the diverse personalities vying for possession of her being. It may or may not be significant that she had seen the movie *Sybil* in which Sally Field convincingly acted the part of a multiple and her struggle to become integrated with the loving help of a psychiatrist. In 1985, Tayja reflects on her personalities as she and I shared lunch in a quiet restaurant.

"1. Jim was the violent one, the person that feels the only way to work through things was to run or hurt others. He felt no one cared and answered with hate and fear and belligerence. He was developed very early. I'm not sure of his exact age." (According to Kluft, "because of the multiple's history of abuse, at least one personality will almost invariably be an angry, hostile and possibly violent alter.")[12]

"2. Jim's opposite was Debbie. She is the sweet street child, the hooker. She was the man chaser, to her sex was all that mattered. Her age was about 13 or 14. She hooked the man, then slept with him for a price, always a price. She was very much confused on many sexual matters. She was the person who expected everything to go nice and gentle. She herself was nice, almost too nice."

Tayja sees these two personalities as mirroring her parents. Debby reflects her mother's love as Jim reflects her father's anger and hate. "I had split parenting," Tayja explains. "I don't remember any gentle contact with my father. My mother gave me love, always gentle; but sometimes the stroking was sexual. You see, my mother wasn't there long enough to hit all the important developmental stages." So Tayja's loving nature was confused by inappropriate sexuality and did not receive parental guidance after her mother's death when she was nine years old. Consequently, the loving qualities present in the Debbie persona were often beaten against and abused by the stronger Jim personality.

"3. Tommy—was a very scared child. He was about four years in age and was very autistic, fear and more fear. He didn't speak to anyone but Jim, and he kept away from others. He was self-abusive physically and hated anyone who might take Jim away from him. He was very upset with any change and didn't care for women. He didn't trust any mother image at all. He felt he had been abandoned at a very young age—as soon as he was born.

"4. The baby personalities were many from infant new-born struggling to stay alive to the infant who died in mind over and over. [This was the baby who, while still in utero with her twin, believed that she would be born only to die.] Then there were the sleeping infants who didn't know the truths of their own being. They were in a drastic struggle to be loved and cared for. [While under hypnosis, Tayja recalls the pleas of Tommy:] What I remember is the words, 'love me,' 'want me!' The babies were always living on the fear and anger of people outside themselves. Always confusion."

Since the fragmentation of her personality started at a pre-verbal stage and even before birth, the number of her personalities was never determined.

"5. Russell. Well, Russell was caught up in being a connector from the negative to the positive, and, I feel, was the one who kept the personalities connected."

The "inner self helper" is a common type of alter personality: "ISHs are exceptionally knowledgeable and helpful personalities who guide the multiple and sometimes the clinician in therapy."[13] Tayja says that Russell was the personality who directed her to her reparenting home. "At the time he was asking for help, whether or not he understood what he was doing."

At the time, Tayja did not understand Russell's place in her personality—or outside of it. If the theory of possessing spirits is used to explain Tayja's condition, Russell could be understood as a spirit guide.

On April 21, 1978, Tayja journaled:

"I told Mom some of my awareness, and she said she's really glad that my personalities trust her and that Jim and Russell are willing to take a chance with her. Jim is not too willing, but he'll have to do it. Debbie didn't want to be known right now, but she said okay too. They didn't want to get rid of personalities because they felt it would be like dying. That's what Jim is scared of. (He says angry, but it is really scare.) Mom wants my personalities to talk with her Tuesday. That will probably happen.

"Russell was the worrier. He was a very smart five- or six-year old, good with experiments, but he had a hard time learning books."

Multiples are usually highly intelligent, perceptive and sensitive people. "I've never met a multiple with an IQ of less than 110," said Dr. Wilber at the First International Conference on Multiple Personality.[14]

Tayja continues:

"Russell was caught up in a lot of fear and confusion. He felt fearful of Jim a lot and tried to help Tommy, but he didn't know how. He wasn't really sure who to listen to. Much that he was told by the others didn't make sense, and Debbie and Jim battled with him. He was so fearful of death, and yet if they all had to die, he would too. He knew he needed help, but he didn't know what kind.

"Russell played a large role—as Jim did. It was like Jim being the negative and Russell being the positive. He knew we would all become love and light, so when people saw light around me at that time, that was Russell. I always felt something different for him. He was the part of me that I really believed in and felt like he was there the day the spirit came to me. I believe it truly was a gift to know that part and live it today. There were more fights that went on personalities-wise than anyone would know. So many parts torn, and yet in a swiftness of just a few years the splits became one. Many times I've had to think of these parts of me and find that they have all changed and been put into the light to never go back where we all came from. Now I can move on and become a humanitarian of the world and give a helping hand to love and honor our Grandfathers; to be a part of the solution and not the problem."

To reveal these personalities and the traumatic circumstances which caused them to split away was, in Tayja's case, one of the goals of reparenting—or was it to keep harmful spirits from entering? "In the end, I had to reparent myself," she explains. "My reparenting home gave me the protection I needed while I was striving for health."

In the day-to-day accounts of Tayja's reparenting experiences from abuse through the confusion of alter personalities, Tayja's story showed the signs of Multiple Personality Disorder—but with one discrepancy which appeared only after she gained unification.

The Institute of Noetic Sciences lists a pattern of indications of Multiple Personality Disorder:

Lost time, blackouts or amnesia. Depression. Mood swings. Self-destructive or suicidal behavior. Headaches. Sleep disorders or recurrent nightmares. Anorexia. Unexplained pain or somatic complaints such as gastrointestinal or cardiac disorders. Auditory hallucinations, the voices often being hostile or critical and coming from within the head. [Here it is important to note that some of Tayja's visions appeared to come from outside her head.] Visual hallucinations or other disturbances of vision. Seizure-like episodes.[15]

To shuffle Tayja's experiences into a logical order would be to give them a quality foreign to the nature of her confused being. The following excerpts from her journals, like shards from an archeological dig, leave one puzzled as to the potentials of the completed whole. Each piece was to be cleaned of foreign material that had contaminated the site, then fitted in its place so that a united vessel emerged to support a united life.

On June 10 at 11:20 P.M., 1980 she writes:

"My throat hurts bad. I feel like leaving right now. [There is an abrupt change to the uncoordinated printing of a child.] It's just too bad, isn't it? It's sick sad, you fucking bitch. It's just too fuckin' sad. Joy is for the healthy people. Don't give me that shit. You're a sad case of the shit. You won't make it, you won't live that long, so forget it, sucker. Forget it. You give me a pain!!! You're a bitch, you really are. You're a cheap tramp and you know that. Tommy."

The next morning, "I awoke only to find scrapes on my right arm, partly dressed and tired. I felt lots of panic around what to do or say. My arm hurts a little. Mamma is going to be mad. After taking razor blades and then this. Well, I'll have to take what happens."

Evening: "I tried to draw pictures of the homo [homicidal] parent, but couldn't put on paper. My hand would shake and picture looked crooked. I can say what it looks like, also the other kids: Tommy, Russell, Bobby. It's crazy, but I can describe each one. 5, 7, 8, their ages. It seems confusion when now I know that they're there. I can feel them, hear them. The Tommy part is silence that happens, Russell is the one who figures out what to do, also feels the confusion. Bobby is the autistic-seeming one, the liar, the sneak, the somewhat explosive one. It was really scarey for me. I feel really upset at times when I don't make sense of things. [Again the handwriting changes.] You crazy bitch, you fuckin sot, stop telling people what's happened stop stop stop! You're nuts you're crazy, crazy, crazy. I'll get you. I'll kill you. No one can stop me. No one. You're a fuckin bitch, you stupid! You're a pig, you're a fuckin cunt. You're going to die, die, die!!! So fucked up! up! up!" He writes, "die" seven times then, "No one can save you." (6/12/80)

The following day Tayja appears to be writing in her own hand:

"I'm sure there is more skeletons in the closet even yet ... I remember saying I wish I had parents who I know love me and car ed ... How could I trust them? I held so much in. Right now I feel I don't know what's a lie from the truth."

The forward slanted printing changes to writing, first straight up, then back slanted as she or he writes, "I feel really frightened, that's all that I am feeling." A transition seemed to be completed.

"Mommy, I feel so scared. Help me Mommy, help! As the tears fell from my face, I feel different again. I feel different. For so long I have had things so bottled up that I feel like all those things were meant to happen. I don't mean to deceive the only family I feel I've ever had. I love those people more than I have loved anyone ever. I know it wasn't going to be easy, but I know I can get well here. I won't hurt myself or them. Please help me, Grandfathers." (6/13/80)

As they switch personalities, it is typical for one persona of a multiple to be shocked by the behavior of another. Tayja writes:
"I've been called a liar before over and over. This part I can handle, but ripping people off is hard. I have ripped myself off, not only physically, my hysterectomy, but also in appreciating my son and other things that people had tried to give me." (6/13/80)

Psychiatrists have found that, since multiples were attacked as children, the violent personalities of adult multiples often attack their own children too.[16]
Tayja recognizes the enemy within herself: "I felt sad and hurt about giving up Jimmy, [Tayja's son] but my thinking is that if I had kept Jimmy, he would of been dead."
When she got in touch with the violence one of her personalities attempted, Tayja wrote in large letters, "God forgive me!"
As was mentioned in an earlier chapter, when anger is released, it uncovers yet another painful emotion. Tayja writes:

"What happens for me is if I give up the homicidal stuff, then the grief is underneath. The fear of dealing with that has hit me tonight ... I am so tired." (6/21/80)

On July 13, 1980 Tayja writes in another mood:

"Sometimes if I think I am going to die, I feel not frightened but envious of others who are already dead. I think what am I on earth for? What's my purpose here? Sometime I will figure it out." Signed, "Debbie Ann." The next day a large childish hand writes:

"Run away, they don't want you . . . you're not alive anyway. Without me, you'll die . . . No one can stop me, Ha! Ha!

July 21, 1980: "Kill is what you need to do, then get away on your broom stick, you witch. Cry for me! I am you . . . I have given you life. You give death, that's what I ask now. 3:00 A.M. Always remember blood, cuts, burns, nothing harms you, you don't hurt . . . Die, die, die. It's me again."

Then Debbie returns: "I feel very upset about the other writing on Monday. It sounds much crazier than before. It feels much scarier." This entry continues with a change to the writing of a child: "Cut your arm . . . no one will know. I help me do it now!!! No one can find you before it's too late . . . Then you don't have to keep feeling their love. [Feeling love threatens the status quo of non-existence.]

On July 24, 1980: "My stomach is so upset, maybe I do need the handcuffs . . . but I'll be okay?" she questions.

Making an adult evaluation Tayja writes, "Something I think of is the homicidal Parent" [the violent parent within her own psyche] "is made up of all the other personalities in the journal." The writing changes: "Help me, help me through this hurt and fear. If you let it out, it'll hurt us all, so don't show it. I can't live here. Debbie Ann."

Tommy responds, "I'll die too, so you can't do that. You want us all to die with you, you forget it. I'm staying right here, you'll not do that to me."

The "inner self helper" or peace maker responds to the others, "You need to take care of all of us. Don't kill me. Russell."

Then "Jessy," a personality who has apparently appeared only once, writes, "You hurt me, and you know you're going to die. It doesn't make sense to kill us when you need us. You know you'll protect us." (7/24/80)

The intense therapeutic work is wearing. At 12:35 P.M. Tayja writes: "The crazy has been bothering me all night, and the dreams are feeling almost real like the dreams are bloody and hunting me even during the day. I don't know what to do any more."

Through July, the intense work continues: "I processed that the cord to belonging was cut when I was born. Hard because the belief is that somehow I will be killed by the homicidal Parent if I allow my two-year-old out. Autism. Sometimes I feel like I am not there at all. [A void when the body seems devoid of any personality whatsoever has been reported by psychiatrists.] I feel very sad right now. I miss the womb. I want to be well right now, it hurts to be sick, it hurts a lot . . . Please keep me safe." (7/31/80)

A child scrawls, "Now I took control of her again." Then later in the night, "Mama, I am buried in the wall of hell . . . Tayja is gone now, it's me . . . I'll kill Tayja yet, you know."

Two days later Tayja recognizes that integration is well on the way: "I know there is a big part of me that is getting well. Other parts will be integrated and get well too. It's to pass through the energy blocks to the homicidal Parent once and for all decathect it." Tayja knew she needed to remove the energy of affirmation from the unhealthy Parent ego state: "I know I need to go through the craziest part and come out the other side." (7/12/80)

On August 16 Tayja went to a day-long marathon:

"It went well. It turned out that I might have decathected the crazy homicidal Parent! excitement, sadness. Something about needing to stay close to Mamma. Survival now. I felt the shock just as I image the homo [homicidal] Parent's neck break, and she exploded into nothing. After, I cried some and felt a lot of confusion, forgot how to tie my shoe even, which seemed funny! Body feels different in structure . . . I feel pretty tired . . . also felt little much of the day, new-born, earlier even. Just think, no more thinking killings, no more hurting myself, that will all be over with!! What a treat. More energy to have fun and play. Even felt hunger pains too!!! Daddy will be surprised a whole lot. I am really missing him too. I have noticed the scare around men is really high. I think I can sleep well tonight." (7/16/80)

The next day Tayja "awoke not feeling angry!! Thank God. I didn't have any bad dreams either . . . I gave away all my horror books . . . I feel like a very young child that is whiny and clingy to Mama's blouse tail . . . I am not fat, I really look thin for the first time."

Tayja's mother realized that Tayja would need time to adjust to the change, and she writes in Tayja's journal, "Give yourself time; you've done so much, and the rest will come in due time. Mama." Tayja continues:

"Well, today was super . . . I put together a tape on the hebephrenic pathology. It sounded pretty good to me . . . Name change tomorrow. [Tayja was looking forward to formally adopting the name of her reparenting family.] I will enjoy being legal. I feel scared around things are going so well, but I am going to enjoy it so long as it lasts." (7/18/80)

A few days later she was warned by Debby: "Tayja needs to be careful. I don't think she's aware of exactly what's happening . . . I wish it was safe enough for us to talk to Mama, tell her what's happening and give her the information that she needs, more protection for Tayja's little Infant. Tommy will want to get rid of that first, then he'll try to get rid of parents . . . "

The handwriting changes, and an autistic child emerges, "The words won't come out . . . " Then later in the same entry Tayja is writing, "Then in Monday's group integrate the other personalities too: Debbie, Russell, Tommy, then be done with it. Break the structure wide open and deal with the healthy infant. Cry. Loud demand. Get those tiny issues met. Also demand time with Mama . . . I don't need to suffer." (8/30/80)

For the last time, Russell writes in Tayja's journal: "They don't know anything about me . . . I help Tayja when it's time. She's doing the things she needs to do now. I love her and won't hurt her, but she's not ready to understand me yet. The things that come will be important. I am crying inside; she won't let go yet. They all need to know if you'll take care of all the parts of us. She will not need me any more. So don't get mad at her for still having us yet. My pain in leg and arm will stop as Tayja intermeets inside . . . The baby, the baby, watch! so it doesn't fall; take care of Tayja . . . you can love, make it come true, Tayja." (11/9/80)

Later that month, on November 24, Tayja is still coping with the turbulence within her: "It is 3:30 A.M. I still feel like I want to kill someone to cover up my own hurt that I am feeling. What to do is the question . . . Debbie wants some of the action. Tommy is making me feel sick, so he needs something. I need to communicate with him as soon as possible. Tommy doesn't talk, so what he needs is lots more tricky. Jim is just violent lately. He feels the need to kill someone. Need to dump the feelings tomorrow in group. I am afraid to. I feel like I am missing something very important—like me."

Although Tayja was still a long way from making sense out of this turmoil, she was in no danger of becoming meek and adaptive to the situation. As she recalls the past over a vegetarian lunch, Tayja explains, "Individuality is so *damn* important to me." Her face is strong with conviction. "I've seen too many people lose themselves, just become robots in the system."

When Tayja left her reparenting home, all of her personalities knew each other. "But they weren't really integrated," she explains. "In the end, I knew I had to take my body back and get it together. I refused to let Jim in, and then all that anger was gone. Debbie and the babies, all the others left too. It was more like a fleeing. They were *gone*. I was free!"

We generally assume that we are one in mind and one in body. Yet, Multiple Personality Disorder challenges that idea and opens the door to a reality that may be stranger than we are able to imagine. When personalities switch, the body often reacts with drastic changes such as allergic reactions, handedness or color blindness, which may be present in one personality yet not in another. The extent to which mind effects body may be seen in this extreme reaction involving sensitivity of the skin:

> Dr. Bennett Braun reports on the case of a female multiple who was tortured by both her mother and brother. One form of this abuse involved putting out lighted cigarettes on her skin. When the personality that received burns took over during therapy sessions, the burn marks would reappear on her skin and last for 6 to 10 hours ... Again, such phenomena have been observed in the hypnosis literature.[17]

Given the rapid appearance and disappearance of symptoms such as rashes and allergies, it is not surprising that this could also extend to more general control of the physical healing process. For Tayja this certainly appeared true. Shortly after meeting her reparenting family,

Tayja was wandering the streets in a daze when she was hit by a car. Although her hip and collarbone were broken, she denied the pain, yet within three weeks, both bones were completely healed.

Are such talents latent in all of us? Dissociation plays a role in the consciousness of everyone, and what Tayja has experienced in an extreme degree, all of us experience in minor ways; for dissociation plays a part in spontaneous fantasy, hypnagogic imagery and dreams. Dr. Peter McKellar says that dissociation may be "a switch into a different gear rather than a splitting."

Were all of Tayja's personalities splinters of herself, or, for example, could one of her infant personalities be the spirit of her dead twin? Where did her "hallucinations" come from—within her mind or outside of it? Or, if time and space can be transcended, does a fragmented personality blend with discarnates so that distinction between them is not possible? Although these questions cannot be answered with certainty, valuable insight can be provided through graphology.

Mary Rowan, the graphologist who examined samples of handwriting from Tayja's journals written while in reparenting at Wiger Woods, was not fully satisfied with the concept that Tayja's personalities were merely splinters of herself. During a week of study, Mary prepared nearly four hours of taped analysis of the various journal writings. After examining nearly half of the samples, she noticed that "Debby," "Tommy," "Russell," and Tayja were signing similar writings. Were they then, true multiples signing each other's names? Or were they possessing spirits? Mary speculates:

> I would guess that they are spirits. I feel spirits can be around you and partly enter your body or aura, be in your energy field and channeling through you, partial possession to whatever degree. That's the way I would react to this. But I don't know, and I can't decide what this is, and it's not my business to do so. But if she sees them and feels and hears them, are they actually a part of her?"

Mary quotes from a journal entry written in a powerful immature hand: "Stop telling people what's happening, stop stop stop!" Mary explains:

> All of a sudden one takes over. To me it looks like an outside personality trying to intimidate her, and she realizes, "Hey, Russell's here, Tommy's here, these people are here."

It's as though she were saying, "I see Bobby, I feel Bobby." So one of them would come in and say, "I'll kill you, no one can stop me." It's as though they were fighting each other for space. That's the way I would interpret this. I can't understand how that can be a part of her.

Now here's another example. She writes, "I think I am going to die." This could be a spirit who is already dead, and is still hanging around, not realizing it's dead. Tayja could hear it and think that it is her. "I feel not frightened but envious of others who are alrady dead." This could be the spirit's thought, something Tayja is picking up from a confused spirit.

Then sometimes it looks as though there could be a spirit trying to have sex with Tayja. They try that sometimes, and sometimes they succeed. There are a lot of genital symbols in the writing that would indicate that.

(For samples of the handwriting, see Appendix I, Mind Patterns.)

Tayja's reactions to looking at her journals soon after her healing support Mary's guesses. "This isn't me," Tayja stated flatly as she read the attacks directed toward "Tayja" written in a violent scrawl. "This is a spirit."

Further support for Mary's suspicions is indicated in Tayja's account of the following experience:

"I remember one day I stayed at a friend's over night in Hastings; and when I was in bed, I saw a Roman soldier standing by my door, covered in blood like he was still in a battle. At the time, I didn't know he had come to be healed by me, and I got very frightened and called my new parents up. They said I was hallucinating, and I should stop it immediately. It wasn't until I finally said, 'Go away, you don't belong here,' that he finally left and never came back again. Many things like that happened to me from the earliest times I can remember. Finally one day my spirit friends told me to bless them and send them on their way. I was told I would be a great healer for those lost souls, but I couldn't tell anyone. I didn't want them to say I was crazy. But I finally knew what path I wanted to take. The spirits told me not to let anyone take me 'off the path we have put you on.' "

Many doctors are now looking at events such as this with serious respect:

Dr. Ralph Allison, who with Dr. Cornelia Wilber is one of the pioneers in the modern treatment of Multiple Personality Disorder, says bluntly that many of his patients have exhibited symptoms of possession: "Repeatedly, I encountered aspects of their personalities that were not true alter personalities . . . In many of these cases, it was difficult to dismiss these unusual and bizarre occurrences as mere delusion. In the absence of any 'logical' explanation, I have come to believe in the possibility of spirit possession . . . "

In keeping with Myers' view that the mind is "open at both ends," Allison has also described benign spirit guides that therapists sometimes encounter in multiples, which he calls Inner Self Helpers. Unlike genuine alter personalities, these beings have no specific date of origin, serve no ordinary function such as handling anger or expressing sexuality, and "know the patient's past history and can predict future actions with great accuracy." They work with the therapist and "serve as a conduit for God's healing power and love."

These questions come up in other areas as well. Included is research in all kinds of altered mind/body perception including trance states and "hallucinations," both visual and auditory, near-death and out-of-body experiences.

Drs. Glen Gabbard and Stuart Twemlow said that experiences of this kind are often non-pathological. In fact, they emphasized that many persons who have out-of-body or near-death experiences report that these experiences have a positive, transformative effect on their lives.

These questions and others squarely pose the question of whether dissociative and related exceptional states are a pathology or a resource. Might they be a key, as a growing number of researchers think, to a greater range of psychological and psychophysiological abilities than we ordinarily command?[18]

On a very practical level, Tayja's reparenting family explored that possibility with their recovering daughter. Tayja was indeed fortunate that her new family put her in contact with people who could explore the development of her talents in directions of healing.

Chapter Eight
Storehouse for Fear

The body is one and has many members, but all the members, many though they are, are one body; and so it is with Christ.
If one member suffers, all the members suffer with it; if one member is honored, all the members share its joy.
Corinthians 12, 11, 20, 85

A purpose behind suffering may be difficult to determine. To feel the physical and psychic wounds she would some day heal, to learn to heal them first in herself and then in others is clear to Tayja today, but on June 2, 1981 when she met "Vic and Lorraine," that purpose was obscure to her, even though at some level she sensed it: "Tomorrow I see Vic and Lorraine to have a psychic treatment which should be interesting and neat. I feel okay but scared about that at some level."

Her fears were indeed justified! When she occasionally touched with her shamanic destiny, Tayja's ideas had been brushed aside by health professionals with the term "grandiose" or referred to vaguely as "unusual thought content."

In her journal Tayja wrote, "I might as well give up ideas about being a great person because that probably won't ever happen—and if it does, so what?" Now she says, "My whole life has been grandiose. With all that was wrong with me, just the idea of surviving was grandiose. Most people in my place would have died."

Now, from a position of respect, Tayja can tell her experiences and expect to be understood by those who know of the free movement of consciousness outside the body and the possibility of communication with those energies and spirits which exist in a non-physical dimension. Tayja writes, "When I got to my reparenting home, I soon

113

began believing down deep that there really was an understanding for all of this. When people kept saying that I was acting crazy, I kept saying to myself, 'What's crazy, the way I deal with a problem or the way they deal with the problem?' I often felt close to higher spirits, and I know they helped me."

At the time of her treatment with Vic and Lorraine, Tayja was familiar with Reiki healing, an ancient form of spiritual healing which included "laying on of hands." Her reparenting mother used the technique, and, recognizing Tayja's ability, took her to study with the master, Ethel Lombardi. Although Reiki is not the technique Tayja uses now, it did introduce her to a group of people who respected spiritual healing and valued her talents. As Reiki acquainted Tayja with words for universal principals she knew instinctively, education in this technique was important to her.

"Rei" is the Japanese word for universal, which includes the soul or spirit, and "ki" is the vital life-force energy which flows through all that lives. A concept of the chakra energy centers as defined earlier in this book is basic to the process. Hence Reiki healing is a method for healing the body, mind, emotions and spirit of a person who opens to the energy and makes an effort to release the emotional experiences that trap illness in the body. In this form of healing, body/mind is regarded as a united entity with the mental energies being the cause of physical ailments. This is in line with the Oriental philosophy of mind and body, which, unlike Western thought (including allopathic medicine) regards the mind as being primary and causal to the physical entity. This idea of ailments being caused by some form of spiritual misalignment or weakness is also basic to shamanism. Shamans usually explain it as intrustion by harmful spirits. A significant difference between the two forms of healing is that the Reiki practitioner serves as a channel, and the shamanic healer takes the illness into his or her body and heals it within. Tayja's potential for doing this can be deduced from her 'game' of body switching with her brother Pony. In her reparenting home she was on the path of using the ability constructively.

Throughout her journals, Tayja writes of many Reiki treatments, but her accounts do not go into much detail. The last mentioned was on January 5, 1982 after her experience with Vic and Lorraine: " . . . tears came even more. I take her hand and put it on my face. The words were, 'Just love me. I survived.' The images I got were head and spine injuries and also feet."

The fears engendered by her experiences in this life would soon make sense to Tayja on a more conscious level. Together Vic and Lorraine were to explore the storehouse of Tayja's body and to find it a cosmic receptacle for pain and fear.

An hour-long tape of the proceedings tells the story as they discovered it. The husband and wife team treated Tayja's bodies: physical, emotional, mental and spiritual. Vic used massage activating the psychic sensitivity in his hands and transmitted energy to Tayja which promoted release of deep-seated causes of physical dis-ease. Lorraine observed Tayja on the treatment table, seeing the path of the soul into the present instant. Her vision included past lives which serve to cause and direct present emotional patterns. Further, Vic and Lorraine together read the soul's purpose, so clarifying and pointing direction in the present life.

The small view of life in a body restricted to the pinpoint of this time and place makes Tayja's painful life seem purposeless. Why should she suffer so, and what could be the good of it? Vision is expanded into the eternal as this couple work together. While he massages her foot, Vic talks, his voice a rhythm for his hands:

> All of the hurts and angers are pinpointed in the body. [Vic concentrates on Tayja's foot which is rigid and curved downward so that the toes seem to be clutching the Earth.] It isn't something really wrong with this foot, it's just emotions tightened up there, so we can begin to get the whole body to relax a little bit. [His voice is soothing with a deep, gentle cadence.] Well, this fear is quite a thing! It comes in a lot of disguises. As we work with it, we might turn it inside out, as we say, and see joy on the other side of it.
>
> You have this thing called free will. You take these fears little bit by little bit, and pretty soon you transform this whole body into joy . . .
>
> Free will is all in our favor once we learn how to use it. When we look at anything, it's our choice how we perceive it. If we want to see beauty, it's our choice. But if we don't move those little pebbles as they come along, pretty soon they get to be so many we gotta use a bulldozer to try and move 'em. More amazing, when we record those little fears, this body holds 'em there in tension, and each one we allow to build up there gets bigger and bigger 'til pretty soon the whole

body just vibrates with it." [Consider Tayja's epilepsy.] So, as we begin to reverse that procedure, then we begin to take it all out.

Vic's deep reverence for the body, or "One," as he usually calls it, extends in the resonance of his voice and the touch of his hands far beyond his words.

It's like God. Each one perceives Him to be what he's most comfortable with. It's the same thing with your body, because this One is the God self for you. No other one like it. God never even made a set of blueprints. This is the beautiful part to me, this body's a miracle . . .

Vic often paused in his running commentary as he became absorbed in the messages from his hands, and he gave much of his views of God, but always with the door of free will open.

We say God is love and God is beautiful—or not. It's your choice. Once in a while we need a little boost along the way. It's like each individual is a catalyst to the other. So each one is God within her own right. When we can love this One so much that we can love no other, we will love all the same. Then you don't need to worry about any other, not even this One.

Tayja's feet, symbolically clutching the Earth in fear, become physical effects, results of powerful causes, mere pebbles in the lava flow of time as June 2, 1981 melts into oneness with the distant past. Lorraine's mind becomes a channel for pictures of another life; her voice, emphasizing key words, projects the awe she feels. She speaks slowly in long, serpentine sentences, as though following dictation:

I was watching a couple of inner movies. Both were experiences in which *fear* was almost a *total* part of that *whole* lifetime. The first one dealt with being a man, being part of a group establishing life on a planet, choosing what people were to take part in that exploration and settlement; but finding when you got there (you traveled by what people would call a craft or a spaceship), then finding when you got there that there were inhabitants you didn't know lived there; and they were extremely huge people; and for you to live there, it would be like putting tiny little dwarfs on the same land as with gigantic people; and you voted to discontinue and go to another different world.

This correlates with Tayja's estrangement from her own body and from life on this earth.

> You were voted down because of the effort, the time, the excitement, the dedication which was involved with the whole group which was about a hundred people. You were voted down, and so you stayed, and you were almost totally afraid during the rest of that life experience on that world. You found that even though they were gigantic beings, they could hear your least movement, and they knew when you were moving near them. You had difficulty gathering food. You had difficulty staying out of the elements, of weather, creating some type of a home the giants couldn't crush. It was a *total challenge* to *every single bit* of knowledge that every one of you had within yourselves. But you kind of went into this fear form, and you were . . . totally living within fear that you would be stepped on and crushed the way you had seen some of them stepped on and crushed. You often asked and wondered in yourself, why, why did this happen? Why am I here? You couldn't walk out in the sunshine because you would be seen. You couldn't sing because you would be heard. It was a totally different kind of life. The learning in that time seemed to be symbolic in that you get thoroughly acquainted with the tiny portion of yourself and love every bit of it no matter how it seemed in relationship to everything in the world about you, and then accepting the gigantic beings as beings of God and learning to love them.

—something Tayja was apparently too fearful to do. Learning to trust and love people who seem to have power over her—people in authority—is something Tayja is working on in this life. To realize her needs as a small being, then become a woman of power is a part of Tayja's path now.

> The major task was creating another home for your people. You were not successful. You were eventually all killed, and you yourself held this tremendous fear because it vibrated in *every* cell of your body by the time that experience was over. You were almost petrified all the time on

that world. You couldn't make a sound, but inside you screamed, "Why did God abandon my people? Why was this allowed to take place?"

Consider Tayja's vacillations between autism and rage in this life. Lorraine continues her story of a soul's progress:

> You raged, you felt all kinds of emotion, but you didn't let the feelings go out of you, so they stayed in your being. You held every one of them because you wanted to make God and man pay for your tremendous fear that you suffered in that time.
>
> But you weren't stepped on. That wasn't the manner of death in that time. You simply scared yourself to death. You became so totally tight in the physical body that you literally bound yourself up in chains. You got so you couldn't move, wouldn't move, and you just starved and died all because of that fear that you held. [Anorexia and bulimia may be seen as present-day manifestations of this experience.] That became your life.

This life makes psychological sense as an explanation for Tayja's strong resistance to looking at her fear, that paralyzing emotion which can kill. To release gigantic rage would surely be safer!

Lorraine continues with a lifetime equally significant when understood against the psychological background of Tayja's present life:

> The second one that I was watching that seems to have an impact on now deals with massive earth changes. Whether you've read anything or not, there was a continent out in the Pacific Ocean of which the islands out there are remnants, a big continent that sank and was broken up. It was called Mu or Lemuria. This was 40, 50, 60, 70 thousand years ago. You were part of that. It was a very evolved group of people who had great understanding on Earth. You were a doctor, a woman, highly respected. You were dealing with your angers regarding man, that you were still carrying, always placing yourself before man as the picture of the capability of woman. You, in your life expressions, wanted man to know that woman was an equal portion, and you had been a part of many learnings in which woman was not the equal portion

but was the abused and frightened and despairing and lonely portion of a team which should have been equal, man and woman, in the sight of God.

As a very intellectual aware being, helping your people to become aware of their physical bodies, you were both a medical doctor dealing with the body and a doctor dealing with the mind, to teach people about the wholeness of the person, the beingness that occupies the physical body, and what the physical body is, and what abilities it has in it that function with the intellect and with the mind. You made very important contributions to man at that point. You brought out the total equalness of all things, not just man and woman, but all things in the universe. You taught people about their bodies and how and what their bodies would do if they communed and used certain techniques with sound and with light; and you also worked with colored stones, mostly the pinks and creamy white and white with yellow and blue, in bringing harmony in physical bodies. That was one method medical doctors used at that time, just one. [Today Tayja is again using color and light in her healing work.] You were very knowledgeable in it, and you were able to teach people that there was a great deal more to life than just coming to Earth and accomplishing a life task in just one little space.

Then you began to have knowings because you were in tune with the Earth enough so that you could get messages that the Earth was telling you that there were going to be big upheavals, and you helped to organize many groups of people who went out to other lands to perpetuate the knowledge and the wisdom that you had helped to bring. But for some reason you chose not to go. You helped to send these other groups so that the knowledge would not be lost. But you chose to stay with those who were too afraid to go, with those who were not believing, with those who, like you, chose for some reason to remain. It was simply because you needed to experience the whole breaking up, to do it on a level of mind and to let it happen on the physical. Tayja is facing a similar challenge in this life.

You knew that would be happening in all of the other different bodies that you were aware of and that you taught people about. You taught people that they had many bodies and that they lived many places and not just where they were aware of in their physical bodies. And you wanted to experience the sensations in all of those bodies, not only the physical body, but the etheric body, the mental body, the emotional body. You wanted to remain behind so that you could care for the people who were still there. On the physical level you reacted to it with stark terror because it was a very terrifying thing to see the land before you shake and break apart, a whole mountain break apart from an energy that you couldn't see well at that time, but that you knew was working in the Earth, and to see that whole mountain just *break apart* and crumble and *cover cities* and break off and go into the ocean. It was a *very terrifying* experience.

Yet you didn't hold on to your emotional situation so much, because you were observing what was going on in all of the bodies, yours as well as other people's, because you were noting mentally, because you were a *very genius type person*. Whatever you noted in your brain, you knew it stayed there permanently. It was part of a file. You kept this universal file going, and you had all these things active in there. You were filing all this information because you knew that you could use it in the spirit body. You could act with it by thought and then use that to help people to see the wholeness of the whole experience. You were being open and busy and doing what you were doing at that time while these various bursts and transformations and volcanoes and earthquakes all happened over a period of several days covering probably two months, (two months our time; it was a different kind of time then) before it was finally under water and you had left that physical body.

But what you did was to take on their fears. You were experimenting. You were doing research again. You were taking on their fears to see how fast you could change and relieve them, but what you didn't do was to let 'em go, to keep an open door in the body somewhere and let them go right out that open door. You followed your own habit of collecting and filing data, gathered in all these fears of people; and you filed them right inside your being. You gathered in *collectively* such tremendous *panic* and *fear* and *anger* that it's almost unbelievable that you could carry that amount in your physical body into the world this time. My feeling is *amazement* that you could keep that pain so long in order to do this thing for the Earth. Yet you weren't aware this was part of what you were doing. You felt you were doing a research, technical, intellectual thing for the race of mankind to find out its responses, how it can be different, how the programming needs to be changed. What you weren't aware of is that you were . . . gathering these fears from all of the people who died, in various ways, at that time, so that you could release fear from mankind.

Lorraine repeated, driving in her point:

You were doing something on a physical level, finding out how man moved, how he thought, how he responded, how the body acted, so that you could deal with that fear on the *physical* level, and you did the whole thing on the *collective* level. I don't know whether you're aware of that or not, or whether . . .

Here Vic broke in:

On a collective level, you're holding it through here. [He was working on her hips and legs.] That's why these points are so sore. That's why it's so sore in the foot and the whole foot's pulled in. It's like you're collectively holding fears for all mankind. Some other patterns are woven in it, but they're minute compared with this collective thing. They'll fall away like little pebbles. It can have a bearing with the birthing experience that you may be going through now. [Vic and Lorraine knew that Tayja was in reparenting therapy.] That's why this is so sore and so tight through the hips. The pain is balanced. Balance says it's collective. There could have been many children involved in it, and you could have been thinking of the children and the mothers. And you brought all this back. That's why you chose the body of a woman, held it in this part of the body [pelvis] which has a bearing with birthing and all the other emotions. Allow faith to see all these bodies surrounded in love. Put this One right in the middle and see what love does to that! Allow love to fill this body and release fear.

Thousands and thousands of people! Look what you

can do for all of them—and all of you! Quite a challenge you put before yourself. A tremendous challenge! What that would do for Earth right now and for all those beings! The effects would be tremendous! It could reach all over the universe.

Lorraine continues the theme:

. . . which is your total aim, to cleanse the universe at this specific time with the energies that are here, to get the job done *now*, and you knew that you could do it.

All this was being predicted for a diagnosed "psychopathic" personality who at this time had all she could do to keep herself alive, let alone save the world! An examining psychiatrist would surely say that for this scarcely literate child of violence, the aim of saving the world was sheer fantasy.

But shamanic tradition would speak with Vic:

My hat is off to you! You really brought in a full load of suitcases! Gee [Vic was excited by what he was feeling], and they're going to open up, not in a horrible or fearsome way, but they're going to open up with laughter. Laughter is one of your keys of release, laughter that will bring tears, that will bring inner knowing and understanding and then go back into laughter again. It's very important. I feel like you've had the feeling you don't want to release these things because you'll have to deal with them all over again, and you just can't bear to see them. But look at the awesome vast thing that you took upon yourself to do . . . There aren't many people in the race who would gather in all those things to clean the universe, . . . so it's a very important thing you're doing, and you can laugh and be joyful because you are accomplishing it.

It will come out, but there won't be agony with it. There won't be screaming that you remember. There won't be terrific avalanches of the land breaking up and going into the ocean, and there won't be the roar of the ocean water as it covered the land: all these sounds and sights are in all this thing that you packed away. You just haven't wanted to open up that Pandora's box, but it isn't going to sound like that, and it isn't going to look like you recall because there's a different set of energies now, and you have a different physical body that can handle this release with laughter.

Praise and thank this One. If you really love it, fear can't stay in your body . . . You're going to have to get used to a *whole new body*. You've held this tension in here so long that this body isn't even going to feel what you would call natural when you drop away all the tension.

As Vic continues to work with Tayja's body, Lorraine speaks of her present life:

You allowed yourself to be in a position with particular people in this lifetime to create that sensation of fear again so that you could connect with what's collectively in you to release. You used it as a point of recognition so that this fear can connect with that deep fear that you brought along to release for all of mankind, so that they could be lighted beings again. As Vic says, you remember working with light. When he said those words, the next image I saw was a glowing person levitating a little bit above the Earth, joyfully happy doing all these different things, creating anything that needed to be created from light. Yeah, you have great understandings.

Surely, not many would see this potential in the limping gait Tayja had at that time!

Vic says:
A lot of people don't realize that God created this world and everything in it from thought. Yet they say there's nothing in the air! Where'd it all come from? You will find that when you start to use thought in a certain way, anything you want in your hand will manifest right there, right out of the air. People are going to be amazed to know they have this capability.

Lorraine adds:
After you get all the unloading done. A few years. Then you can release fast. You don't force it to do anything, but you can allow it to do all things.

Vic says:
People run around looking for this guru and that guru in

a state of confusion rather than open their own doors and let this One out. We've heard the phrase, "guardian of the gate." He's sittin' right here. When you accept God's gift of the body, you won't have to prove anything. The glow around you will speak for itself.

You've got free will. If you want to get a gun and kill yourself, he won't say "no." He gave you free will, and you can do anything.

Lorraine says:

Every day you could image yourself opening the gate, because you're the gatekeeper, and you get to let these things out, one by one or two by two, however you choose. So you open the gate, and you let out two or three children with a couple of mothers, and you see them there, and you say, "I love you." You watch them walk away into a great big huge glowing light, and then you know that they are where they need to be. The next day you can open the gate again and let out a man and his wife. Little by little you can let things out. You gathered them in, so you get to let them go, and all you have to say is, "I love you," and your love directs them into God's light which is where they need to go, and they'll have understanding. Every time you open that gate and let somebody out, you are freeing cells in yourself, lighting them up, taking off a great big weight. You already did your research, so it doesn't need to happen again. You have understanding of people, their emotions . . . and you can use it in many ways . . .

Vic says:

Maybe you'll wake up some morning and find that you left the gate open, and you don't have any more left. You can clear this whole beautiful house, mansion, cathedral, temple, whatever you want to term it, and see it filled completely with love. Then you'll know the meaning of "My cup runneth over."

Lorraine explains:

Then you'll be at the top of the mountain. This shirt with the mountain on it that you chose to wear is quite symbolic because you've been at the foot of it for a long time. But when you let all this go, you'll be at the top, and that's where you're headed. I would say by September there would be a massive change. [It was in September that Tayja chose to move into her own apartment.]

Vic takes over:

Let that gate be a two-way thing; get that love going out and see it coming in. See this mental body out there tell this emotional body you love it, and then see what happens to the physical body caught in between. It'll just float around then!

. . . This physical body does not have to die. That's all a state of confusion. It can function so beautifully that we can take it anywhere in the universe. You can walk right through walls and everything else. Man doesn't have the knowledge and interpretation that can stop this God self. How can we stop air? What we see in air is what this body is when it is clear.

Lorraine sees the Earth a play of life:

This is such a tremendous school here on Earth, all the stages dealt with: all the stage hands, writers, actors, everything's all here. We go through all these different acts for learning, and we take on different costumes, and we become older or younger to act out a certain part, and that's what our plays and stories are all about, to show us that physical life is costumes and acts.

Vic continues to work, commenting on the changes he feels coming to the reproductive organs.

This is so beautiful and so gentle in here that it goes beyond words. It would take more than the light of every star you can see to express the love that lies within this self. You don't have to forgive the people out there, you can forgive this One, 'cause that's the one that's holding it. Those people, they were the catalyst to let you see what you were holding in here.

If a person does something that makes us feel hurt or angry, we can actually thank that person for letting us see that we are holding that feeling within ourselves.

Now you stand there at the gate, and if you see anything but love or beauty walk by, you say, "I don't need you, you walk on down the road. I'm only going to let in that which I am." Then everything will change.

The healing was finished, and Tayja remembered deep in her body. But her journal entry was simple: "Went and seen Vic and Lorraine. They said some interesting things about two past lives: one a space person with fear connected, then a doctor with fear connection. Severe pain and fear, but I felt, somehow, if I loved me, I wouldn't have to deal with any of the other things. Afterwards I felt good, my feet were flat on the floor."

Less than a year before seeing Vic and Lorraine, Tayja had drawn this "self-portrait."

August 31, 1980

> The violated crown,
> The divided brain,
> Pain in the wavey lines of the eyes,
> Visual confusion in the crossed eyes,
> Anger, obsession with blood flowing from the mouth,
> Autism: "Won't talk, you not make me."
> "This is me. It."

Chapter Nine
Star Story

While ALL is in THE ALL, it is equally true that THE ALL is in ALL. To him who truly understands this truth hath come great knowledge.

—The Kybalion

I always got up very early to see the rising of the daybreak star . . . Many would get up to see it with me, and when it came we said: "Behold the star of understanding!"

—Neihardt
Black Elk Speaks[1]

What the ancient Greeks said in a mystical way and the American Indians said in a natural way, Tayja's reparenting mother says in a scientific way: "Every cell of our bodies really is a hologram, and more and more we're aware of that. We are microcosms of the whole cosmic universe." Her statement brings to mind the "Bohr model" of atomic structure. This concept won for the physicist, Niels Bohr, a Nobel Prize for a concept of atomic structure which had come to him in a dream of the solar system in which the celestial bodies formed the model for the atom.[2] Now, in the modern world we are coming to recognize the wisdom of Hermetic Philosophy as the ancient Greeks conceived it: all creation one in unity. The Native American, Black Elk, realized this union as it reached to the stars. So from *The Kybalion* to the modern concept of the cell, we and the stars are one.

Through thousands of years of scholarship, astrological relationships have been refined, and now, with modern computers, natal charts can be compiled in minutes. Like mathematical principles, astrology operates at a level of consciousness where time and space become an eternal instant. In this consciousness, the solar system (the macrocosm) and human beings (the microcosm) become one as surely as the atoms are a part of the cell. As the atomic scientist probes the mysteries of the cell and discovers the power locked in the tiny quarks, the astrologer probes the solar system discovering its power in conjunction with men and women:

> The main centers of man's physical system bear the same relationship to each other as the planets in the Solar System bear to each other. Each glandular center, therefore, is probably a receiving station for one particular form of solar energy, transmitted via the transforming agency of the corresponding planet in the Solar System.[3]

The chakras, energy centers in the human body which have been related to the glands, may be instrumental as receptors for this solar energy. As Alexander Pope writes: "We are but parts of one stupendous whole, Whose body nature is and God the Soul."

Our union with the planets of our system leads us now, as it did Black Elk, to seek the "star of understanding." The term "morning star" is actually applied only to the visible planets, Mercury, Venus, Mars, Jupiter and Saturn. A planet in this group is typically in the position of morning star when observable in the eastern sky before sunrise and in the position of evening star when in the western sky after sunset. These planets, therefore, may be evening or morning stars depending on their relationship to the Sun. It is Earth's planets in conjunction with the Sun and Moon on which astrology is based. So Black Elk's "star" does indeed transmit astrological understanding.

Modern shamans maintain astrological tradition. As Agnes Whistling Elk explains it to the writer, Lynn Andrews:

> Do you know how noble Grandfather Sun is? All of the children of Grandfather Sun, the planets, revolve around him . . . A star has a great and noble spirit . . . Pray to endless space. Pray to the sun. Pray to the seven: Earth. Jupiter. Mars. Neptune. Moon. Venus.[4]

Astrology is often believed in by those who know little about it and scorned by those who know even less. When Sir Isaac Newton was challenged about his belief in astrology by the astronomer Halley, he replied, "Sir, I have studied the subject. You have not." It is indeed a complex subject.

The configuration of the zodiac in relationship to a person's pre-cise time and place of birth give nearly infinite variety to individual astrological charts; so the interpretation of charts is a profession which demands years of study. A casual observation that a person's seasonal birth time indicates Aquarius or another of the twelve signs is as fragmentary as an isolated equation in Einstein's relativity theory.

Although a complete theoretical understanding of astrology is beyond the reach of a lay person, the use of it is certainly available. The uninitiated citizen can drive a car down the highway without understanding its construction; similarly one can steer one's life course using astrology as a tool without a technical understanding of it. Tayja, drawn like the tides by the Moon, responded to an astral magnet, and turned to an astrologer to further open that doorway be-tween her conscious and unconscious mind. A friend told her of Moonrabbit, a practicing astrologer in Minneapolis, Minnesota.

Tayja, in a period of transition between her reparenting home and independent life, was beginning to recognize that the purpose of living is to discover the purpose of living. More specifically, she wan-ted to know: "What abilities and talents do I have? At what time and in what ways can I manifest them?" These were questions astrology could help her with, and she felt an affinity with the sky that prepared her to make use of it. "At night I would go out to the sky and sit for hours moving and turning in the four directions, praying and getting answers from the wind people and my spirit friends, White Feather, Sacagawea, Crazy Horse and so on. I liked the feeling of being with my dead mother. I could sense her around me."

Moonrabbit prepares carefully before each consultation. The first step is to do the calculations, measuring the placement of planets relative to geographical location on Earth and configuration of the heavens. This can be complicated by differing time zones as well as the constantly changing distances and positions of the planets (the wanderers) in relationship to the Earth and to each other. In Tayja's case, Moonrabbit's task was complicated because Tayja knew only the day, January 26, and year, '54, of her birth—not the hour.

The Zodiac (wheel of life) which includes most of the bodies in our solar system which are significant to astrology, is a term derived from the Greek word *zoe* which means "life," an appropriate deriva-tion for a system which can be seen as a template for our lives. The

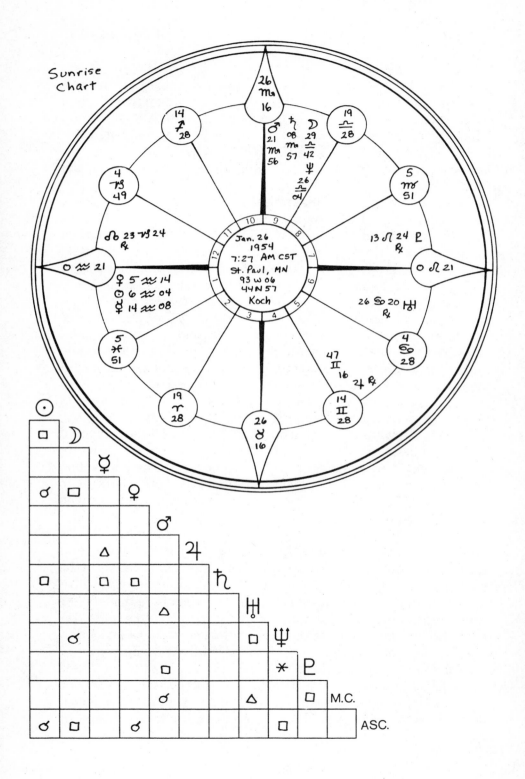

Zodiac is an imaginary belt in the heavens wide enough to encompass the paths of all the principal planets except Pluto. As the eight planets, together with our Earth and Moon, orbit the Sun in a single plane, the Zodiac with the Sun as its center may be thought of as a disc or saucer. This saucer is divided like a pie into the twelve astrological signs. It takes one year for the Earth to pass, in a counterclockwise direction, through all twelve signs. In the course of that year, influences will change in accordance with the positions of the planets, including their relationship to the Sun and Moon. Like a human community, all have influences on each other. Each planet can be said to have its own personality which reacts in certain specified ways to influence the bodies with which it comes into proximity. Season and time of day change these influences in predictable ways through changing angles and distances relative to the Sun, Moon and planets.

These astrological signs relating to the Earth's annual orbit around the Sun are divided in several ways, one of which applies in an unusual way to Tayja's chart. This is a division into the four elements of Fire, Earth, Air and Water, energies all of us carry within us. This ancient division can be conceived of as energy (Fire), matter (Earth), gas (Air) and liquid (Water). The first sign, Aries, is a Fire sign, the second, Taurus, an Earth sign and so around the Zodiac with Gemini—Air, Cancer—Water, Leo—Fire, Virgo—Earth, Libra—Air, Scorpio—Water, Sagittarius—Fire, Capricorn—Earth, and ending with the Air sign, Aquarius, followed by Pisces, a Water sign and so back to Aries.

These signs are grouped in several more ways in accordance with geometrical laws of nature, but since application rather than theory is our purpose here, we will return to Tayja when she first mentioned her plans for an independent life. Both the scare of leaving the parental protection of her reparenting home and the will to succeed on her own are evident in her journal entries nearly two years before she actually left treatment. In the fall of 1980, she was already dreaming of moving out on her own.

"Before, I was willing to put up with almost anything . . . Now I feel stress from the things I have to put up with, D. wetting his pants, all the crazy behavior. It's very hard for me to not be crazy because I know that's how I can get [the reparenting mother's] attention."

signed "Debby." (10/29/80)

At the time of Debby's writing, Tayja's journal entries were signed by several of her personalities, and she was in regression, getting her bottle, and frequently in touch with her "homicidal kid" with desires to hurt herself coming from that portion of her personality. As Tayja continued to work with these issues, part of her yearned for a healthy environment in which to continue her growth. In December, 1980, she writes, "I am at a point where I know that I am dying fast and feel like I don't even want to live here anymore . . . I told him to stop throwing things, and he said, 'stuff it up your ass.' I want our house to go back to a family and not a hospital or institution . . . Maybe I can't live here anymore, but I know that I can't live alone yet, kinda in a double bind." She signs off with a large, angry period like a cannon ball.

Tayja, then in her late twenties, was at a point of tension between her past and her future. This situation can be explained with reference to the nodes of the Moon as shown in her natal chart. The nodes mark the point at which the path of the Moon intersects the path of the Earth round the Sun. The nodes of the Moon set the life of an individual in a larger spiritual context with the South Node indicating the past and the North Node indicating the future. The past as reflected in the South Node represents the sum of the karmic residue with which the soul enters the present life, while the North Node shows growth possibilities. Cause from the past together with effect to be realized in the current life point to world evolution. In respect to her nodes as in other ways, Tayja touches the extremes. Her Cancer South Node tells of the perennial infant wishing to maintain the focus of parental attention, her sensitive feelings shattered by rejection. She must learn to let go of the past, for the North Node in Capricorn points to a life of honor and respect. When she identifies with a cause greater than self, she is destined for a life of splendid accomplishment. Even today as she moves into her life of "splendid accomplishment," her mother's attention is a factor in Tayja's life.

At the time of her visit to Moonrabbit, Tayja's "hallucinations" are still troubling her. As she works with the psychological paradigm which defines them as symptomatic of insanity, she has a fearful love/hate relationship with her visions which makes their content often angry and violent, corresponding to her mental/emotional attitude toward them. Shortly before Christmas she writes, "God help me from leaving treatment!" The temptations to run are very much with her. "I still feel angry . . . is it worth staying freezing with the cold and paying $250.00 per month—listening to all the crap—sometimes I hate people—their slimey bodies around me. I hate being told what to do . . . I hate second seat to people acting crazier than I." Then, more philosophically: "We all get tired of it off and on." (12/2/80)

A year later in September of '81, Tayja writes, "If I left here tomorrow, I don't think I would even have too much problem adjusting to it." Then, on December 9, Tayja is preparing for her apartment. "Bought stuff from Joyce for my new apartment, feel so excited, fun planning."

Along with the fun, there are still apprehensions, "It's a hard thing to decide to move out right now, but I really need to do that. I want to know if I can make it out there on my own, and that's hard to know if I'm still living here. Got trouble with nights and spare time, but I've got to figure out how I'm going to deal with that eventually . . . "

Tayja was lonely with her decision: "I felt very angry that Mama didn't say 'good bye' to me; felt separate and lonely . . . I've got so much different feedback around my moving out." (12/11/81)

On December 13th, 1981, "Mama held me a few minutes . . . Moving tomorrow. At house meeting [I have] fear of them all saying it probably won't work.

"The next day at house meeting, they confronted me about my icky energy . . . I told them anyway, upset and scared." She resented not getting time time to be held later in group.

Today Tayja writes with mature understanding: "I think it was hard for my mother to say 'yes' to my moving out. But I had to go out and experience what I had learned. It was hard for me too, as I had experienced leg surgery and could hardly see. There were some hurt feelings and very similar things when every child leaves for the first time."

Tayja was ready, and her spare time was taken up in school at The Society for the Blind. She continued to take the bus to her reparenting home for work in groups. "It's been good at school, much harder at Wiger's. Hard to get back in once you leave. Haven't felt much need to do heavy work [in therapy]. Think I've been doing very well on my own." (3/23/82)

Tayja was ready to expand to a larger source of self-knowledge. Moonrabbit was a good choice as her discipline could determine potentials and possibilities from an impersonal perspective, and she could observe signs in the future that were not manifested in Tayja at the time.

Like any other technique, the manner in which astrology is applied determines its value. Moonrabbit, as a caring counselor, attempts to show her clients how to realize maximum personal growth through utilizing the guidelines shown in their charts. The chart is carefully interpreted and preserved on tape so that the client can review it. As there was much going on in Tayja's life at the time, it is well that she did not have to absorb the entire pattern of her life in one sitting.

As Tayja was not able to give Moonrabbit a birth hour, a sunrise chart was used, thereby measuring positions of the planets the morning of her beginning on Earth, her physical, emotional, mental and spiritual starting point. The signs at this significant time influence all of life which is a concept held also by the Sioux:

> At birth each of us is given a particular Beginning Place within these Four Great Directions on the Medicine Wheel. This Starting Place gives us our first way of perceiving things, which will then be our easiest and most natural way throughout our lives. But any person who perceives from only one of these Four Great Directions will remain just a partial man.[5]

The beginning sign can be seen as a sort of astrological family, a place where life positions are learned. But, like a family, it is a place of departure when an individual achieves adulthood. We are not locked into our beginning signs on the astrological "medicine wheel."

Recently an astrologer looked at Tayja's chart and, seeing her beginning place, exclaimed, "With this chart it's a miracle she's alive! What a will that woman must have!" Her chart showed clearly that death was Tayja's close companion from the beginning when she and her twin were struggling in a life/death position. Moonrabbit saw this, but she started in a different place:

> You have no planets in Earth signs, and the Earth in astrology has to do with being very practical, materialistic, dealing with laundry and checkbooks, all that mundane stuff. People who don't have many planets in Earth tend to

go one of two ways: one is to be very chaotic . . . But I also have met people who are extremely orderly. It's almost like they knew if they weren't extremely orderly, everything would be completely chaotic. So it is not natural for you to get your head out of the clouds and your feet on the ground, because Earth is the component that keeps people grounded.

Tayja, born with a broken hip and cerebral palsy affecting her legs, has had trouble with her connections to Earth since birth, and she still has some difficulty walking. She is clean and orderly in her housekeeping and an excellent painter, clean lines and no spattering. She pointed out to me, that since she learned to paint when she could scarcely see, she needed to know where every drop went, otherwise she might step in paint and track it all over. Not only could she not keep her feet flatly planted on Earth, she couldn't adequately see the matter of which it was made! With those complications, it would indeed be easy to give in to chaos. But she does not want to do that any more than she wants to give in to death.

Water is of paramount importance both personally and cosmically. Over ninety percent of our body weight is water; most of our home planet is water. It can erode earth, put out fire and displace air. Moonrabbit has more to say about it:

> You have a lot of watery energy in your chart. Water is more the emotional, the sensitive, the creative, the nurturing, the intuitive. So it's very easy for you to relate to the world around you through emotions, through intuition, through feeling more than practical means. Water's like a sponge . . . Water people generally love swimming, love being in water."

(It has always given Tayja comfort to sit beside the water, and while at her reparenting home she spent many hours easing her tensions in the hot tub.)

> Water in and of itself lacks structure . . . so you spend all this time sort of flowing and seeking. It's harder for you than for most people to make long-range decisions and to feel a sense of purpose in your life. You have much more ability to be in the moment, in some ways to deal with people, in some ways to deal with your own inner self and to develop intuitive, spiritual, creative qualities.

> Your Sun is in Aquarius, and you also have Venus and Mercury in Aquarius.

On January 26, when Tayja was born, the Earth's position relative to the Sun put her birth sign in Aquarius, an air sign. This was her starting point on the wheel of life. Moonrabbit continues:

> Your Aquarian Sun is in the house of Pisces (the 12th house) so it's a watered down Aquarius. Aquarius is the sign of the rebel, of the innovator; it's the sign of a person who sometimes feels special in a good way and sometimes feels like an outsider. People who have a lot of planets in Aquarius can look back on their lives and feel like whenever it comes to a group situation or even their family, that they were different than the others . . . So Aquarius is the sign of doing your own thing, of being free. What motivates the masses of people does not motivate you, and at times you even choose to do something different because you don't want to be part of the masses.

"What is crazy?" Tayja asks, "the way they do things or the way I do things?" Her refusal or inability to accept consensual reality is key to her shamanic abilities. She sees herself as a sensitive maker of reality, not one of the ranks in humanity's mass march.

Moonrabbit continues:

> Aquarius is an Air sign, and Air basically relates through intellect, so gathering information and putting bits and pieces into patterns gives you that "ah hah!" reaction when all those seemingly irrelevant pieces fit together. When Aquarius is working at its best, it's like everything you know goes somewhere. Most Aquarian people have extremely good recall.

True to her Aquarian and Piscean influences, Tayja uses her intellect with a unique blend of intuition and emotion. She very literally reaches into the air for spirit contacts and into the seas of her unconscious mind for her free and unconventional approach to life.

> On a more personal level, Aquarius is a hot-cold, on-again off-again energy. You also have Aquarius rising [coming into influence on the eastern horizon when the person,

or "native," draws the first breath. The rising sign is the native's window to the world. Through it the world is viewed, and the world looks back]. So you tend to do things in spurts . . . intensely enthusiastic . . . for a time. Then you'll need more solitude or quiet time for introspection, or to look at the larger pattern in your life . . . I compare Aquarians to a zigzag pattern. They have to take a 180 degree turn every once in a while to get to the goal and check out the other side . . .

You also have Venus, which is a sign of love and romance, in Aquarius, so you have this side of your nature that says "I want to love people, but I want to be free." When we get to relating to people, this can be a hassle.

So here's all this Aquarian energy: intellectual, rational, innovative, and it's in a part of your chart that has to do with intuition, inspiration, emotionality, going with the flow, kind of feeling your way through life. They're very contradictory energies, Water and Air. Like a big lake, and the only way the air and water meet is through a little bit of evaporation right on the surface . . . The Water relating to a deep part of life, and the Air more superficial. It has to do with keeping things light . . . Aquarius is easily friendly with lots of people and knows lots of this and that to talk about, whereas the Water component—!" The splits in Tayja's personality certainly manifested in an extreme manner! She can be, as Moonrabbit says, "on one level, intensely emotional, on another playful, humorous, objective.

Moonrabbit gives advice on how to deal with these extremes:

Sometimes you can be in the pits dragging through the mire, and the Aquarian, because it's objective, can step back and say, "Now I'm really depressed, but maybe I can find something to enjoy." Sometimes Air is a nice balance for Water because Water tends to be depressed, overly concerned with the past. Air gives distance and humor. That's really nice, but not always. Sometimes you can be getting into something really deep and feel a different level of what's going on, and then the Air says, "It's time to get distracted, time to get away from this heavy stuff." So in your personal development, Air can be a hassle. (Throughout her therapy, Tayja would alternately immerse herself in group work for a time, then become fed up and retreat from it completely.)

Tayja's destiny as a shaman is reflected from the cosmic medicine wheel:

I want to talk more about that Aquarius/Pisces balance. They're both humanitarian, humanistic, or transpersonal. So they give you energy to relate to large groups of people, to humanity as a whole, to social situations. But both those signs make it hard to relate personally because they tune you into the higher causes, interpersonal causes, mass consciousness or social kinds of problems rather than tuning into more personal, selfish kinds of life involvements. They get involved in a cause that is larger than themselves. It could come out on a real personal level, "Other people are more important than I am."

As the twelfth house on the wheel before recycling to the first, Pisces is the culmination of the eleven preceding energies of the zodiac, so it is possible to become either confused or enlightened by access to all the other energies.

As Moonrabbit explains:

It can be a very self-sacrificing position, almost a martyrdom, to play out the role of, "Oh, poor me!" There's a strong element in your chart of the whole Pisces struggle. The Pisces or Neptune struggle (both Water signs) makes you this incredible human being, so sensitive, sometimes, that you feel everything. You can be feeling just wonderful, then this person you care about can come up and say, "I've got some problems, can I talk to you?" and you'll be sympathetic and understanding and nurturing, and they'll feel better, and you'll feel just lousy like you absorb what's going on into your body. Typical response: "I'm tough, I can handle it, just put more weight on my shoulders." So you're in there trying to fix everybody, and you don't have time to think what's ailing *you*. And then the last way, "Oh, I'm just so sensitive, I try so hard, but nothing changes. Oh, poor me!" The blessing is to have that much sensitivity, but the curse is what you do with it, how do you use it productively?

Because all three: the martyr, the rescuer, the victim are all non-productive solutions. A possible solution in your chart is the intense amount of creative energy.

Although this tendency to absorb the emotions of others often made life difficult for Tayja during her reparenting years when she was surrounded by troubled people, she now has learned to use the ability creatively in her healing practice. In typical shamanic fashion, she takes the problems of others into herself, then cleanses them from her body and psyche. Thus she first becomes one with her client, then heals by healing herself.

The planet Venus has to do with beauty, with art, with music. That planet is right next to your Sun, so you can iden-tify strongly with something in life that brings harmony, that brings a feeling of making things better by making them more peaceful, more harmonious. That strong Venus is generally an indication of artistic talents, but what we have to talk about in your chart is a block in that part. To talk about that block, we have to talk about your family, your natural family.

Moonrabbit knew she was dealing with an emotionally charged subject, and cautiously she attempted to bring clarity to the con-fusions in Tayja's parental relationships.

Mostly I can just see your mom and dad. I'm going to start off by talking about your father, but sometimes it sounds more like your mother because they switch roles. If this hap-pens, just tell me. In your chart your mother and your father are very close allies. It looks like they had a joint role and collaborated in some ways. They both come out as very se-cretive, very distant emotionally, cold, withdrawn, rule-oriented people. So a lot of emphasis as you were growing up was on being conservative (according to the family struc-ture), playing the game by the rules. With your father there is very deep indication of disappointment and rejection. There's a tremendous feeling of hurt in your relationship with your father, and the thing about that is that at one time you may have felt that there was a real special relationship, so you may have felt that something you had got taken away. It's not like he was always real cold, but there was something that changed, bringing deep disappointment. Then there's something that's kind of confusing to me. I'll put this out to you: there's all this repression of emotion, but there's all this underlying real inappropriate sexuality. I have no idea how far that went. I have no way of telling, so I don't know if that's covert or overt. One of the possibilities is that it could have come out through violence.

Tayja confirmed in her deep, flat voice. "Right. There was a lot of incest."
"And also there was a lot of physical abuse."
"Yes."

. . . 'cause I see with your dad things building up and building up, and then kind of a lack of control on his part and a lot of explosion, but this real thin line, it looks like he felt intensely sexual when he was violent, and that's why I get all these mixed feelings about that. One of the things on your dad, going along on this theme, is that he controlled everyone incredibly. He really controlled your mother and repressed her too, but in some ways she really stood by him.

Your mother comes out in your chart as playing out the victim or the martyr, somehow being in that role of being powerless and helpless. She tried to be a friend to her children and talk to them, to treat you as an equal. She may have confided in you things you had no business knowing. In some ways she was a sympathetic, understanding woman, but she was so trapped in her own powerlessness that there wasn't much she could do. She also had a lot of weird confusion about her sexuality, so boundaries are all mixed up in your family, and especially your mom's. It's like your dad had boundaries in kind of cruel ways, but your mom just didn't have any.

Tayja's mother, confused as she was by alcohol and her husband's abuse, was certainly confused sexually as in other ways. Although Tayja appreciated her gentleness, she also referred to her mother's inappropriate touching.

The early part of your childhood was almost like a desert, real dry, and here you are, this incredibly sensitive human being, so it's very very difficult for you, and your chart shows that basically what you did was survive by withdrawing into yourself. It makes it so hard for you to reach out to other people who can help you. For a while that was survival, and now it can be damaging. One thing I see in charts with this kind of configuration is this incredible fantasy life as a way to deal with things. So this is part of the whole Neptune-Pisces thing that can come out in this incredible creativity. It's almost like you had to create a different reality to survive. [Tayja did indeed go to extremes to create her "separate reality."] So in some ways, that's where your power lies, but it's so mixed up with all that yucky stuff that it's hard to feel you can unblock creativity without having these horrible consequences.

Now I want to go back and tell more detail about your family. It's unfortunate, but we all seem to inherit certain patterns from our upbringing, so we'll talk about some of these things that show in your chart and go into ways to use them more productively. We'll start with your Moon in Scorpio. It is at the tail end of Libra but enough into Scorpio to give you a Scorpio Moon. [Because Tayja's exact birth time is unknown, it can not be positively deduced from her chart whether her Moon is in Libra or Scorpio.] I have developed the theory that a Scorpio Moon is a sign that deals with shame, and the Moon symbolizes your needs, how you get them taken care of. People with their Moon in Scorpio seem to inherit this legacy of being ashamed of what they need and also of their feelings. It seems to me that both your parents, but especially your father, had a big role in making sure that it happened. He was so good at shaming people, probably good at shaming your mother too. One thing that happened to you in your growing up was that you really learned to bury your wants, especially things that felt important to you. [Tayja had journaled, "I need to learn to ask for what I want.]

Now I'm going to give you a different kind of thinking that goes with this Moon in Scorpio. Some of it may fit; some of it may not. One of the things that typically goes with this Moon is that you think that if you want something too much you're never going to get it, so you better learn how not to want things. The other thing is that if you care about somebody

too much you're not going to get what you want, so you better
not care about people too much. Also, if you need something
from somebody, you think you have to repay the favor ten-
fold. So under all this is a kind of undeserving mentality. This
is one of the hardest things to change because its big. [The
need to give, a natural part of Tayja's personality, is amplified
through her association with Indian tradition.]

Let's talk about some of the more positive things in
Scorpio to get a little better feeling in here. Scorpio is the
energy that has to do with rebirth, regeneration. It's the
energy that has to do with sinking into the darkness, then in
some way reemerging reborn from deep, dank places somewhere within your own self. So the principle of Scorpio is the
principle of death and rebirth.

As well as being implicit in Tayja's chart, death and rebirth are an
integral part of shamanism.

Because of this strong Scorpio you have, it's in you to
experience some of the worst possible things and also the
best of life. Scorpio people sometimes feel that they have to
die in order to change. So there's this real intensity of
experience and of emotionality. Scorpio rules all the negative feelings like jealousy, vindictiveness, cruelty, revenge
and anger; but it also rules all the transcendent kinds of
emotions: intense love, intense joy. It's the power to trans-
mute yuckies into the beautiful stuff, but it seems like a lot of
the Scorpio people I know will get involved in the real negative for a period.

Before her reparenting, Tayja went through a time of being
involved with black magic.

It's almost like riding a wave until you bottom out before
you start to reemerge or resurface. So there's a whole process for you of rebirth and renewal, but you resist it as long as
humanly possible, and you punish yourself to the point of
pain where you can't do anything but let go and give in.
Then you get on the other side and think, "Oh, that was
really a good change." That's Scorpio. Underneath that
feeling of resisting change, there's fear of change, and
underneath that, there's a fear of death. With your Moon in

Scorpio, you have to work a whole lot harder to know what you're feeling than most people. It's kind of like things will build up to a crisis, and then you know you're feeling something.

It is interesting to compare this Scorpio trait with the denial of feeling and even existence which is a part of the hebephrenic diagnosis.

Sometimes you think everything is fine until you get to a certain point, and then you think, "My God, this has been bothering me for months, but I didn't know it," because Scorpio is underground. It's like an iceberg where only one eighth of what is really there shows up on the surface. And the rest is so internalized! So you have an incredibly active inner life, subconscious, whatever you want to call it.

For Tayja, it proved to be the wellspring of shamanism.

Stuff is building and dying and rebuilding all the time, and only a little bit of that shows on the surface, so periodically you're finding things about yourself that you didn't even know. People around you are surprised, and you get surprised too. So much happens internally before it gets to the surface! You process everything before you come to the realization, and then it's total, and you can move with it really fast. Change may seem slow because so much precedes it.

Scorpio is an intensely stubborn sign, and so is Aquarius. Scorpio tends to be an all or nothing sign. So Moon in Scorpio makes it really hard for you. It means you tend to give in totally to somebody and do things totally their way or to be totally stubborn and do things your way.

At the time of this astrological reading, Tayja was capable of flipping from independent young woman to defenseless baby within the space of a few hours.

One of the lessons with Scorpio is learning to compromise, and it's like you're not born in this world with any sense of how to do it. Certainly there was no compromise ever in your family. So you have to learn to meet somebody fifty percent of the way rather than bend over backwards and get walked on or to be completely stubborn.

What I want to emphasize is that this chart gives you incredible power to regenerate with intense *major types of changes*. Even now if you look back on the type of person you were in your teens, you will feel like you're totally different . . . It's kind of like walking down the path of life in a rut, then standing in front of a door for a real long time. Then in a short period of time opening that door and getting on the other side and closing it. Also, you have the power to make the best of things when horrendous things happen to you. You say, "I can learn from this." So then it's valuable, even if this intense learning doesn't always feel good. I'm sure you already know that.

The planet Saturn is next to your Moon. Saturn has to do with karma on one level and on another with rules, with structure, organization, doing what's right. On the emotional level it has to do with fear, with blocks. So all three of these levels are relevant to you.

Let's start with karma. What you have to do in this lifetime has to do with emotions, needs, sexuality. Those are parts of life where you have most to learn and where you may experience the most intense struggle. You can't run away from your karma. The sooner you take responsibility for being emotional, getting what you need and being sexual, the sooner you get to leave that karma behind. During the first twenty-nine years of a person's life, they generally will work out karma from past lives, so some of the struggles with emotionality and with sexuality you may be clearing out from other lifetimes. As you get to be over thirty, that may change for you.

Let's talk about the fear element of Saturn. This is a strong planet for self-protection, saying "You could get hurt." From an early age you learned not to trust people, so now you need to take chances . . .

On the practical level, Saturn has to do with Earth, but you don't have any Earth, so it's good Saturn is close to your Moon. This makes it easier for you to be organized and practical, to set up goals and get things done. It grounds you. Some of that suspicion and fear is good because otherwise you'd be overly naive and idealistic. Saturn gives you capabilities of being pretty good at telling other people what to do. It also gives you inner authority. With your Aquarius, this is an important balance.

This is interesting. You have the planet Neptune close to your Moon, and you have Saturn. Neptune and Saturn are as different as day and night. Neptune has to do with going with the flow, with the spiritual side of life, with intuition, emotionality, that spongelike sensitivity we were talking about. Saturn has to do with the most practical, mundane, hard-working, responsible, structured, limited approach to life that there is. Neptune says, "I want to do it all, feel it all, be part of it all." Saturn says, "You have to do this first, this second, pay attention to this detail, that detail." Saturn is total structure, total limitation. Neptune is lack of boundaries as in cosmic consciousness. Saturn's the business person, the organizer, the developer. There's so much conflict around that part of your nature! The potential exists for you to integrate the two. What happens is you take the mysticism, the dreams, the visions, and you make real practical plans for them. People like this can go into massage where they can take feelings and then use their hands to make it practical. Or they do sculpture or Reiki healing. So anything that brings the spiritual to a concrete focus is a wonderful way to integrate them.

This type of integration is exactly what Tayja has moved into.

The other thing I have to talk about is that people who have this will feel real confused about their role in life. The Neptune will make you feel like you want to be a healer, a dreamer, a searcher on a path that's flowing; and Saturn says, "I have to fit in, I have to hold a job, it has to be respected." Saturn is so worldly! So typically people will go from one extreme to another trying to find a balance, a way to be in the world.

One more thing about the Moon. You were born when the Moon was in its last quarter which means that when you believe in something, you believe in it very, very strongly, and you're good at convincing other people about what you believe in. Areas that have to do with teaching communications, getting out information and affecting other people are capabilities you have. Practical use of inspiration is good here too.

Now I want to talk about your Mars in Scorpio. Mars is the planet that has to do with anger, sex, how we get what we want. Mars is Fire. Scorpio is Water. They do not go together at all. Together they steam! It's a very hard placement to have; it's a configuration which adds additional stress. Mars is the raw energy to get going, but the way Mars has to express itself is through watery energy. So you have this Fire meeting this Water, and that tells you to slow down, go inward. So this emphasizes the hot-cold, on-off energy we talked about. Then you go from being a steam roller to plain old passivity. One of the lessons of Mars and Scorpio is not to be so attached to what you want . . .

Let's talk about your Mars in Scorpio, the anger part of the Mars. What happens typically is that feelings build up to the point of explosion, and the person feels totally out of control, and they do things they will regret later. That's the worst way; the best way to use the energy is probably to be angry all the time for a while. You've probably discovered that the angry part of your nature is just like a bomb. [This is exactly right as Tayja has journaled that she feels "like a bomb waiting to explode."]

But there will come a time in your life when that isn't so intense because you can deal with things in your life as they come up so that anger won't have a chance to build up. That Scorpio influence in your life—there it is again—the power to transform your anger into creativity. The part of your chart that has to do with philosophy can help. So as you go into difficult, angry parts of your life, you can learn and teach.

The last way to use that Mars energy is sexual. You have both Mars and Saturn with Scorpio, and they both have to do with sexual repression, growing up with that repression. What's hard is that Scorpio is the sign of sexuality, so you have an intense amount of sexual drive. Then there're all these rules and inhibitions about it and a lot of fear as well. So you may go through periods of being intensely disinterested in sex, then go through periods when you can't get enough. One of the lessons about Mars and Scorpio is to find balance about your sexuality. For you it goes much deeper because of all the abuse and fear that make sexuality and intimacy of any kind all tied up with power. For better or for worse, the people you are attracted to tend to play out your battle patterns, so you'll have to work to change all that. Always you will be attracted to powerful people because your essence is very, very powerful . . . You have the potential in your chart to have very equal relationships. It looks like you want that, but part of you gives a lot of struggle about jealousy, ownership, control—all those things in a power relationship.

Let's talk more about struggles in relationships. Venus and Aquarius has confusion between love and friendship, between friendship and sex. Also, you may have very different standards than society, so you feel good with freedom in relationships. You may have had a tendency earlier to get so wrapped up in a person that you would do everything together, but that was devastation because Aquarius says, "I have to be my own person." [This comment from Moonrabbit could have been quoted from Tayja's journal.]

The work part of your chart talks a lot about dealing with people. If you were a counselor, you would be real good. You have a unique ability to know what's motivating people. You can see through them real well, so if they're playing games, they're not going to play them on you. There's a strong motivation to do some kind of work that's of service, something tied up in education, educating in the large sense. It doesn't have to be in the school system.

It seems like you will get to a stage in your life when you will get firmly established. In the early part of your life you will try out a lot of things. Then your potential blossoms when you are 42.

Tayja comments, "I've always had a fantasy that I wanted to be 30. All my life I've wanted to be 30, so I must have picked that up subconsciously that some of the other things were going to change."

Moonrabbit agrees:
Let's try and get a little perspective on this. During your middle 20's—24, 25, there was a lot of expansion, then a lot of getting away from things . . . Now, (28) you're in a phase of breaking free, leaving a lot of stuff behind. As you get farther into your 30's, you'll get in different types of

relationships that will give you a new lease on life. Then in your 40's your profession will really come together.

Tayja explains, "Right now I'm in school learning braille. My work in the past had been working with autism. A lot of teaching. I teach at reparenting workshops."

In your career there will be a lot of people to help you.

"What I wanted to know was in early birth. I was born with a broken hip and stuff. Is there anything in the chart around physical?"

Yeah, there's a couple of things. One is that you were born with the planet Pluto prominent because of its angular position. Pluto has to do with life and death. To me Pluto is pretty much of a karmic planet; not *the* karmic planet, but it brings in things you have no control over. I said the early part of your life was devoted to survival, I mean from the moment you popped out. One of the interesting things is that you have an incredibly strong will to live that pulled you through the early part. I would be curious, were you ever suicidal?

"Yeah."

But something inside you said, "No way," 'cause there's a fire in you.

"There was a lot of violence that we grew up in and had to learn to survive through; the eyesight and the birth, all that."

Mercury is the planet that has to do with vision. Mercury was in with Pluto . . . I don't have very much experience with the medical aspects, but I can see that it's tied in with birth and this whole thing about 'are you meant to live or die?' . . .

Are you interested in being a mother, what that would be like?

"I've had children."

We can talk about being a mother from your chart. One of the hardest things is boundaries. Because you are so sensitive it's as though you'd want to feel your children's pain for them. There's part of that whole rescuer mentality that would come out with the kids. On the other hand there's a lot of support, sensitivity, caring, nurturing. You have a lot of that good stuff. So the biggest struggle you would have is getting boundaries straight and trying not to control them, or being the same as your family, obviously. The other thing that you have is the feeling of having to do everything on your own, all the responsibility. One of the things your children taught you is that you can't do everything, that you needed to get other people in there to help you. It seems that the experience was very difficult and draining.

"Yeah, I've had three babies that died," Tayja says.

So that explains it. Let me tell you this. There are two different points on the chart that have to do with karma, and it has to do with letting go and the whole thing about death and rebirth, so with that strong a Pluto and the strength of the circumstances, it almost forces you to see things in a much deeper way than most people, and it makes you really good at helping other people as they go through difficult times. It's almost like there isn't anything that you haven't experienced . . . That's a more constructive way to use that negative energy.

Let's talk about now. Lots of the things in your chart are in the part having to do with intimacy. So a whole lot of what you are doing is changing emotional patterns, changing especially father-type things. That's going to be going on for the next couple of years. You're in a long period right now of shedding a lot of illusions, of having to focus on more practical, concrete ways of doing things . . . There was a period, practically all of 1980 and 1981, of tremendous upheaval in your life where you were almost forced to break out of certain patterns, and things felt totally out of your control. Even starting in the fall of 1979 that was going on. [Moonrabbit pinpoints Tayja's reparenting experience.] Now you're on the other side of that intense disruption stuff. You're more in a period of new structure, new responsibility. It's kind of like putting the pieces back together. It won't be really back together until almost the end of 1983. Then you'll be on a whole new leg of life. [This "leg" culminated in June of 1984 when Tayja regained her vision after a winter of exercising her psychic skills through regular participation in the Blind Awareness program.]

You're entering a period called your Saturn Return, what happens when people turn thirty. You're already feeling it now. During the month of November of 1983 you will be doing your most serious Saturn Returning, and actually a little bit into July and August. It's time to get rid of a lot of fears that have been inhibiting you. It's time to make reappraisals and set long-range goals . . . Saturn Return is a time of getting rid of everything you don't need in your life, whether it's fears that inhibit you, whether it's people who are no longer good for you, whether it's possessions, whether it's losing weight, Saturn has to take everything down to the bare bones and make you deal with who the inner person is, where you really get your strength. This will be a major turning point.

It is putting karmic debt behind and moving into spiritual potential to be realized in the present life.

One of the nice things that happens is that Jupiter goes into Scorpio first . . . It's making you feel much more positive, more renewed. It's giving you a sense of faith. For the whole year you're going to feel like you're expanding and growing in all sorts of positive ways. It will help prepare you for some of the struggles that are coming that are very difficult. But you will have a sense of faith in your self that will really help you during that time.

The other major thing that is happening starts in 1984 and goes all through the year. It's a change in relationship to career. [After her recovery of sight in June of '84, Tayja began her career as a shaman.]

It could be a change in relationship to home as well. This planet comes up and says, "time for a change." . . . You could get involved with something that takes you traveling. [Tayja went to Montreal in the fall of '84.] So 1984 is a big year of change, but you're together, you're stabilized, and you know where you're going, so it doesn't seem as disruptive as the past changes you've been through.

There are a lot of professional opportunities coming into your life in the fall of '83. It may have to do with teaching or traveling, and then in the winter of '84 there are bigger changes.

In '83 Tayja developed her psychic potential to a high degree among people who respected it, then in the early spring of '84 she began to teach.

This November, actually the end of September and the beginning of November, you go through a period of becoming more disciplined, more practical about some of your ideals and dreams, so it's kind of like putting things in order.

This is a wonderful time for you as far as healing goes and really developing the psychic and the intuitive. That goes all the way into the fall of '83, and you may find that when you are giving healings, a new kind of energy is opening up for you.

In answer to a question about Tayja's family, Moonrabbit said,

What you're in the process of doing is becoming an adult and, in that situation, taking your power back. With your new family, there are really good energies for expansion and trust. '84 will be the time when you stop living with them. That's more conjecture than absolute, but it's a real possibility. When you get into the fall of '82 and the winter of '83, you may find things are harder with them, more struggles as you assert yourself into being more grown up.

Tayja left Moonrabbit with one of the strongest confirmations of her being she had ever had in her life. There is great strength for all of us in the knowledge that the stars hold a purpose for each one of us and for our age as well. Like Tayja's life, our age may be seen as suspended between a self-centered inner focus of the watery Piscean age and New Age Aquarian aspirations into space. The old must be washed away to make room for new evolution.

Chapter Ten
Vision Without Sight

We are now becoming aware of more and more things of which we have no direct sensual experience. One reason for this stems from scientific advances in measurement techniques; the other, in part a result of the first, is an increased awareness of our psychic abilities. Through more sensitive instruments, science has pointed the way to a vast increase in our observations of the complex world beyond our direct experience. To take just one example of this interaction between science and psychic sensitivity, the ability of some people to see auras can be accepted by scientifically oriented people after they have been shown a kirlian photograph of the energy field which surrounds all living things. In humans this energy field is profoundly affected by the mind, and with the sense extender of a kirlian photograph, both physical and psychological states are clearly pictured. Psychological disturbances such as schizophrenia will be indicated by a ragged picture of the corona surrounding the fingertip. In severe disturbances, the light disappears almost completely. Conversely, healers may show a flare of light coming from their finger tips.[2]

Less than two hundred years ago, most people believed our eyes could show us a complete picture of our world. Now we realize how much we are missing. On a circle showing the full spectrum of light rays, those which our eyes can see make up a tiny fragment which disappears into ultraviolet on one end and infrared on the other. Our sense of hearing is also limited. Although science has but recently measured our limitations, its findings are not new. As Confucius taught, the greatest obstacle to hearing is the ear; the greatest obstacle to seeing, the eye, and similarly with the other senses. Plato had an equally limited respect for human sense perception. He compares the universe humans perceive from within their sensual cave to shadows of reality thrown on the back wall of a cave from a source of illumination the cave-dwelling human is unable to see directly. Are we truly limited to this incomplete perception, or can we cultivate other methods of sensing or perceiving energies? How much more can we see and hear and know?

Tayja and I, through our joint association in a program teaching ESP techniques to the blind, were to have a role in bringing answers to these questions into light on a practical level. We were soon to be working with others of like mind in a program reaching beyond our sensually perceived world toward a vision without sight. The inspiration for the project was Carol Ann Liaros's work with the blind which showed us the successes which are possible. In her book, *Practical ESP*, Liaros wrote: "Modern physicists, as well as mystics, tell us that solid-appearing objects are not really solid at all; the material world is an illusion. Individuals who develop psychic ability learn to see the world as moving molecules, or fields of energy, while others cannot see beyond the illusion. Who is more in touch with reality?"[3] This recalls Tayja's question, "What is 'crazy,' the way I see things or the way they do?"

Our project was to begin in the spring of 1981 after Joyce Anderson, Joan Washburn and I attended the Midwest Spiritual Frontiers Fellowship Retreat where we met and learned from Carol Ann Liaros. We could not then guess what joys and responsibilities that gleam in our eyes would lead us into.

Meanwhile, as our plans were incubating, Tayja was aware of her growing blindness. To her this was not of major importance as the other problems in her life were so much greater. Also, she was long accustomed to relying on psychic or intuitive abilities for many things the rest of us use physical vision to perceive.

From the time Tayja and Pony attempted to play baseball, Tayja pitching with her face a bat length from her brother, her eyes have deceived her. This difficulty is reflected in her medical records and occasionally in her journals. In April of 1977 Tayja's medical report stated, "The patient had tunnel vision on confrontation fields." Laboratory findings in March of the same year reported, "EEG [electroencephalogram] revealed mildly delayed responses bilaterally which may be due to diseases of the eye or to psychological problems."

In February of 1980 her psychiatrist reported, "visual inconsistencies: (These neurological deficiences have been described to occur in deprived or schizophrenic children by Lauretta Bender, M.D., New York, N.Y.; and several years ago multiple sclerosis was suspected but not confirmed.) During her current treatment (reparenting) these signs have almost completely disappeared, and her dyslexia is much improved."

In August of the same year Tayja journals, "I am aware my eyes hurt, also there is a film over them—not focusing very well right now. I felt a lot of panic being by myself downtown, and maybe it isn't good for me to be alone."

On August 3rd, her pain pours out in poetic images:

"I have to see the scare that rides upon my head, the rope that hangs from me to the ground, the embrace that hurts the body, the rape in my eyes that goes on, the smell of death that comes over me . . . The dreams are there, the fantasy is also fact, blades of pain hit the sex parts, bleed with pain and cry until the end."

In September of 1980, Tayja again mentioned her eyes, this time when she was reliving a painful period of infancy during her reparenting: "In evening group I decided to work on the two-year-old tantrum. But when I started to go to it, I felt really little. What it was was abandonment issues about mama being gone, I am sure . . . Just before I got really little, I wanted to say, 'Wait for me! Wait for me!! My eyes burned like it was the first tears I had pushed out. I felt sad, and my body felt like the first time I felt the air on my skin."

In October, 1980, Tayja's dyslexia was evident, and in large scrawling writing with words and letters upside down or omitted and punctuation confused, she wrote, "Having trouble focus my eyes." In addition to the burning and focusing, Tayja also complains that they are "jumping-feeling."

A report from Diagnostic Testing Services in March of 1981 states:

> Legal blindness [and] She is a complete non-reader, essentially blind and cannot deal effectively with any type of

printed material. Her range of general academic knowledge
is naturally restricted . . . I do not believe her reading han-
dicap is amenable to typical educational procedures and, in
all likelihood, the client would have to be treated as blind
and exposed to a Braille system of reme-diation or talking
books as a means of upgrading her now lacking academic
status.

A month after this report, on May 27, 1981, Tayja writes, "Well, a
lot has happened since I last wrote in this book . . . I've been talked to
on Monday evening about not being able to write and see color and
how I've taken that away from myself after being able to do so well.
I've got to give up my fantasy world and live in the real world, and
that's what I've decided to do no matter how it hurts. I've had my T.V.
taken and also my records (crazy records). I feel the most sad at me
and how others had told me all through my life, but I didn't listen.
Must not have been ready . . . Right now I've got small headache and
feel kinda good at the same time. The headache is in the third eye
area . . . I can write and see more of the colors than I am letting me
do . . . I am glad I didn't burn up my journals. The whole lay out for
hebephrenic behavior is shown in every one of the writings, and also
the blocking in my eyes also hurts too . . . I'll be able to read my
own stuff."

It may be implied from Tayja's writing that she is being told that
she has the mental power to regain her sight. On May 28, 1981, she
again writes of her vision: "I still am not putting things together. The
reading of words is not all there, but it's coming . . . The reading is still
hard even if I can write because I still don't understand. Hope I can
maintain the writing that I am doing. Anyway, the fight goes on. I am
still going to take help from The Society for the Blind because of the
tapes, and I don't see well enough to go places by myself, and it's not
because I don't watch myself, but I don't see cars well. The color is still
not back, and the grayness, how I see other people is still there, but
slowly it's coming . . . I know that there is a lot of work ahead and that I
do have the courage and motivation to stick it out no matter how hard
it is for me. Tayja."

There was work, also, for Joan, Joyce and me and the others
who joined us in establishing Blind Awareness Project of Minnesota.
As Tayja's darkness grew, so did potential for light. Carol Ann Liaros

is a practical psychic with a direct, logical approach. Joyce, Joan and I heard her tell of her work in a lecture at the Spiritual Frontiers Fellowship Retreat in June of 1981. Carol Ann gave us a clear, matter-of-fact account of her dramatic experiences during eight years of working with the blind. It all began when Carol Ann was teaching a psi (psychic) development class near Buffalo, New York. The class practiced techniques designed to teach skills in psychometry, telepathy, clairvoyance, aura scanning and other means of cutting through sensual barriers.

Carol Ann's audience at the Carleton retreat listened with rapt attention as she described the start of Project Blind Awareness, a program she designed to develop "second sight" for the blind after what, on the surface, appeared to be an accidental event: While teaching

her psi class in Buffalo, Carol Ann had been particularly impressed by the performance of one of the men in her class who accurately "saw" the colors of auras and noticed irregularities such as form, color and intensity. In one of the practice subjects who had a diagnosed cardiac condition, her gifted student picked out a dark area in the chest around the heart area. After the class was over, his wife came to Carol Ann, proud of her husband's prowess. "The interesting thing is," she said, "my husband is completely blind."

Carol Ann was as surprised as the student's wife. "How did he do that?" she asked.

"That's what we hoped you'd tell us."

Carol Ann asked him, "How did you see the aura?"

He considered, then answered, "I did with my *mind* what you told the others to do with their *eyes*. It is as though I saw it from the middle of my forehead."

After another similar experience with a second blind subject, Carol Ann enlisted the help of a clinical psychologist at the Human Dimensions Institute of Rosary Hill College, Buffalo, where a comprehensive testing program was conducted. At this time, in 1974, Carol Ann began her three-month pilot training program, the first Project Blind Awareness. It was soon realized that all blind people could profit from this experience.

The first essential step was to train the students in relaxation: "Fear, tension, and interference by the intellect are all barriers to the unconscious mind, and also the most common problems experienced by beginning students of ESP."[4] This is especially important for blind people. It is as though they expected their environment to step out and hit them—which it often seems to do, so a state of relaxation must be induced. Guided imagery from the instructor combined by the willing cooperation of the student bring the result. Carol Ann's often-repeated, "the body follows the commands of the mind," is the key to success. And success she certainly achieved. The three-month program she agreed to conduct continued for eight years.

Carol Ann used volunteers from her ESP classes to work one on one with blind students while she directed the class as a whole. It proved to be important for the volunteers to be able to tune into the blind person they worked with, accurately sensing their difficulties, whether it might be trouble from home, a physical difficulty, fatigue, or some other problem interfering with their relaxation.

Sessions for new students began with a review of the scientific literature so as to prepare their minds to know what could be accomplished. It proved to be a great deal. Carol Ann described to us her well-tested, step-by-step techniques as she showed slides demonstrating the class procedures. Since feeling energy is basic to progress, the first exercise is to feel the energy from a partner's hands. Once the person distinguishes this, he or she may be asked to feel his or her own aura. Then an energy circle is formed by the blind and the volunteers taking hands. The energy in the circle may be changed by asking the students to think of someone they love. Awareness of the subtle feelings and sensations is encouraged by asking the students for feedback: "How has the energy changed?" "What do you feel?" "Where are you feeling it?"

With all of the techniques, these questions were asked, and the volunteers kept careful records of students' results. Partially sighted students were blindfolded in accordance with scientific requirements.

Although Carol Ann does not consider it the most important technique, color discrimination is frequently reported by the press, perhaps because results are so easy to quantify, and it is easy to get a 'Wow!' reaction from people when they hear about or see people with glass eyes distinguishing colors by variations in the feelings their hands sense when held over different color cards. With some of her students, this developed into an ability to scan clothing and so select appropriate combinations.

Other abilities developed through training were: discrimination among shapes, positions of objects, and aura scanning by moving the hands a few inches from the body of a partner. This technique may indicate scars or other health factors. Carol Ann noted that this technique is the only one in which the blind excel over the sighted because they are not diverted by shiny hair or other visual indications of health.

Mind travel is another technique which can be extremely valuable to a blind person. Realizing that a person can relax and go in their mind to a far location is a great help in orientation. The hour it takes for a blind person to acclimate to a new environment can be reduced to a few minutes by using this technique.

One man in Carol Ann's class reported that he can walk down the street without a cane because he can now sense the positions of walls, curbs, or lampposts, "out of the side of my forehead." On one evening, an excited woman reported to Carol Ann's class that the night before, she woke to a golden glow filling her apartment. At first she thought her home was on fire, but there was no heat. Next she checked to be sure there were no lights on (later laughing at herself because she couldn't normally have seen either fire or a light). It was really happening! In gold and white light, she could see all of the furnishings of her apartment. For two hours, she just sat and enjoyed the "sight."

No wonder Project Blind Awareness excited our interest! Surely a useful and creative way to "act out our visions," as Black Elk would say.

Joyce Anderson talked to Carol Ann and arranged the first meeting with her the day after her lecture at Carleton. Then, after our return home, Joyce called eight interested people to a meeting in her living room. David Elton, Max Swanson, now our chairman, Stew Webb who handled the legal work for our corporation, and Joan, Joyce and I attended. Blind Awareness Project of Minnesota, Inc. had begun.

After a full summer of planning and fund raising, we were ready with over fifty volunteers and twenty-three would-be instructors (also volunteers) to receive Carol Ann's training in September. With so many reinforcing our faith in the viability of Blind Awareness, our confidence increased. We could use it! We went into the project with the tottering steps of a baby moving toward a glittering object not yet understood. Like the baby, the hardest part of the experience was not in taking the step but in gaining the confidence that we *could* take this step beyond the accepted beliefs of our society. We knew there was something bright to reach for—a new way to see. We knew we were made to travel toward it, but to most of society our goal was as visionary as "reaching for the moon." Yet we had seen the reality of human boots on the moon. Why not travel to inner space through teaching blind students to use awareness beyond their senses to perceive a light their eyes would never show them? We were to wait through three years of growth for Tayja to show us the far reaches of our journey, beyond anything we dared to hope for as we started toward our "moon."

"I may be blind, but I have tremendous vision," one of our blind students told us in an orientation talk she was giving as we started our training program for volunteers. Her words could have come from the Master Puppeteer who was pulling our strings with a synchronicity beyond our comprehension. In the beginning we were cautious, and when our first publicity came out under the headline, "New Program Gives Blind Sight," we were upset and perhaps a little frightened at the sensational tone of the article:

> Can the blind be taught to see?
> "Yes," says Carol Ann Liaros who has been doing just that in her classes in Buffalo, N.Y.
> "Yes," say local women . . .
> In fact, they're so sure of it they've formed a new nonprofit organization called Blind Awareness Project of Minnesota.

The body of the article contained good information about the program we were about to start:

> For years now, scientists have been telling us man uses only a small part of his brain. We hold vast, untapped resources within us . . . Recently, researchers began nibbling at the edges. Biofeedback helps people to eliminate or control pain. Other programs enable people to increase memory, read faster, be healthier. Blind Awareness is one more step.
> Everything around us contains energy. Every color vibrates on a different wavelength. Scientists measure these

energy vibrations. Now, people are being taught to feel them and to see them.

The article ended in a blaze of optimism evoking an image of our blind students tossing their canes into closets and striding into a visual world shoulder to shoulder with the sighted. But we were practical people with a dream, not exhibitionists seeking notoriety. Only one of Carol Ann's students had given up his cane. It was not something she often mentioned as it could be dangerous for the blind to go without their accustomed aids because psychic sight is *not* infallible. The slow alpha brain wave frequency in which relaxation reaches a level permitting the necessary change in consciousness is a fragile state. A honking horn or sudden awareness of personal problems can break it without warning. Then, back in normal beta consciousness, the faculty of vision may be returned to the inadequate optical system so that the person again functions as blind. We would be happy if our students could see a few lights in their minds, sense a little of the energy from the auras of their friends.

As we were locating space for classes and tending to other organizational details, Tayja was working with her blindness. On September 7, 1981 she writes, "Well, Mama and I had conversation in the hot tub about my blindness. She says she thinks it is hysteric kind of blindness. She doesn't think it is physical at all. She says she thinks it is hebephrenic way of dealing with stress." (Jeanne Wiger states that she did not diagnose Tayja's condition.) "I believe she is right, so I can deal with it and heal myself. I feel it has a way of staying with me even when I clean up one mess, soon it starts in again. I decide that, yes, I can read and write, then it goes back to old way. Why I don't know. I have many hunches. Part is around recognition and the other is around I am not supposed to be smart or anything. Part is probably hanging on to old crazy in case I am going to leave Wigers. The other is, how will anyone know that I exist if I don't make them know me one way or another? I know a part of me knows how to read, not well, but part of me knows how to write also, but I can't let people who are on the outside know. How will they help me get what I need then? I don't know how to read well enough to go to school any other way. I don't know how to take tests or anything else. I think eyes deals with existence. I think if I don't see, then it can be a goal never to get completely healthy, get attention, love or companionship. Then the end will be to die!"

Tayja continues to analyze, going back to her childhood. " . . . reading in front of the class and reading too slow. Teacher would finish the story before me. Tough! Tough! Finally stopped reading all together in fifth grade. Even back in grade school I got the teasing others gave and stood there and took it much of the time . . . I know I can read, write and spell. It's not too hard, only words that are small. Need to stop lying to myself. I can heal myself. The color blindness is real and unreal. There's a reason for my belief around it. Can I discover what?"

For all of us, beliefs influence perception, and they do so beyond our consciousness:

> Our lives and our behaviors are much more profoundly affected by the beliefs we hold unconsciously than by the beliefs we hold consciously . . . to reach the breakthrough state we must make a fundamental shift in consciously and unconsciously-held beliefs we all have about our own limitations . . . *knowing* the possibility of reshaping one's beliefs is the necessary prelude to *doing* so.

> Of all the stimuli that impinge on the sensory receptors of sight, hearing, touch, smell and taste, only a small portion ever reach our conscious awareness. Some "inner observer" . . . selects which inputs should reach awareness and shunts the rest to some other part of the mind. This selection is influenced by people's expectations, particularly as they are conditioned by beliefs arising from previous experience . . .

> The effect of beliefs and attitudes on visual perception even appears to extend to the pupil of the eye, which tends to dilate (and thus increase perception of light) when we are presented with something we want to see, and contract (thus decreasing visual input) when there is something before us we want not to see.[5]

At the time Tayja made her next entry, she was at a point of visual darkness between the pain of her history and the hope of her destiny: "Carol Ann's workshop 7:30 to 10:00 P.M. The workshop was fine. It felt fun and also felt I hope I could pass for it. I hope I have strong enough ESP and also psychic powers."

I first met Tayja in Carol Ann's evening instructors' class. Tayja came with her reparenting mother and two sisters. From time to time she left the room to breath into a paper bag because of her tendency to hyperventilate. Other than that, I don't remember much about her as I was never paired with her in the one-to-one techniques we practiced, usually wearing blindfolds. The exercises always began with a relaxation technique which resulted in an alpha state of attentive consciousness. We then went on to exercises in energy sensing and color discrimination which are accomplished with the hands a few inches from the person or object to be sensed. There was also shape discrimination in which we held marbles or die over the third eye area, psychometry using objects and pictures, sensing male and female energies from photographs, aura scanning, healing, viewing the aura, and mind travel in which we journeyed to one another's houses where we had never physically been. The experience felt like imagination, yet when we compared notes, we found that often we were correct.

In the mind travel exercise, I was paired with one of Tayja's reparenting sisters, and I "noticed" things about her house. (Although I had been in the school, I had not been in the house.) I sensed the presence of rugs rather than carpet on the floors, a striped quality to the couch (it was corduroy) many books, etc. Most of the others achieved similar numbers of "hits." As we worked in a state of non-competitive relaxation, we felt a bit like kids playing a game, loose, expansive, free. (Carol Ann's step-by-step guide, *Practical ESP*, explains these techniques in depth.)

"I know this is for me!" Tayja exclaimed. She was interested in all of the techniques we practiced as they reinforced the mind outside the body which had been a reality for Tayja all her life.

But "they opened the program in St. Paul," Tayja laments, "and I was so angry because transportation was a problem. [Tayja had moved out of her reparenting home and was living in an apartment in Minneapolis.] So I didn't get involved, but it was still in my mind, and I was still doing the things Carol had taught."

Unity Unitarian Church offered us a large space at a very low rent, so in the fall of 1981 our classes began with Darcy Bauer directing the program and Kathy Messetler and Bill Mitchell doing most of the teaching. We followed Carol Ann's techniques, kept careful records, and our students got results.

Peggy Thiel, one of our volunteers, wrote of our progress:
To Max [an intelligent and sensitive musician with a

philosophical bent who had been blind from birth], the color blue seems to give "a feeling of compassion or justice in the highest sense." It feels like pressure or a tingling in the palm of his hand. White feels like a "sticky echo," and is felt in his knuckles . . . Maggie (sighted) can distinguish all colors with ease and without much practice, Ruth (blind), on the other hand, increased her accuracy to ninety percent by practicing regularly."

[Mind travel was a favorite technique from the beginning. Participants exchanged home addresses with their partners.] Philo traveled to Jeanne's address and pictured in his mind a fairly new house with a metal outside door with windows in it. In the living room he saw a statue of a lady, landscape pictures, a fireplace, a blue cushioned chair and a small dog. All of these things were accurate except for one. Sorry, Philo,—the small dog is a cat.

Students also did well in aura scanning. In Peggy's aura, Randy felt a difference in the energy field at the nose, the right ankle, and around the back of the neck and shoulders. The nose felt hot, which seemed logical, considering it had undergone surgery less than a year ago. The ankle felt colder than the rest of the body. It had been broken about twenty years ago. The neck and shoulders radiated the accumulated tension of the day. Once Randy brought it to her attention, Peggy could concentrate on relaxing this area.

In scanning photographs, most of our students progressed far beyond determining male or female energy. In a laughing photograph of a man in pajamas and a cowboy hat, Highrise Joe (blind from birth) correctly picked up family tragedy, sadness and emotional repression in the laughing man, accurately demonstrating the point made in *The Course in Miracles* that "perception of form" may indeed "mean understanding has been obscured." As sense perception varies, so does psi perception. A blindfolded artist sensed a large white cap over a small face as "a snowy hill."

It usually takes dedicated practice to focus attention with accuracy. I got an unforgettable demonstration of that from Max Swanson one evening when we were scanning landscape pictures. He completed one picture with complete accuracy except for confusing bright flowers for "laughing children." But I was confused when he continued his description with, "There is water in the foreground, a wooded hill behind, and a tree with bare branches in the left foreground." Max's description had nothing whatever to do with the picture in front of him. Then I chanced to look at the other end of the table. There, about six feet away, was the picture he had accurately described.

Finally, with two eventful years behind us, we moved to Minneapolis, and our successes continued there.

I recall the Tuesday evening in September of 1983 when Tayja first walked into Awareness class after we moved to Hennepin Avenue Methodist Church in Minneapolis. Our new home was in a large basement room, warm and comfortable with wood paneled walls and furnishings of glowing reds and golds. Tayja walked over to me, her white cane in front of her, not flickering like the nervous whiskers of a mouse, but straight and steady just a few inches off the floor as she made her way through the twenty or so people warmly greeting each other. She stopped beside me, "I know this energy!" I told her my name as we had learned to do when speaking to a blind person. Tayja nodded. "I remember you from instructor's training."

Her voice was deep and flat reflecting little expression. It was also strong and gave one the feeling that there was an iceberg of power somewhere in the depths beneath sight. But Tayja was certainly not physically strong, and she complained about her legs, saying that it was difficult for her to stand for the ten or fifteen minutes it took to complete the energy circle.

Tayja did well from the beginning, as did many of the others. Most of our students were good with psychometry, and their ability gave us novel ways of sharing experience. For example, after returning from Southeast Asia, I tried an unusual method for gaining information about objects I had collected on the trip. A quote from an article I wrote which was reprinted in Carol Ann Liaros's Project Blind Awareness report in the national SFFJournal follows:

> Philo Frykman recognizes "a religious figure" by hold
> ing in his hands the plastic bubble enclosing a small gold
> Buddha. Max Swanson said of it, "Very, very bright. An
> unusual color. It means a lot to its owner." That owner, a
> woman lawyer from Bangkok, told me, "It is a good one. It
> will give you your wishes."
>
> On that same evening, Highrise Joe found some new
> pieces to a puzzling "magic book" I bought from a Batak
> tribeswoman on the shores of Lake Toba in Sumatra. Was it

made merely as a novelty for tourists? Were the ancient spiritist feelings from which it originated still viable? High-rise Joe told us, "It was made with a lot of care and a lot of love . . . I see a dark upstairs room." (In Batak houses all rooms are upstairs as the homes are built on stilts and usually without windows. As to the "care" Joe referred to, it certainly must be a part of the bark book inscribed with mysterious symbols, then folded like a Chinese fan between carved covers of wood.) "But there's something here I don't understand . . . a lot of fear. It doesn't make sense with the love. I'd like to spend more time with it." Our games were beginning to yield interesting information.

Awareness meetings are always open, and many of the visitors with whom we shared stayed to become regulars. One evening, Katie, instructor Bill Mitchell's eight-year-old daughter, was part of the group. Bill (a banker in his "other life") stood, eyes closed, voice melodious, mesmerizing, leading the group in an energy circle.

As we stand, hands joined, eyes closed, the feeling of oneness grows strong; we feel the union of our shared fields. Time melts away. With the rest of us, Tayja's consciousness is freed from her body as her mind does the things the rest of us usually do with our eyes. Katie steps into the center of the circle and Bill asks the group, "Who is in the center of the circle?"

Tayja recognizes a child's energy.

Bill then asks, "What color is her coat?"

Philo and Tayja both recognize red. Then he asks the color of her boots. Tayja "sees' white. It is not such a big thing to us. We have grown used to such demonstrations of sensitivity.

But some things still surprise us. Another of our instructors, Kathy Messetler, brought in some colorful posters illustrating a variety of scenes, animals and people. I was sitting at the table adjacent to the one at which Tayja was working with Joyce Anderson so that I could see Tayja move her hand softly over the picture just a few inches above it as Kathy directed the exercise, her voice clear and gentle. "Hold your hand above the picture . . . Experiment with the distance . . . What feels best to you? . . . What are you feeling? . . . Where are you feeling it? . . . Ask for the feedback you want."

Although I couldn't see the picture in the dim light, I was close enough to hear Tayja's responses. She said she'd like to be there and smiled as she began feeling the picture. First she recognized "animals." Tayja has a strong affinity for all kinds of animals and tunes into them easily. When asked what kind she was feeling, she answered "ducks or loons." She said two of them were just landing or taking off. She pointed out the lake, the marsh and the reeds. She pointed out the mountains in the background.

"How many ducks are there?" asked Joyce.

Slowly Tayja ran her hand across all the ducks and stated—correctly—that there were twelve.

Joyce pressed for even more information. "There is one more animal."

Tayja pointed to the moose in the background and named it correctly.

Was this a fluke, or could Tayja do this again? She was given a second picture.

First she pointed out a large brown area. "This part is darkened," she responded. Next she picked up a feeling of curiosity, then a warmth that felt like animals. "Kittens?" She was correct.

"What color?"

She answered, "Peach," and saw the eyes as blue, again correct.

"What letters are in the left-hand corner?" She was able to 'read' "C," but the printer's name was too much for her, and she could pick up only that it was "swirly."

"She told me that she thought the picture had a title. When Joyce asked what it was, Tayja replied, "Double Trouble." Although Joyce has excellent vision, she had to take the poster under a light to pick out the details Tayja was seeing psychically.

Tayja laughed in appreciation of the picture seen in such an unusual way. "It's my way of saying to the world, 'You do it with your eyes. I'll do it some other way.' "

Other students in our group also did it "some other way." Connie David, blind since birth, says in an interview for the Spiritual Frontiers Fellowship Newsletter:

> I really like to do psychometry (object reading) probably because I do it well.
>
> Developing this part of me that could have gone totally unrecognized, has really made a difference in my whole life and the way I look at things and events. It has been an enlightening and opening-up experience for me for the two

and a half years that I have been involved. I have added a whole dimension to me as a person and to me as a spiritual self that I hadn't recognized nor found before.

I've never been able to get names of artists of pictures that we're trying to describe physically, but at Christmas time, I did describe a fireplace mantle with stockings hanging on it which was in the background. It wasn't the main part of the picture, but rather in the background so you had to look closely to see it.

One thing I noticed the last time we scanned colors with our hands—I was wrong about fifty percent of the time. When I just let the color come to me psychically, I was right nine out of ten times! When we did "aura seeing," I didn't see the colors, I just "knew" them! I can't explain it. When we were checking the color of Katie's boots, white slid into my mind really fast. And I thought, "no" who would put white boots on their kid in the winter time? But white was right. I have a tendency to discount my impressions and logically think things out. And this is a really dumb way for me to do it, seeing as I am blind! When you discount your impressions like that, you're really going to miss!

I think this group is really unique. We accentuate the positive. There is such a feeling of love and warmth and acceptance.

A few months after this interview, Connie came to Awareness class in a high state of enthusiasm. "I've got something to tell!" We shared her excitement as she told us her story of a frustrating attempt to mail a letter. She was on an unfamiliar corner, and she had no idea where to find a mail box. She asked a pedestrian and was told that there was no box on the corner. Not knowing what to do next, she stood quietly, then, feeling an assurance she was learning to trust, she directed her dog across the street—straight to a mail box which her sighted informer had failed to see.

No one could question Connie's psychic progress; she has been blind from birth. But Tayja's condition was not so clear cut. Not surprisingly, questions came up. "Can Tayja see?" some asked. As one of those who had responsibility for the program, I called in the skeptical side of my mind and wondered. Although a Russian woman who had been extensively tested was able to read, oddly, through her elbow,

Carol Ann, after eight years of training with the blind, had only one student who could pick out a few letters. The probability of Tayja's being able to read so naturally was not high. Although I didn't doubt Tayja's honesty, I thought it might be possible that she was seeing physically yet thinking her vision was psychic, or "derma-vision" as the parapsychologists term it. (I do not like the term as it implies a simplistic "eyes-in-the-skin" explanation of psychic sight.) I decided to check out my questions, so called Tayja's reparenting mother hoping she would end my doubts.

"You are asking the same question we have asked," she answered.

At that time, February 29, 1981, Tayja received an extensive University of Minnesota eye examination which was given to gain objective information about Tayja's blindness. The tests included an ERG, electro retinogram. In this test light is shined into the eye for the purpose of detecting a retinal response. Since Tayja's diagnosis, retinitis pigmentosa, usually results in "tunnel vision" rather than total blindness, the ophthalmologist wanted additional information so as to better understand Tayja's condition. I quote:

> Cooperation good; though unable to keep eyes open and gaze directed straight ahead; even with eye held open by tech, patient rolled her eyes either down or way over to one side, such that mostly the white of eye was showing. Functional loss, possible RP [retinitis pigmentosa] vs functional NLP [no light perception]. Comments: The patient is described as legally blind and cannot distinguish light from dark. Because of blepharospasm [forceful shutting of the eyes, either voluntary or involuntary], eyes are held open by technician during testing. The patient did not look straight most of the time during testing but deviated her eyes to either side. The ERG is present bilaterally. [Retinal response was present in both eyes.]
>
> The visual evoked potentials as recorded from the mid-occipital region during repetitive flash stimulation are bilaterally present and somewhat reduced in amplitude although symmetrical. Repeat FEP [flash evoked potential] testing . . .

The flash VER (visual evoked response), can assess retino-cortical function in infants, demented or aphasic patients, and it can distinguish patients with psychologic blindness from those who have an organic basis for poor vision. Measurement is taken from electrical recordings made of the occipital cortex of the brain to determine whether light is being perceived. This technique bypasses the conscious knowledge of the patient.

> ... testing with eyes closed reveals a better defined, higher amplitude response on both sides. [Simply put, Tayja sensed light *better* with her eyes *closed*.] The ERGs are bilaterally present. The latencies of the P100 (wave IV) are bilaterally prolonged. [This means that the electrical recording indicated perception in both eyes.]
>
> *IMPRESSION*: The flash evoked potentials are suggestive of bilateral optic nerve dysfunction. There is no evidence for significant retinal disease. The moderate degree of evoked potential latency prolongation, however, does not seem to be consistent with the patient's complaints of total lack of light perception.

In a long letter accompanying this report, the doctor observes:

> She states that she sees nothing and that that has happened over the past year and that her visual disturbance began with poor vision since second grade. She noticed severe disturbance in her night vision by age 15 and that her peripheral vision was enough limited by age 17 so that she stopped driving. Now she sees nothing and states that she tries to open her eyes but gets tremors in them. Her eyes roll up. She is aware that her eyes are rolling around but cannot open her eyes. She said she has been able to see light and dark "shadows" until three months ago. She was sitting at work on an assembly line and her vision decreased down to a haze and then her eyelids closed and began to twitch all of the time and even when she opened her eyes she could not see anything . . . It is our impression that this patient has some degree of functional visual loss perhaps on top of an organic problem. [Emotional problems appeared to be making the physical, "organic" problem worse.]

Tayja explained to us that "the doctor was going to put a needle into my eye ball." [Actually the doctor wanted to temporarily paralyze the *lids* so as to perform an additional test. Contrary to Tayja's understanding, the doctor had no intention of putting the needle into the globe of the eye.] Tayja told me this had been done to her brother, Pony, and he went blind because of it. "I got out of there *so fast!*"

The week after Tayja had identified the contents and title of the kitten picture, Greg, one of our volunteers who is a picture framer, brought in a print by a mystic Russian artist which he had framed. A sky of reds and oranges appeared to smoke against a black ground, and a white haze surrounded people streaming etherically from the backs of white horses. Tayja's face radiated appreciation as she moved her hand above it while looking off to the side. She "saw" the colors, recognized the horses. "I like it. It's exciting, spacey," she said.

One evening Bill started the class off by setting a red book on the mantle. Several of the participants "saw" the color red even though it was a good fifteen feet from them. Tayja recognized the book as a hymnal. Next Bill opened it, showed the page to several volunteers, then passed the book to Tayja. She put her hand over the page and picked up the word "joy" immediately. We waited in silence while she "studied" the book through her hand. "Joyful, Joyful, We Adore Thee," she said.

"How do you do that?" one of the volunteers asked her.

"First I got the image of children playing, and that means 'joy' to me. Then I saw a mother and baby, and that means 'love.' After that the name just came."

Toward spring, we did some psychometry using objects in closed boxes. Tayja felt hers. "Old," she said. "It's a decorative object." It was an old cob of Indian corn used as a table decoration for about five years.

Late in the winter Tayja got her first Leader Dog. When she came home with the beautiful golden retriever, Daisy Mae, we gave her a "puppy shower" at the Blind Awareness class. She told us about the training procedure she and Daisy had gone through. Because of her leg and hip problems, Tayja got very tired and her legs were painful much of the time. The trainer was a driving taskmaster, and Tayja stuffed a good deal of anger during her month's stay.

"Were they surprised at the way you could tell where things were and see colors?"

"I didn't do any of that there," Tayja answered. "I couldn't be that relaxed." But with us, it was different. As she opened the presents, she "read" the cards and identified the flowers on the wrapping paper. We asked her what kind they were. "I can't do everything!" she

exclaimed. But with a few hints she guessed they were, appropriately, daisies. She always read with her hand covering the words. Also I was aware that, when she had been able to see, she could read a newspaper only when she held it upside down and then very haltingly. She had never at any time in her life read with fluency.

In May, Tayja and I had a brief but decisive conversation before awareness class started. "I've been thinking of starting a psi development class," she said.

"Really!" Surprise must have sounded in my voice. "So have I." We agreed to work together.

We started the next week with three people attending. Our decision to hold it in Tayja's apartment was a good one. The rooms were supplied with interesting Indian objects, and the atmosphere was clean, but most important there was a charged feeling of energy in the air. One of the first exercises was one Tayja conducted in psychometry. Into my hand she put a small lump. I heard myself saying, "It's very heavy," although it could not have weighed as much as an ounce.

"Yes," she said, giving me the immediate feedback which helped so much in keeping up our confidence in the cues our subconscious gave us.

I went on to identify "coldness, a ceremony with other objects present," and the object I held as "of central importance." When I finished, Tayja told me it was a miniature replica of an iron pitcher used for cold water in a sweat lodge where it was surrounded by other ceremonial objects.

The subject of our second class dealt with new life and rebirth, although we had not planned it that way. Tayja had been given an almost-new-born jack rabbit who was struggling for life. She had nursed it through the day, feeding it every few minutes.

In the class we discussed healing energy and the importance of continuous warmth and love being funneled to the new life in our hands. When we took the tiny youngster from its box, it felt cold and still, but after about a minute of exposure to the heat in Tayja's hand, the little rabbit was warm and squirming in its eagerness for life. Tayja managed the medicine dropper of milk by feeling the mouth with her finger, then inserting the glass tip with the other hand. It was certainly not a class we planned, but it gave us a reverence for the energy of love as we felt our hands heat up and saw the quick response of the little Jack.

We didn't know then the new life into which Tayja was about to leap.

Chapter Eleven
The Birth

I Am the Light!

Spiritual Frontiers Fellowship,
Carleton Retreat theme, 1984

I first knew Carleton College during the final years of the Second World War. As a student I watched uniformed men in olive drab march to their classes, perhaps singing the Air Force song: triumph or heroic death.

It was different now. "Going down in flame" had become "rising up in light" to those of us attending the Spiritual Frontiers Fellowship Midwest Retreat. SFF, a national organization incorporated in 1956, draws membership from many churches and is open to those of all faiths. To quote from its "Principles, Purposes and Program":

> SFF is *spiritual* in that it is concerned with nonphysical phenomena which relate to God, the human spirit, and the future life. It is *frontier* because it explores matters beyond the usual range of church worship and activity, the paranormal. It is a *fellowship* of those who, having accepted the validity of one or more of these phenomena, would encourage each other and ultimately the whole Church to seek for further light and greater reality in the spiritual life.

Soldiers marching through snowy streets were far from my mind. It was June! With the explosion of new green, spring is an exciting time in Minnesota. For all of us who were going to Carleton, our inner "swelling of the buds" kept pace with the plant growth around us. Participants had selected classes, two per day, from a list of subjects such as "Practicing Spirituality in a Psychological Age," "Esoteric Numerology," "Jewish Mysticism," "Becoming Earth Healers, and

Co-Creators of the New Golden Age," "Practical ESP" (taught by Carol Ann Liaros), "Tapping Your Own Spiritual Power," "Transformation," "Mediumship for Personal Development" (taught by Marilyn Rossner), "Touch the Earth" (Native American religion taught by Tsonakwa), "Promise of Light," and many others. The instructors were among the best the U.S. and Canada had to offer, so choices were difficult.

Alight with anticipation, I drove to Tayja's apartment as we were going together along with Carol Smith, another friend of ours from Blind Awareness (and now the artist illustrating this book).

Tayja was ready with suitcases, bags and a carton bulging with sacks of dog food, her clean shirts and blouses on hangers, and her long, red ceremonial gown. "I hope we have room for all this stuff," Tayja said, letting her high spirits out in a laugh. "Now with Daisy, I'm packing for two. And of course I have to bring my Indian stuff."

"Don't worry, we've got miracle space," I said.

There was plenty of room, and we were on our way. Tayja and Daisy shared the back seat and floor with suitcases for the week's retreat.

The first person I spoke to on arriving at Carleton was—significantly—Marilyn Rossner. I first took a class from her in the late 1970's in New Albany, Indiana. The following morning I would again be working with her, this time in a class for mediumship development. "Rev. Marilyn" was someone I very much wanted Tayja to meet as I had great respect for her combination of psychic and intellectual abilities. But there was more to it than that. They were alike—alike in very different ways, like two separate pieces of the same puzzle. Tayja, the sturdy, dark Sioux woman with a deep, masculine voice and a halting walk appeared to have nothing in common with the small, blond, feminine woman who (in contrast to the jeans-clad Tayja) always wore long dresses brightly splashed with color.

Marilyn is under five feet tall, delicate, childlike, with a full face. Along with a playful spirit is a sharp intellect. She earned her master's in behavioral psychology and her Ph. D. in special education. She is a college professor and president of The International College of Spiritual and Psychic Sciences as well. She currently spends most of her time traveling and teaching trance and mediumship development.

Her spiritual background is even more eclectic. From a Jewish family, she became a yogi at 14 and about the same time saw a vision of Christ. Subsequently, she became a Spiritualist minister. Just before I met her for the first time, she had married an Episcopalian priest (now a canon).

The only thing Tayja and Marilyn obviously had in common were their guides, both Daisys. Marilyn's Daisy was a child guide who directed her when she was in trance, Tayja's guiding Daisy was a golden retriever. Why did I feel so strongly that Tayja and Marilyn should meet? Although I ask now, I wasn't questioning at the time. Harmony in diversity seemed natural at Carleton. In fact, diversity was seldom noticed. The husband of one of the Carleton Retreat participants commented that, "all of you look alike." When pressed, he went on to say that everyone's eyes had that same luminous look, and they all had the same warm smile and open expression of affection.

Tayja and I didn't spend much time together as we weren't sharing a room and were taking different classes. Her dog, Daisy, led her surely, so she had no need of a guiding elbow. Also, she ate in the smoking section of the cafeteria. However, I frequently saw her sitting under a lamppost smoking and talking, usually with a group of people around her laughing and chatting. Her sensitivity seemed to be responding to the growth energy at Carleton, and once when I was beside her, I heard her call out, "Hi, Bill." Bill Mitchell, the instructor she knew from Blind Awareness, was nearly half a block away, and her back was toward him. As well as instructing her in the Blind Awareness class, Bill had given her MariEL healings, and she felt close to him.

I finally had an opportunity to introduce Tayja and Marilyn after the evening lecture and service late in the week. Bill and I were together at the time. Bill asked Tayja to read his name tag for Marilyn. Tayja laughed exclaiming, "I don't need to read that!"

"Go ahead," he urged. Tayja reached over to him and located the tag above his left shirt pocket. "It's hot!" she exclaimed. Bill took it off and handed it to her. She held it in her cupped hands, then suddenly burst into a rich laugh, "Billy! Nobody calls you that!"

She went on to scan Marilyn's clothes, her hand a few inches out from them. "You've got a shawl on like a grandma. It's green, and it's got flowers on it." Although old ladies are usually more conservative in their choice of colors, Tayja was essentially correct. Marilyn then gave her the program with the retreat theme, "I am the light" on the cover to read, but she said it was too hard to make out the small type.

Photo by Brad Armstrong

She did better at reading the boldly printed posters that were on the wall of the entry hall. Marilyn watched with interest, focusing on her eyes as she identified clothing and "read." They were, as usual, tightly squinted shut.

The healing service was to be the following evening. I saw Tayja briefly in the afternoon, and the meeting was memorable. We were standing under a tremendous elm, wide across its ancient crown, great branches sweeping downward to brush the Earth, a tree such as I've never seen in another place. It formed a leafy tent above us, shimmering in the sunlight. "I've got something to tell you," Tayja said. She smoothed her pink blouse over her belly. It was definitely distended. "Good heavens! Is she pregnant?" I thought. But I knew she had had a hysterectomy.

"It's a spirit baby," she explained.

Is she going to tell me she's going to have a virgin birth? That's too much! Even Mary had had an intact uterus.

"Here, feel this." She put my hand firmly on her belly. My mind was racing too fast for me to tune in right away, but it didn't take long before I could feel a fluttering inside. "Feel the heartbeat?" she asked. I did, but it felt more like a wing beat, very light and quick. I was still feeling awed and lightheaded when she said in her usual flat voice, "It's about time to get on my Indian stuff." I heard later that Tsonakwa had told her to ready herself for the healing service. He was not the only one who felt something happening in connection with Tayja. We found out later that Highrise Joe, one of our blind students, had a prophetic dream the night before: someone was going to see. I was aware of a strange tension in the air as were many others.

When on the way up to my room to get dressed, I felt a drawing toward Tayja's room. Responding, I stopped at the second floor and walked into her room. She was alone, dressed in her red Indian robe with a bright pattern, front and back. She was sitting on a chair in front of her "Indian stuff" which had been carefully arranged on a book shelf in front of her. I felt the ceremonial atmosphere surrounding her as though she were a bride. "Hi," I said softly, not wanting to interrupt, although the only thing that appeared to be going on was Tayja's struggle to clasp a small gold bracelet on her left wrist. "This is the last one," she said. "Can you help me? It takes me 45 minutes to get dressed," she said as I fastened the bracelet. "I have this Indian ritual. I have to bless everything I wear and pray." I didn't know then what she had prayed for, but I heard later. "I don't pray for what I want. I pray for what I need," she explained. Although she didn't know what that was, she was certain that she would get it.

"Can you braid hair?"

"Yes." As I put my hands over her head, I felt a strong, gentle energy from her crown chakra and a warm, electrical "halo" around her head. I brushed and braided her heavy dark hair, softly scented with shampoo. She told me that, in her tradition, an older woman usually braided the hair of younger women before a ritual. She stood up to exchange a hug, and I noticed she was barefoot. "Is that all right in the church?" she asked.

"Of course. You know what you need to do." Then I went up to my room, telling Tayja to go on ahead as I still needed to dress.

I reached the chapel only five minutes before the service was to begin, so there were few seats left, and I took a place in the second row from the back on the far left side. In addition to the five hundred people registered for the retreat, over a hundred more had come to Northfield for the healing service. The colors of the people warmed the gray stone walls of the chapel and vied with the rainbow light pouring through the stained glass windows. The music for the occasion rang with an open joy. No room for lugubrious hymns there! The healing service was a celebration of recovering wholeness, not concentration on dis-ease. With the focus on the joyful objective, we were in for a gala celebration—what a far cry from a doctor's office or a hospital ward! I found my belief in disease dissolving even before the service began. Although I felt close to Tayja without seeing her, I wanted the addition of eye contact, but I couldn't find her.

Ethel Lombardi, a healer with whom both Tayja and I had studied, had given her message, "The Keys to Spiritual Evolution and Healing," and the chorus was singing as the service progressed. I watched the orderly procession as ushers guided the assembled people to the healers, perhaps thirty. The healers stood at the front of the church in two rows with empty chairs in front of them. As I watched, still looking for Tayja, I felt a growing tension, and for some reason I couldn't explain, an ache was developing between my shoulders. It puzzled me as I felt no reason for it within my body. Where was Tayja? I searched the audience, feeling intensely drawn to her, but in the crowd of people, I couldn't pick her out. That tension in my back between the shoulders was beginning to be a real pain.

Later Tayja told us her side of the event. "I didn't even imagine this was going to happen, but I knew something was. That whole week things opened up, everything. I could tell what people were wearing, I could tell how people walk, I could tell strangers. Daisy and I had much more of a connection. It seemed I was wide open to whatever was going to take place. Saturday afternoon I told Cynthia, 'I gotta go up and do my thing,' my Indian ritual. Before the healing service, I blessed everything and wore my gown. I even went barefoot because for me that's right to the ground, right to the Earth. When we were sitting in the pews, I knew something was going to happen. There were some weird energies. Then I got soreness on both shoulders, and the woman sitting next to me got a sore arm, like her arms started aching, and she felt she should grab me and take me down. So we both kind of went, 'Yeh, right.' When I got out of the pew, and it was our turn to go down, we decided to get in the line for Marilyn. It was really cute 'cause one of the ushers said we can't do that, and the other one said, 'Never mind. She knows what she's doing.' So it was like we went down to the front, and Marilyn was busy, so we stood behind her waiting."

Tayja waited just long enough for me to be guided to a place in the aisle from which I could see her sitting on the chair in front of Marilyn. Of course! How could it be otherwise? All week I had been wanting the two of them together, but except for an introduction, then the quick meeting with Marilyn in the entry hall the night before, this was the first time they had been together.

As I stood waiting to be guided to the next empty chair in front of a healer, I saw Marilyn working on Tayja in a completely uncharacteristic manner. Marilyn usually healed very quietly, but now I saw her energetically shaking Tayja's head. One of the choir members said that her head was moving so fast she couldn't even see it. Although I could see it, I was struck by the feeling that Tayja was completely relaxed, going with the movement as though her neck was a rubber band or maybe a wet noodle. I found it hard to take my eyes away from the dramatic scene in front of me long enough to go to the chair the usher pointed out for me. It turned out to be directly in front of Marilyn and Tayja! What's more, my healer was our Blind Awareness instructor, Kathy Messetler. With some thirty healers, how could I be so lucky? Kathy started to focus on my energy, our backs to Tayja and Marilyn; but neither of us had our hearts in sharing a healing for me, and we soon turned around to watch the scene directly in front of us.

Tayja describes it, "When the other person left and I sat down, I went right into a trance; it was that quick. Then the healing started. It was like I didn't even hear what she was saying until she sat down on the floor in front of me . . .

Kathy and I heard Marilyn's intense voice exclaiming, "You can see! You can see." Over and over again, "You can see! You can see!" Marilyn's yoga-trained being was intensely focused as she looked up into Tayja's face, into her gray-blue eyes (not brown as I would have thought). Marilyn went on speaking. "Keep your eyes open, let go of the past. It's over, it's all over."

Later Tayja described, "Then my eyes seemed to pop to the front of my head, and it was like, Yes! I can see! Ah, I don't know how to describe it—seeing for the first time. And it was getting brighter and brighter and brighter until I could see everything, the lights, the people, and then I just turned around and yelled, "I can see the light."

Over and over again Tayja shouted out in her strong deep voice, "I can see, I can see, I can see!"

"It was like I didn't care what anybody thought, you know, and I was always the one who was taught to be respectful in church, and I was yelling out, and it was such a good healthy feeling to be able to tell the whole world."

In contrast to Tayja's immediate explosion of joy, Marilyn sat crosslegged under her long white dress. She began to cleanse, using pranayama breathing, a yogic breath exercise employing explosive breathing through her mouth, in preparation for the next healing.

Yes, many denominations, Christian, Jewish, Buddhist, Hindu and probably others, were gathered together to celebrate the healing, or 'wholing' of a Sioux-Caucasian by a Jewish-Yogi-Spiritualist. But not all the "people" were actually seen by those attending.

Tayja explains, "My spiritual guides were there, Marilyn's were, everybody's were, and it wasn't like Marilyn was the one that accomplished this for me. Everybody accomplished it: Ethel, Carol Ann, and Tsonakwa, even if he wasn't in the church. It's like—you know, I could feel the energy from *every* one, from this direction, from the back, from the front (where the choir sat), just everybody's energy. Some people think Marilyn did it. No. Marilyn was the *tool*. She helped with it. She was the guide, and the rest of the people were the pushers. They all pushed and put that energy there and gave that energy freely. I think, without *all* people's help it would not have happened, because it was necessary for everyone's energy to be there. It's a unity; it's a togetherness thing. The peole who were sitting right behind—I was yelling, and people were saying, 'send, send, send,' and the energy was just enormous, just like a big bubble around everyone. That's the important part, that everybody sticks together and says, 'Yes, this does happen.' It says in the Bible, Jesus healed blind people, Jesus healed lame people. We are all part of that. We're his chosen kids. That's the way it is, you know. We help. We're his tools. The unity of One."

The "Hallelujah Chorus" that exploded spontaneously at the end of the service was an instrument that, for many, literally removed the material roof of the church. They were in a transported reality; seeing not people, but lights.

Chapter Twelve
New Vision

The power to change people comes from confronting our own adversity. Wounded people are the best healers. We heal ourselves by virtue of our wounds. Through healing others, as the shamans know, we keep our own selves healthy.

—Rollo May

Tayja had indeed become a healed and healing light. "You're glowing!" her friend Donna exclaimed. Joyce and others also saw the golden glow around Tayja's head and shoulders, shining as though there were a lightbulb inside her. She was standing against the gray stone wall in the side entry of the chapel waiting for Tsonakwa who had been at the art exhibition during the healing ceremony. The door was open, and the night birds and insects had replaced the "Hallelujah Chorus" with their serenade.

Again and again my gaze returned to Tayja's wide open gray-blue eyes. What a contrast to my intellectual graduation so many years before when we graduates were initiated into adult life with mortar boards forming a black shield over our crown chakras.

Tsonakwa came quickly. He had not been far away, and in spirit he was not away at all. His religion is not enclosed in a church building but is most intense when his feet are on his mother, the Earth, and his eyes looking up to his father, the sky, shining as it was that night, with the eternal eyes of the Grandfathers.

When her friends returned with him, Tayja gave Tsonakwa a hug. She described his silent reaction as, " 'Oh, yeah, I knew it was going to happen,' " but Tayja was thinking, "Come on, act happy! Everybody is dancing for joy."

187

Tsonakwa was in that space where 'even the Great Spirit knows to take his moccasins off and walk in silence,' and in the presence of spirits, he does the same. He told Tayja what was important, "Tonghak is gone. No more." He didn't stay long in the midst of that volcanic celebration. "But I can just see him thanking the Grandfathers all the way back," Tayja said. Tsonakwa could have been hearing his own words repeat in his mind: "For the spirits intrude upon our world, and we intrude upon theirs, and we need not be amazed at all. We can invoke them through the doorways in the tops of our heads and in the channels of our hearts."

Later Tayja said to a group of friends, "Those words from him were so reassuring! All the pain, all the craziness, all the schizophrenia *gone*. That door will shut. Now I'm free."—It is no accident that "freedom" is the meaning of "Tushi," her middle name.

"In Tsonakwa's class we talked about shamans and what they had to go through in their lives to become a high priest, a high healer. That helped me so much because all of my life I have been on this journey and could not figure out where I was going."

Tsonakwa's description of the human spirit as "a great light beamed into the sky," had taken on solid meaning, and the usual capitalist view of U.S. "consumers" bound in material concerns seemed unreal. The rush-hour view of human turmoil was far away as we absorbed the joyful reality in this place where seeing the light-bodies of our friends was not only accepted but admired. The positive power of the mass elevation of consciousness after Tayja's healing awed nearly all of us.

"A psychic simply touched her ... and all her ailments had vanished forever," is the kind of "quickie coverage" events like this often draw from people who are not themselves involved in healing. Such superficial treatment of such a profound spiritual experience leaves out one half of the equation, one it takes courage to accept. Each individual is ultimately responsible for his or her own health; for those illnesses which we can cure, we can also cause. *A Course In Miracles* uses blindness as a symbol for the shroud of evil through which we so often judge the world: "Judgement will bind my eyes and make me blind. Yet love reflected in forgiveness here, reminds me You have given me a way to find Your peace again."[1]

This integrating rebirth within an individual has far-reaching consequences for the integrating of the "split personality" of our planet. As Krishnamurti states in *The First and Last Freedom*:

If we can transform ourselves, bring about a radically different point of view in our daily existence, then perhaps we shall affect the world at large, the extended relationship with others . . . to be is to be related . . . If we can transform our relationship in that narrow world, it will be like a wave extending outward all the time.

Tayja had first to integrate her new perceptions of the world, then to push outward to teach what she had become through transforming and integrating her personality. The immediate practical task for Tayja was to make sense of sharp visual perceptions flooding into her wide open eyes.

As we left the church, I automatically gave her my elbow, and she took it. We both laughed. "It feels okay," she said. "It's hard to walk with the ground so close and sharp looking." As I guided her for the last time, I thought of Daisy and the beauty of the intimate relationship the two had formed. Even in the loss of a limitation, there is pain; and there is a form of death in every birth. I thought also of Blind Awareness. Would Tayja continue to come? Would she maintain her highly developed psychic sense now that her eyes could do it for her?

The silent questions flowed by unanswered as others joined us on the way back to Tayja's room. Quickly the room filled with joyful friends listening to the replay of events and filling in their pieces of the story. Tayja told us the details.

"I want to stress the power of Everyone, that's the important part: that everyone sticks together and says, 'Yes, this does happen.'

"I have four guides, they're all Indian. I have three male and a female. While I was standing in the aisle waiting for Marilyn's chair to be free, I worked with my guides on opening me up so that I could accept whatever healing was going to happen. I have neat guides that stay with me no matter where I go or how I get there. They appear a lot, usually standing behind me." (Bill Mitchell and others in Awareness class have seen them.) "So my guides are very strong and very protective. I've had two of my guides since I was about eleven. When you grow up and you take on guides in my Indian way, some you have to turn away because they aren't good for you any more. So then you gain new guides. Since I was so young when I got mine, I've had to gain several new guides. The problem for me, for anyone who's had guides for a long, long time is that they can be hooked into some negative things with you. They want to take control instead of your higher self being the control. So you have to let a few go. I'm very excited with the ones I have now."

Although she did not know what her life was designed to be, Tayja trusted that it had a purpose, and she prayed, not for what she desired on a conscious level. Rather, her prayer was an offering of faith, and she put her prayer into the unknown, asking for "what I need." Tayja's trust had been answered with healing beyond anything she would dare to ask for.

The questions flew: "How does it feel?"

"Wonderful!"

"What color is the bedspread?" Bill asked.

Tayja reached out her hand to feel its energy. "Yellow."

For that evening, we existed in our laughter, our rejoicing in the miracle we shared. Only one seemed sad. It was Daisy. Her tail gave a few tentative thumps at the floor as she lay behind Tayja's chair a little apart from the joyful scene. Her dependent friend was gone; her life's purpose altered. Daisy loved her work, and it was clear she perceived the alteration. Tayja's movements had changed. Had her scent also changed? Whatever the case, Daisy *knew*.

Marilyn had asked Tayja to Watson Lounge where the speakers and workshop leaders were having a party. Tayja changed back into her comfortable jeans, then she and I left the group in her room and walked to Watson Hall. Marilyn was sitting in the corner of the couch, her legs stretched along the seat, as she enjoyed a foot massage from one of her students. Again experiences were shared. Marilyn said that she had been aware even before she entered the chapel that something unusual was building. "Normally I'm a quiet healer. But this time it was very different. The second I touched her, I felt a bolt of energy. There was a frequency in my body—a motion that came from elsewhere. I placed my hands over Tayja's eyes. I found my breathing perfectly synchronized with hers, as if we were one. Then I went into a complete trance, which I'm told lasted ten to twelve minutes.

"Suddenly, I could hear Tayja yelling: 'I can see—God is real—I can see.' "

Then Marilyn asked Tayja how it felt.

"It felt funny like there were two eyeballs in the back of my head." Tayja put her hands behind her head and circled them forward to the third eye region. "Then real suddenly they came around to the front and joined, and I could see."

It was certainly true that looking behind had frozen Tayja into a body that was both physically and psychologically frozen to past injuries. Looking ahead was to change all that.

We didn't stay with Marilyn long. A few people were ignoring us, only one or two; but in our open state, we were sensitive to it. For then the feeling stayed in the background, and neither of us let the particulars enter consciousness.

I returned to my room as Tayja went back to continue celebrating in hers.

After meditation on Sunday morning, Tayja explained how the healing seemed to have happened. "During the struggle [when Marilyn was shaking Tayja's head], one of my guides had taken on Marilyn's body to help, and then he couldn't get free of her body until Eve [one of the healers] came over and said some blessings. Then during meditation this morning I heard my guide say, 'Little woman, powerful, powerful.'" We laughed with Tayja at her picture of the surprised guide.

Just as it takes a courageous leap of faith into the unknown to heal oneself, it takes a leap of faith to accept the healing of others. The awesome power of the mind to rule over life, death and disease gives added responsibility for selecting the focus of our thoughts.

Talk of whether Tayja's was a mental healing or a physical healing is irrelevant to me as to most other spiritual healers. I have over and over again seen evidence that physical and mental healing are one, and in guiding energy circles as one of the Blind Awareness instructors and participants, I had spoken or heard over and over again, "the body follows the commands of the mind." As Tayja once chose blindness, she now chose to give it up. Her first choice was fraught with pain and difficulty; her second, ecstatic with joy. Yes, of course it is possible to find a physical explanation for Tayja's healing. Perhaps a doctor could trace some neurological rearrangement or change in the corpus callosum [connecting bridge between the hemispheres of the brain] to the energetic head-shaking that was part of the healing. But how had Marilyn come to do the shaking? That Tayja's brain cells were shaken randomly into place sounds a bit like exploding a bomb in a print shop and creating a Bible. Surely there was creative direction.

After Tayja returned home, events moved quickly. "I have another road to go, lots of things to do, lots of things to see."

Tayja called me the Sunday after we came home to ask if she could come to our house for a few days as she felt the need to be with people who had shared in her healing. It felt good to have her and reap the continuing joy. As did Tayja, I wanted to go on living in the miracle.

But not everything about her recovered vision was easy. We live in the country, and there were a lot of new things to see. We started the first evening by showing slides—safe enough. Tayja described the experience: "It's so different! I've milked a goat before, but I've never *seen* one. Is *that* what I milked!? I worked on a pig farm, and people told me they were ugly, and now I know. They *are* ugly. To see a grasshopper for the first time—I never saw a grasshopper! People told me, but you get such a different idea when you can't see.

"I took Daisy out to meet the horses. My goodness! I trained horses, but when I went out there, it was a surprise. These big things?! 'Cause when you don't see, you imagine something a whole lot different. Daisy was scared. She was on her leash, and I was trying to hold her, and the horses came in between us, and I thought, 'I'm done for, I'm going to be crushed'."

I shouted to Tayja to let go of Daisy, but her instincts made her hang on to that leash like some sort of umbilical cord to life. She and Daisy were still one.

"So then something just said to let go of Daisy, and she'll take care of it, and she did. She ran away in a hurry! Cynthia was trying to keep me from the hot electric fence. I finally got out of there safe, but I haven't yet taken the risk to ride them. Things are so different and so big! It's going to take a while to sort it all out, put it together and understand it all. Maybe there just isn't any way of understanding all that happened."

On July 17, 1984, Tayja had her eyes retested at the same ophthalmological clinic which had pronounced her blind seven months previously. She called me from Minneapolis after her eye examination and read the evaluation from the same doctor who had written her previous report which evaluated her as legally blind:

I am pleased to report to you that I reexamined [Tayja] on July 17, 1984 and discovered that three weeks ago she had regained all of her sight with the aid of a spiritual healer and help of an Indian medicine man. Since that has happened her acuity without correction was 20/200 and improved to 20/20 in either eye with prescription of -2.00 + 1.00 x 72 right and -2.00 left. Dilated examination was unchanged and normal. Confrontation visual field was full. I am delighted that she has regained her sight and is doing so well.

Her epilepsy, too, was over and she gradually discontinued her Dilantin with no ill effects.

Tayja joined the Course in Miracles group which I attended once a week with some light-minded women in our neighborhood. Sandi, one of the participants, was instantly magnetized toward Tayja. Her smile, expressing a kind of volcanic joy within her, was especially radiant as she caught sight of Tayja entering Becky's living room. "I know you!" Tayja and Sandi exclaimed in unison. They recognized each other through acquaintance in many lifetimes, and for more than a year they lived and shared spiritual growth together.

No one expected a woman who had been either dyslexic, blind or both ever since birth to be much of a reader. Yet, when it came Tayja's turn to read, she opened the Bible Becky loaned her, and with only slight hesitancy, proceeded to read—with her hands covering the print. Although it seemed somewhat impolite, I leaned over her Bible to make sure she was actually reading through her hand. It was indeed the case as I read the words both above and below it, certainly not what Tayja was reading. This was not a one-time occurrence.

Becky also saw Tayja do this, and when Tayja was at home with us, I watched through our living room window as she sat on our patio reading from *The Course in Miracles*, again with her hand covering the print. However, now that her eyes have become less distracting to her, she leaves her hand out of it as she reads.

I read *The Course in Miracles* to her as she painted the front of our house. "All right!" she frequently exclaimed, recognizing truth for her when we shared passages such as, "My condemnation keeps my vision dark, and through my sightless eyes I cannot see the vision of my glory. Yet today I can behold this glory and be glad."[2]

While she was with us, both my husband and I enjoyed healing massages from Tayja. A busy summer passed quickly with the inclusion of many friends who called Tayja or came to share her joy. However, in a healing as dramatic as Tayja's there are bound to be people who accept it as a kind of lightning bolt out of the blue and others who regard it as fraud. The unexamined position in either case fails to break through limits to the true meaning of healing, which points, not to divisions between mind and body, but to their union. As spiritual healing unites an individual with energies beyond the body, it carries the potential to unite the medical fields with channeled healing, prophetic insights gained from astrology and even the legacy from past lives. Medical diagnoses may be amplified by handwriting analysis or psychic insights, then checked against our advanced medical technology. We are only beginning to tap the possibilities.

Tayja continues to write in diverse voices, her handwriting changing when one of her guides channels through her. The following is a letter written to Marilyn shortly after her healing:

Marilyn (Little Feather) and John (Bearer of Water) I want to thank you for helping Tayja Tushi through the healing. Using you as a tool helped. She had to come to you, and we guided her to you from the beginning. We know you were the shaman we had been looking for for Tayja Tushi.

The shaman Tayja has been working very hard. She has spent many moons on her journey to meet you. She is kind of tired right now and she is seeing many visions we have been sharing with her.

The next time we talk, I want to speak to you through Tayja Tushi. I hope you don't mind me calling you Little Feather. Good name for you. Shows strength and power among my people.

Tayja Tushi needs much teaching. With her knowledge she has to now travel on a much higher journey. She has much to understand and needs good teacher as you and John are. Tayja knows much and yet has much to learn. She now sees in both lights, she now sees in all light. Tayja Tushi is High priestess . . . and has always been on her way. She has never lost faith or trust in herself. Makes me proud man to see her move into the highest Shaman Woman . . . To know her presence is dear.

We have not talked to outsiders of our being here because of Tayja Tushi's past history. Glad to know that now she can share the stories that are bursting to get out, so Tayja Tushi can become a whole person. Tayja Tushi knows the direction she is going . . . Knows to help her path blossom and grow with people of her understanding.

I need to speak and say what my mind means, John (Bearer of Water). Tayja Tushi needs a man outlook on God and the spirit. Never had from a man—physical man. Needs good man to show her and teach her. She can learn good many things from man. She never had a friendship with physical man, good understanding. Hope I no offend you or Little Feather for writing this, but have to say from my ♥ the important messages that I get and give you. Hope you can understand this.

Hope to see you before too many days pass. I have said what I need to say. Bless you both and much friendship,

White Feather

Not long after this letter was written, Tayja and I went to Montreal where she gave healings, and we co-taught a class in shamanism. Tayja had begun to give what she had been given, and she writes of her purpose through a guide:

"God says, 'Bring thy selves together and speak as one. Jesus, my son, was a human man serving his destiny, and he got a lot of resistance but still accomplished much of his task. Now it's starting to come together for all mankind! We have a gift, all of us' . . . Many people have the understanding but are afraid to express the oneness. God says, 'No fear is needed to do your job as human people of mankind. Fear only stops the fruit of the trees and the bushes.' "

Some of the fruits from Tayja's bushes in Montreal are told in these letters written in November of 1984.

I would like to certify that I have received spiritual healing from Tayja Wiger on two occasions during the month of October 1984.

On the first occasion, Tayja completely healed me of a sinus headache. My sinuses then continued to drain for the two days following.

On the second occasion, I received an emotional healing from Tayja, when she released a lot of sadness and pent-up emotions that I had been holding on to.

I shall always be very grateful to Tayja for sharing her spiritual gifts with us.

Yours truly,
Nicole Moronval

On Friday, October 19, 1984 I went to a healing workshop given by Margaret Curtis, and assisted by Tayja Wiger.

On that day, I noticed that the pain which I have had for quite some time in the solar plexus area was worse than before. I felt that pain was a nervous condition as I had been through a lot of stress, and thought this blocked my development.

We were practicing healing on one another. The man who was giving me healing, at one point, came and stood next to me and to my right. Suddenly, I became extremely uncomfortable. I felt this man had exactly the same vibration as my former husband and I had a very hard time staying on my chair. I felt that if he had touched me I would have screamed. It was as if I was with my ex-husband all over again, and I did not want that. I wanted to cry, and my stomach felt as if it was tied in knots.

The next part of the workshop consisted of Tayja giving us healing so we could witness all the different forms of healing that she is using. When my turn came, I stood in front of her. My eyes were closed so I could not see what she was doing. At one point, I became aware of her voice saying: "Let it go, let it out." I suddenly started to cry. The pain in my stomach left me completely and I felt as if a big load was taken off my shoulders. I felt free. There was a physical drawing out that took place and a definite release of fear and anxiety.

To date, two weeks after the healing, the pain has not come back, and I know it will not come back. I realized I was holding on to some fear which, with Tayja's help, I was able to get rid of . . . [end of letter]

In October of this year I had occasion to open my door to Tayja Wiger. I soon realized that I not only opened my door to a very beautiful soul, but I also opened my heart.

I first experienced her healing in my home, for when she arrived I was suffering from a severe sinus infection, within minutes I felt release from pressure and pain. On the second occasion I was relieved of the anxieties of an underactive thyroid. Most symptoms have disappeared, and I am now awaiting confirmation through a blood test.

The experience of having Tayja living in my home has been an ongoing healing in mind, body and spirit. I consider Tayja one of the most gifted healers that I have had the occasion to meet.

With all sincerity,
Margaret Curtis

Tayja, My Dear One,
I thank you and your beautiful spirit Guides and Helpers for the wonderful healing you gave me in my throat area and chest while here in Montreal in October and November. I still do not have any more dry and scratching throat. My breathing is also nice and clear. No more struggling for my breath.

Now for my Grandson, Ameer Atari who will be four months old on Nov. 29. He has no more infant shock syndrome which he used to quiver and shake so much from every time we moved him or picked him up. He is so calm and beautiful and just getting nicer every day.

I will have some pictures for you at Xmas time of all of us.

Thank you and thank God and all your Angels. God bless and love,

Marion B.

Dearest Tayja,
. . . You are a beautiful soul and a wonderful healer who gives so much to so many—God Bless you—I do want you to know that not only have you healed my osteoarthritis and legs but I am a happier Being altogether.

Also I wish to add that I am not a naive person but have been on the path the past 30 years in this incarnation and am old soul in others . . .

I am well aware of the various degrees in one's capacities—Yours is very close to the ultimate. We look forward to a speedy return . . . in loving gratitude, I am Yours,

Roseanna

The following October Tayja did return to The Spiritual Science Fellowship in Montreal, and again she healed.

Soon after she returned from her October Montreal trip, Tayja came to the Blind Awareness group and conducted a healing ceremony. Her face had a soft, glowing look. More gentleness flowed from her, and new, higher notes danced in her voice animating her expression. She was now "intuneative" as her guides taught her to say.

She called on the highest spirits before beginning, then went to the center of the circle. It was beautiful to see her moving quickly, almost dancing as she worked. One by one she called the thirty people around her to the center of the circle. Her lips moved as she worked, and those beside her heard her whispered Indian prayers. It meant a great deal to me as I had shared healings with three or four of the people so knew something of their physical difficulties. In every case Tayja's hands moved truly to the trouble spots.

It was Kathy Messetler, one of our instructors, who had the most surprising reaction. When she felt the heat of Tayja's touch, her consciousness appeared to melt away, and Tayja caught her under the arms and let her gently to the floor. After she regained consciousness, Kathy said that, even as she was falling, she told herself, "I'm standing up!"

Those who followed Tayja's progress from the first days at Blind Awareness to her success as a shaman have also written her. Grace from Blind Awareness writes:

> . . . Thank you, Tayja, (and you, too, God, for using Tayja as a channel). My life has been blessed through my contacts with you. My health has improved, my spiritual life deepened, and I have an increased reverence for ALL life. Your deep well of faith has strengthened mine (and I hope that sense of humor and enthusiasm have also rubbed off on me!!) . . .

The thank you letters continue:

> . . . Thanking you for healing my feet at your home. It is so wonderful not to feel any pain anymore . . .

Sept. 2, 1985
Dear Tayja,
At work on August 21st Wed. I cut half of my finger tip off with a razor edge while cutting industrial rubber material.

I was rushed to the hospital. The doctor couldn't sew back the finger tip and said that I would have to wear a large over-sized bandage for 8 weeks. He also said that it would not grow back, but I would have only scar tissue on my finger. On August 22nd, Thursday, I came to your healing group for a healing. I felt no pain after the healing. On August 23rd, Friday, I went back to the doctor and he said he couldn't believe how fast it had grown back, and I wouldn't have to wear the large bandage, only a small Bandaid.

Now a week later, I have a finger tip again with even finger prints. All the tissue was healed remarkably.

Thanks to you and to the spirit.

Todd Wolf

Tayja had a busy winter which included studying for ordination. She was now a lay minister in the Spiritualist church. Her remaining time was filled with lectures and workshops for the Theosophical Society, Present Moment, and other places in the Twin Cities area and Rochester. She conducted a guide group in which she trained her students to get in touch with spirit guides and lost souls. An ongoing healing group met on Thursday nights. As one of her students told me, "She is so warm and so giving and yet so humble." Tayja intends to keep her humility. We talked about the pitfalls of charisma, and she said, "Being on a pedestal only hurts in the end. You're like a statue instead of a person, so you can't make a mistake or they knock you off, and you break." She enjoys "teaching people to laugh and know that so much is illusion except for the present."

Just one year later, in June of 1985, Tayja was back at Carleton, this time as a healer. The SFF Retreat theme was, "We Make Our Own Reality." Daring to interpret Christ's direction literally and take on the responsibility of actually doing "all that I do," is frightening to most of us. After all, in our culture, doesn't it mean we are insane? Yet with its acceptance we give up our small identities—our split personalities—to become, not tiny drops in the eternal ocean, but the Ocean itself.

In the vision of One is the world reborn, not in fantasy, but in truth. As Tayja instructed in one of her meditation tapes, "Go beyond existence, beyond the word, to be born into the universe."

Chapter Thirteen
Carry the Light

When pain is to be borne, a little courage helps more than much knowledge, a little human sympathy more than much courage, and the least tincture of the love of God more than all.

—C. S. Lewis

In a gentle voice, strong and deep, Tayja tells of her dream for all people "to live as one being throughout the world because God has chosen it to be that way." Her words came to me on tape from Phoenix. I thought of the legendary bird, emblem of the city which is now Tayja's, and recalled its unique way to face death. When the phoenix sees death's face come near, it makes a nest of wood and sweet-smelling resins, which it exposes to the full force of the sun until it is burnt to ashes in the flames of its own nest. Another phoenix then arises from the marrow of its bones.

Tayja spoke through the tape, "It is time for giving birth to that new sense of feeling and to that new sense of direction, because birth is what it's about: a new coming of the Christ within us. This light brings our harmonies together, and the energies from each cell of our earth bodies comes together as one, and I know that we can do that. We can do it because, from this light within we will all receive new directions, and my hope is that we will follow those directions so that we can be a part of that eternal mechanism of our own souls, our own hearts, to be able to understand and know that we will survive, to know and understand that we are eternal. We don't need to make those nuclear things; they are not necessary. They make fear, and that doesn't help. God's plan is peace. Life is a learning tool for that plan, and we will continue to learn from now until eternity and

201

beyond eternity.

"Because of the strong energies speeding change, some people will fall off balance, and they will have to struggle to regain that part of them that they have lost. But those who haven't lost, who have continued to gain and stay in harmony with their God, they will be there to show the others. The freedom will become the kind of freedom that no one has ever experienced before, and the butterflies will fly."

As I put Tayja's tape back into its box, I thought of how the light in the bulb is tightly surrounded by the cocoon of a glass sheath, yet the light shining purely within its vacuum may reach for many miles. "The least tincture of the love of God" within a human being seems to me like the light within the bulb—the light switched on within Tayja. My experience during Tayja's healing when I saw light from her on physical, emotional and spiritual levels had quelled my residual skepticism about healing in others. Also, I had seen healing in many of the clients with whom I had worked. Yet I was reluctant to turn that healing love energy toward myself, so recognizing my responsibility for switching on the light within me. We skeptical moderns often look at the weathered cocoons of ancient traditions with no concept of the bright young wings within. Yet all of us have them. Each of us can become our unique version of the Modern Shaman.

Did I see the modern shaman in myself? Had I truly healed my own body/spirit?—Not exactly.

My own unfinished work showed up for me in the fall of 1985 when I went to a doctor for the first time since the retirement of my previous physician over four years before. My purpose, as I thought, was not so much for the doctor to check me as for me to check out the new doctor. The switch came when, as he palpated my neck, the doctor located a lump on the right lobe of my thyroid gland. He recommended an x-ray and an ultra scan.

It was March 6, 1986 before I followed through with the x-ray. The small town hospital was a friendly unhurried place. I was the only patient in for x-ray, and the technologist, a pleasant young man who worked with methodical care, took time to explain his procedures. As I watched the heavy, black-framed eye descend to my neck to record with its magical insight, I relaxed, letting my human insight function. Deeper levels of my mind told me it would not show a normal picture, yet I didn't feel anything negative about it.

I continued to relax on the table as the technologist developed his battery of films. An image I had seen in meditation some months before recurred to me: I was looking down on my neck as I lay back in a reclining chair. A dexterous pair of hands were delicately working at my throat. I saw them sharply, somewhat dark of skin and with black hairs growing from the backs of them. From the healing work I had done with others, I knew the throat chakra was the seat of will. Then how should I go about "willing" in a stronger way? Although I knew I needed to reform my body in some way, I had no idea at that time how to put my energy into the spiritual seed from which the new body could grow.

The return of the technologist from the dark room put an end to my contemplations. His attempts to explain the image shown by the ultra scan were meaningless to me, but the x-ray showed clearly that the right side of the gland was approximatley three times the size of the left.

After examining the x-rays, my doctor recommended removal of the tumor and with it the right lobe of my thyroid gland. He then referred me to a surgeon who, after performing a needle biopsy of the thyroid, confirmed the first medical opinion. After examining the slides, the surgeon pronounced my growth "A 'cold' follicular tumor," and told me that, in such tumors, cancer could not be ruled out. The cancer, if any, was of a slow-growing type, and I needed to be in no hurry for surgery. Of course, I wasn't, and again I procrastinated.

About three months later I found an M.D. who practiced therapeutic touch (although quietly), and I changed doctors. She (a family practitioner) referred me to an endocrinologist who confirmed the diagnosis of a follicular neoplasm in agreement with the other two doctors, and, after explaining the difference between "hot" (benign) and "cold" (possibly malignant) tumors, she told me my chances of having thyroid cancer were about thirty percent and recommended, as the other three doctors had, that the right lobe of the thyroid be removed. On her recommendation, I selected a surgeon practicing at the University of Minnesota Hospitals, but again I put off making an appointment. Christmas of 1986 was "almost at my throat." I did not want surgery to compound the breathless festivities.

Tayja was coming home for Christmas, home for a festival of lights. The phoenix had again turned Tayja's past to ashes, and the new Tayja I met was sixty pounds lighter. She was slender, bright and beautiful. Makeup colored her face, and her strong hands were tipped with long, painted nails. Yet it was indeed the same Tayja powered by the same rich laugh and with muscles ever-stronger to meet the growing challenges of her life. She knew her destiny and moved into the future with a strong step trusting in the wonder of herself and in her union with the universe.

"What spirit is telling me now," she said as we drove through the countryside toward home, "is that we need to get away from beliefs and into *knowing*. Beliefs come from others, but knowing comes from the Self. It's sure, and we need the courage to follow it. The spirit who is giving me all this stuff is called 'Ki.' "

How significant that her new guide's name is "Ki" which is the Japanese word for "life-force energy!"

We went on to other subjects, but somewhere inside me I was asking, "Do I really *know* that I can heal myself? For over two years now I've been working close to Tayja through her darkness into light. But has my belief and trust in healing yet turned to positive *knowing*?"

Tayja and I spent the afternoon in happy conversation, much of it in the car as I completed last minute Christmas errands. One of them was a trip to the vet's to pick up some thyroid extract pills for our dog. As Tayja stood there beside me, the technologist told me, "Her thyroid has regulated itself now. You won't have to continue giving her pills."

Even my dog was doing it right! Although my thyroid function was normal, it certainly wouldn't be if it had to be removed. But all that would wait until after Christmas. I had an appointment with the surgeon scheduled for the afternoon of January 7, 1987. I also had a tentative date for surgery on January 9.

After Tayja and I arrived home from the vet's, we talked about setting up a meeting with our publisher. We had no agreement with him, but Tayja's belief in Llewellyn was within a breath of knowing, and mine was nearly as close. Tayja took out her engagement calendar saying, "I know it can't be on the weekend 'cause I'm giving a workshop in Rochester."

I leaned over her shoulder to check the day. "What's it on? I asked, hoping to be able to go.

"It will be about the new messages I'm getting about going beyond just believing with our heads to really *knowing* with our whole lives."

"It would be fun to get a group together and go down."

My plans for attending the workshop came to an abrupt halt. Tayja shook her head. "It's already full." Tayja returned her attention to our planned meeting with our publisher. "Our lunch should be on the 7th," she said.

I checked my calendar and was face to face with my 2:30 doctor's appointment. Lunch here in Afton at 11:30, then the University Hospital in Minneapolis an hour away by 2:30? It wasn't reasonable, but "knowing" didn't ask confirmation from a puny human brain. So the 7th it would be. Carl Llewellyn Weschcke was invited, and the date was set.

Another party intervened. Tayja's birthday was on January 26, but she would be in Phoenix then, so her reparenting family planned a celebration for her on January 1. It would be a perfect way to start the new year, and I looked forward to the event.

From the beginning it was no disappointment! Poignant wafts of garlic chicken greeted me as I entered the kitchen, and I exchanged warm hugs with two of Tayja's sisters whom I had come to know quite well. One of her sisters was frosting the cake while others got out plates, broke up lettuce for the salad, or hurried on mysterious missions to other rooms. The feeling of Party laughed through the house.

Tayja came downstairs looking as festive as the Christmas tree behind her. Her usual jeans had been replaced by a long skirt, its broad vertical stripes of pink and white emphasizing her new slender figure, and small flowers decorating the pink stripe showed her feminine side while in no way obscuring her power.

"Would you like to see the house?" Tayja asked.

Three of us went with her through rooms artistically furnished with graceful antiques. Tayja pointed out the paintings her mother had done and showed us all the way to her mother's sky-lighted studio on the third floor of the attractive Victorian house.

The meal tasted as good as it looked, and the four chickens were soon reduced to skeletons, the salad bowl empty, the punch drained from the Santa mugs, the candles blown out in one breath, and the cake demolished.

Tayja unwrapped her many presents unveiling much needed clothes. Her old ones hung on her like the dress of a scare crow. When the presents had been passed around and duly admired, it was Tayja's turn to give. She had promised her family and friends a healing service.

In preparation, Tayja called on one of her sisters to braid her hair and went upstairs to change into her robe.

When she returned, she was wearing a long white gown which she had decorated with decals of Indian motifs and painted with "liquid embroidery." The lights were dimmed, then, to the background of Indian flute music, Tayja began the healings. She stood in the center of the circle as she had at our blind awareness services in the autumn after her own healing. She took each person with her in turn to the center of the circle.

This time was for me. Dimly I felt my body swaying in a spiral as I sat in a comfortable chair. Dimly I heard a woman cry. Then I felt Tayja's touch on my shoulder and followed her to the center, lay down on the floor as she bid me, glad she had not asked me to stand. My eyes were closed. I felt her hot fingertips reach to the right side of my neck, pointing against, then apparently into, my thyroid gland. The wave of energy, like electricity, passed through my body until I felt it prickle my feet. Next I felt my breath controlling my body, and the quick bellows-action in my lower abdomen seemed entirely disconnected from my conscious will. Within five minutes it was over, and I had returned to my chair.

The Biblical caution, "Test ye the spirits," is never far from my consciousness, and I wanted the proof. It was only six days away.

At 2:30 on January 7th, I was skimming the highway both actually and metaphorically. The meeting with Carl Weschcke had been a happy occasion on all sides, and my belief was budding into knowing almost as fast as my car was going.

As I drove into the parking ramp, the strains of the "March Triumphant" from *Aida* blasted over my car radio from the University public radio station. To me it spelled out graduation, and I saw again the Carleton chapel, my academic graduation, then in the same place, Tayja's graduation into the seeing world.

The words of a hymn we used to sing at our high school graduations hummed into my mind:

Be thou our ruler, guardian guide and stay:
Thy word our law, thy paths our chosen way.

The path had been given, yet chosen, destiny and will joining hands in the synchronies of life-designs. Very literally I had seen it "at my throat": my will must be joined with the hands of a larger destiny.

Although I was a half hour late—How else would I have been accompanied by the destined music?—I waited over an hour in the reception room of the surgery clinic in the Phillips-Wangensteen Building. When at last I met the surgeon, I liked him immediately. My aunt had been the wife of the late Owen Wangensteen, chief of surgery at the University School of Medicine. The name of the building we were in opened mutual connections, and the doctor inquired about my aunt, my father, and gave me news of some relatives of his.

After examining the x-rays and the ultra scan, he confirmed the opinion of the other four doctors.

I was relaxed, free, as the surgeons hands felt my neck. "It feels soft to palpation," he said.

He decided on another needle biopsy, and, with the expectation of change, I was in favor of a new look for the new year.

As I prepared to leave he told me, "The tumor doesn't feel hard to palpation, so I see no need to operate at this time. I'll send you a report on the biopsy in about a week, and I'd like to see you again in four months."

I came home late, time to feed our little dog, Blue. As I prepared her food—without the thyroid pill—I thought of the way our pets, like so many other elements in our lives, mirror ourselves showing them in new guises. Surely Blue showed me my own neck, then demonstrated the natural healing of our bodies. I smiled as I put Blue's dish on the floor, and I smiled again as I glanced at the wall hanging above it. It was a linen print of a girl with long blond hair—like Marilyn Rossner's—and dressed in a multi-colored skirt, looking much like one I had seen Marilyn wear. She was feeding doves, and I was sure her Joy Guide was named "Daisy," as Marilyn's was. I wondered, what was Tayja's Daisy doing now? Who was she guiding? Mirrors of life were playing a crystal light show of reflections back at me. I felt the rainbows of light laughing around me with the same throbbing light source that put healing in my body. Or was it always there, only my vision that had changed?

(The doctor's report which arrived two weeks later was anti-climactic: "No malignant cells seen in aspirate but insufficient for diagnosis.")

I was to see Tayja only one more time before she returned to Phoenix. It was at her healing service in Minneapolis. The room which would have been crowded with 30 people in it was bursting with nearly 40 by the time my husband and I arrived. The service was in progress, and we squeezed in between two chairs and sat on the floor in the semi-dark room where Tayja was working between two large paintings of angels, one with a glistening jewel over her solar plexus chakra. I looked away from Tayja as I felt healing hands on my shoulders and turned to see Kathy Messetler, one of our blind awareness instructors and a treasured friend. Again I was taken in memory to sight regained at Carleton. Then too, I was seated in front of Kathy and feeling her healing hands on my shoulders.

My husband and I had to leave the group early, but not before Tayja had channeled her energy and a message, "Spirit tells me to say you should trust yourself more." My last view of Tayja is of a powerful healer giving what she has received.

The ink Tayja has used in the writing of this book is her own life blood. I have done my best to translate her blood to words where I put you—as she put me—in healing hands working as One with our own wills.

For ways and means to reach our deep-mind power, turn to Appendix II.

Appendix I
Mind Patterns

Graphology is a complex combination of science and art designed to read in the form of the writing, the form of the mind that directed that writing. The professional graphologist, Mrs. John Rowan of Minneapolis, analyzed Tayja's handwriting while she was in reparenting at Wiger Woods. Recently Mary Rowan reexamined samples of Tayja's various writings from the journals.

In keeping with a holographic concept of mind and action, handwriting illustrates the physical, emotional, mental and spiritual position of a person at the time that person is writing. Total changes in writing such as Tayja displays are almost unheard of in the annals of graphology.

The following guidelines will help the reader to better apply the analyses which follow. It is, however, important to keep in mind that writing characteristics, like characteristics of a personality, do not exist in isolation, but form a network. Any indicated trait may be either augmented or diminished by the presence of conflicting indicators.

Handwriting with a right hand slant indicates a warm, emotional response to situations and people. This trait indicates a person who is emotionally involved and sympathetic, especially when the lower loops are of generous (but not excessive) size. These people usually care about others and often express it openly. They are all heart and may give so much of themselves that they become easily drained. A professional analyst such as Mary Rowan will, however, look beyond the slant of the writing to discover qualifying traits. For example, very emotional people who were badly hurt could have resentments which cause them to be bottled up or angry and blocked from

211

expressing concern for others. "One could observe five traits in a writing sample," Mary explains, "then see another five traits which neutralize those first five." Traits observable in writing include indications of stubbornness, inhibition, caution. "Being easily drained is a *tendency* for those whose writing slants to the right, but if the person writes with a lot of pressure, that means they have a lot of energy, so they won't get so drained. Also, a naturally open heart may be blocked by so much bitterness that it is not expressed." People with an extreme right-hand slant tend to be emotional and a little too impulsive at times. This can color their judgement, and they may leap before they look.

A vertical writer (writing unslanted) is often cool and reserved. These people tend to be excellent judges of people and situations. They don't get as emotionally involved with others. Their heads rule, and they think before they act, yet the wisdom of their actions may be influenced by their intelligence. Also, irregular lines which indicate imbalances could be evident in their writing.

Backhand writers can be introverted. Often they may be filled with fears arising from past hurts so have difficulty trusting others. Their concerns are closed in toward themselves and their problems, and they often prefer to be alone.

Small writing indicates that the writer may live in a small world. Often little social life intrudes on home and the job. A qualifying sign here could be large lower loops in the writing which indicate that the person would like to get out but may be confined because he or she has to be, as in the case of a student who must stay in to study. It's possible that the retreating person may be an accountant or perhaps a brilliant scientist. If small writing becomes abnormally tiny, it can indicate mental problems, a desire to disappear.

Big writing shows that the person needs a big world, a place to expand. Such a person looks for variety, change, people, activity, especially if the lower loops are large. They are usually extroverts.

The "t" crossings indicate goals in life, higher ones showing confidence and achievement, lower ones self-doubt. "t" crossings which stop at the bar indicate procrastination.

"There is so much more!" Mary exclaims. "We are all showing in our writing a variation of traits plus a variation within those traits that let the world know we are all different and individual."

The following samples and analyses are excerpted from four hours of tapes which Mary Rowan has supplied:

4/24/77: Sample One

"In the first sample, we see evidence of a nervous condition. There is a feeling of simplicity in the strokes, but with an adult strain of getting right to the point. She shows a little feeling of satisfaction in the 'r', then sort of an aggressive stroke. There's some frigidity showing she is hard to get along with. Also, there are rounded strokes showing a gentle, yielding kind of person, one with many mood changes.

"I see a tenacity stroke here, also self-doubting and a trace of introversion. She appears to be under pressure. She shows a desire to learn.

"She feels she has to go upward for answers. I am seeing a trace of psychic ability, and a little ability to prophecy the future."

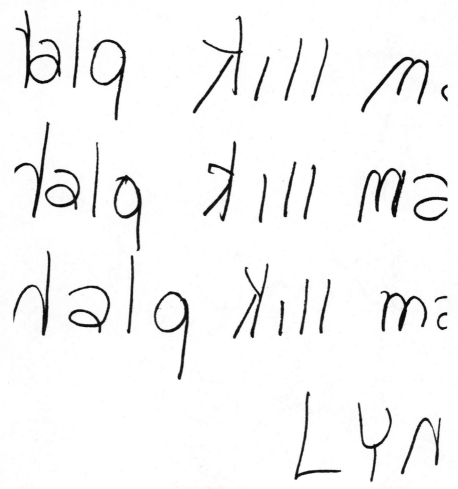

5/7/77: Sample Two

In the dyslexic writing above, Mary saw in the heavy pressure, "a lot of energy, also fear and deep feeling. She can't adjust easily to new things. Her senses are very alert; everything has such meaning! Any terror or worry is very strong. She is like a blotter, so she is going to hold the terror, the worry and feel them very strongly.

"There is also evidence of some shrewdness and cunning. She shows that psychic ability again, and there is evidence that she is very hard on herself and others too. She shows little attempt at self-control."

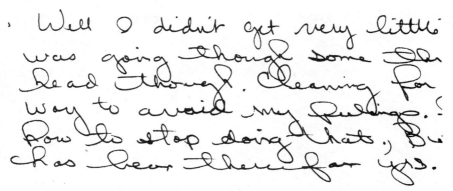

12/6/77: Sample Three

"Good power of concentration, tendency to be a hermit. But also she can be overcome by a desire for change, for travel, excitement and action. So there is a conflict here. Those wide lower loops show wild ideas. Some of the books would say they indicate schizophrenia. Although those lower loops show a fantastic imagination, there are conservative strokes as well.

"The way the letters are leaning show that there is a wall up. You can't get close to this person.

"That same wild imagination shows up in the philosophical realm as well. Those fat 'l's' indicate wild ideas in her thoughts on God and religion.

"She shows planning and organizational skills, but she can be touchy and bothered if criticized and can be nitpicking toward others, also tactless at times.

"Although she has the capacity to be a funny, humorous person, she has too much of a wall to let it out much.

"She is a sharp person with a logical mind, but moody and goes from cool to emotional. There is no crookedness or dishonesty.

"She shows a lot of self-interest, 'me and my problems.' Yet she is warm and caring at times.

"This writing shows secretive thoughts including unusual ideas about sex.

"I see some marks in the a's and o's which could indicate that she is a smoker. [Tayja has smoked since she was 9.]

"Her goals are practical, and she indicates the ability to achieve them most of the time."

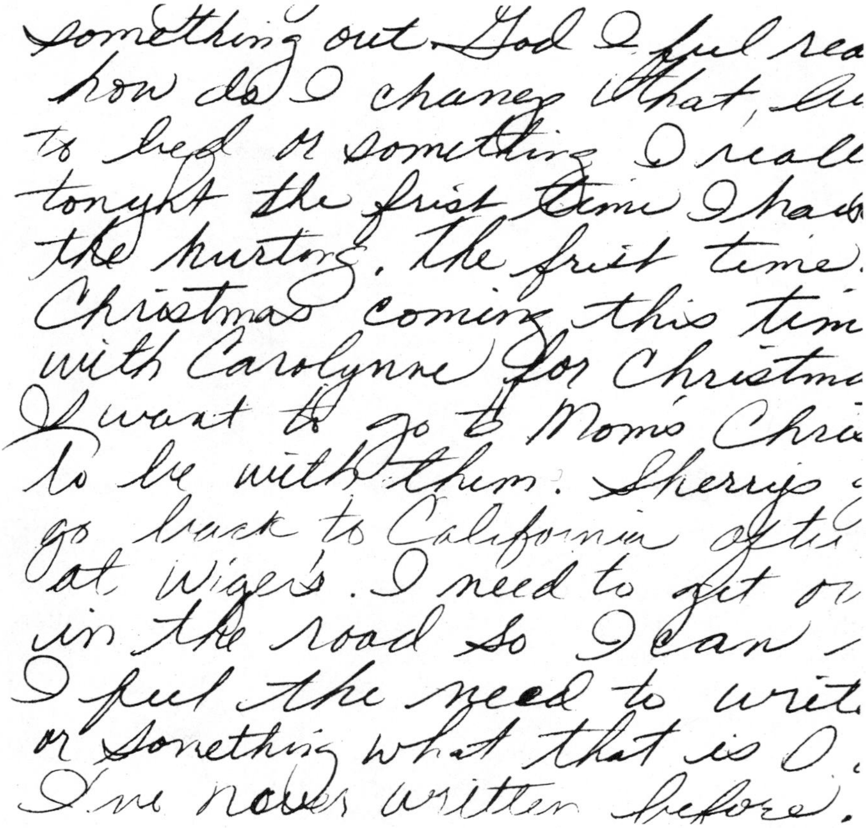

[handwritten text]

something out. God I feel rea
how do I change that, Are
to bed or something I reall
tonight the frist time I had
the hurting. The frist time.
Christmas coming this tim
with Carolynne for Christm
I want to go to Mom's Chris
to be with them. Sherrys
go back to California ofter
at Wigers. I need to get on
in the road so I can
I feel the need to writ
or something what that is I
I've never written before.

12/13/77: Sample Four

"This is pretty good normal writing. Here she is more talkative, and the tops of the 'l's' and 'h's' are narrow which shows she is narrow-minded in religion [note contradiction to previous sample] and does not have the wild mood swings. Confusion shows up in the mixing of two lines of writing. Here she is more emotional, kind, loving, caring and responsive, a different person. She is more mature. She does her job with pride and dignity. Although generous, she is cautious. Here she looks as though she would make a good counselor. She appreciates words and shows literary ability.

"But she is self-concerned and shows a need for attention. She has a tendency to procrastinate. Energy and power are missing from her everyday life."

Ball's and it went pretty

fun. I felt pretty good about

, I was dreaming and woke my self

ther, I wasn't sure where I was,

ne And one together. Mom came into

bed, but I was really out of it

+ went to bed.

12/23/77: Sample Five, "The little printer."

"Spaces between the letters and words show that she needs more space, more time for herself. She feels tiny, very inhibited. She is reserved, logical and pretty independent. 'I can take care of myself.' She does show a lot of conflict here: 'I feel pretty good about myself; I'll never make it.' She shows a fear of following through with her ideas."

5/8/78: Sample Six

"Something is obviously wrong with her nervous system as the shaky strokes in her writing show. She is self-involved and aggressive, but lacks the strength to implement it. This is indicated by the weak pressure in her writing. Here where the writing becomes disorganized, an entity may be influencing her. She appears to be ailing; there seems to be something wrong with her physically."

In the summer of 1978 her writing shows improvement including an increase of energy.

7/2/78: Sample Seven

"She shows too much psi ability for her to control, but she does show increasing maturity. There seems to be some worry with her psychic and prophetic ability."

10PM and that I probably know
what the block is but I
won't let me know. That
I should stop the secrets
and tell what I am blocking
I felt like busting me
by braking the windows
in the library It was so
cold in there. I was upset
because I couldn't go anywhere
because I was tied to the
bed. The blocks are Anger,
the bruises, pain, hurt.
Having to burie my mother.
I need to set up how to
bury her proper.

1st mother

Burial Words:
Nia Nia Nia 12+A 12+A
YKA YKA YKA 12+A
2KA 2KA 2KA Yua Mo Yua Mo.

12/5/78: Sample Eight, Burial of 'Old Mom'

"This writing shows she is very insecure about the future as shown with the large right border and the incomplete capital 'r'. Her small 'p' shows she is a peacemaker and doesn't want to argue.

"On this date (right before Christmas) she indicates, as many people do, a wish to acquire as shown by the hooks that start out the words."

Tommy, 6/10/80; Tayja, 7/13/80; and Debby, 7/22/80: Samples
Nine, Ten and Eleven

"These three are signing similar writings. They show a back-slant that indicates that she is putting up a wall, not trusting many people. It shows that she was hurt in the past and is running from authority. The extra-large loops indicate an over-active imagination, and the way they interefere with the line below indicates a lot of confusion."

6/13/80: Sample Twelve

"Oh my, look at the 'g' on frightening! It shows that she can bluff her way out of a tight spot. Then at the bottom of the page we see a much younger person showing a lot of pressure and tension. This person shows a lot of hurt. 'I've got to hide; I can't get along with people.'"

mama's and daddy's return from Can , my stomache feels sick again this I am so tired of feeling this way. So I think I am going to die I feel not but enevous of others who are already think what am I on earth for what's here. that sometime I will figure out, all for now. Debbie Ann

Well I thought I would write some n I am sitting here cout a top which f really good it is so hot + unconfor anyway Jeff said it wouldn't bother If Eliz were here I couednt do it at ae feels free. I have a feeling of

7/13/80: Sample Thirteen

"Debby Ann is controlled, immature, childlike, secretive, lying, insecure. 3:45 P.M. "God, I am so tired of feeling this way. Sometimes if I think I am going to die I feel not frightened but envious of others who are already died. I think what am I on earth for. What's my purpose here?" Could she be picking this up from a confused spirit who is not aware that it is free of its body so does not move on to other dimensions? Bottom of the page, Could a spirit be trying to have sex with Tayja?"

7/23/80: Sample Fourteen

"This childlike sample shows a tendency to lie in the double looped 'o's' and 'a's'. An interesting point about this is that positive and optimistic affirmations which may be used in therapy can be untrue when they are first spoken, so may show up as lies in the writing. Here Tayja's 'm's' show worry loops, and this also indicates psychic ability. This psychic ability can cause worry as one senses in advance that something bad is about to happen. One moment she has a rounded 's' and can be influenced and easily pushed around while the next moment she stands her ground as is shown by the pointed top on the small 's'."

7/24/80: Sample Fifteen

"This sample shows increasing psi ability and worry connected with it.

"It looks to me as though between 3:00 and 5:00 o'clock she was taken over by a resentful entity. These repulsive orders appear to me as being given to the Child personality of Tayja, and it's like they stuck there. She wants to get rid of them, and they come up now, and maybe she can release them and be free of them."

*That much. Help me Help me &
hurt and fear if you let it and itll hur*

7/24/80, 10:30 P.M.: Sample Sixteen
Can personality change so fast!?

"In the first part of this she is out in the world. Then within half an hour or less, she is shy and small within herself. She is writing desperately, "Help me, help me." This one is signed, "Debbie Ann." There isn't one writing for one person.

"Russell shows underdeveloped will here and lacks push and enthusiasm. Finger dexterity is also evident."

*I was ever going to get there the
to meet Barb O'leary downtown
and was 20 min late, panic! +*

8/21 & 22/80: Sample Seventeen

"Here she is showing wonderful organizational ability. This is sensible writing showing that she is functioning really well."

But on August 27, 1980

*! Well today I stay in bed until 10³⁰/pm didn't
... ...*

"She writes in a pinched backhand. This writing shows great fear and sadness. Again she is asking, 'Am I going to make it?' She feels too much pressure and is withdrawing. Then on the next day, it's as though she were hiding from fear. 'I might not make it.' Then, at 10:30 the very same day she shows extreme control and a state of over-optimism."

I feel things are close
on me. I feel violant
inzibe like the the yr

did a piece of work with mama on
that I put the other underneath u
and I dont allow myself to feel the

10/6/80: Sample Eighteen

"This example shows dyslexia at 9 A.M., and apparent recovery from it at 12:15 P.M. on the same day. The right border at 12:45 shows extreme fear of the future."

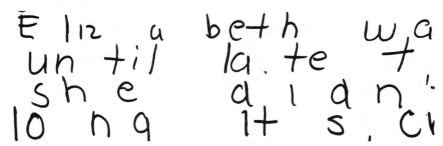

E liz a beth wa
un til la te t
she a i an
lo ng it s ci

11/9/80: Sample Nineteen

"Here Russell is signing a childish writing which indicates confusion in the spacing of letters together with a strong need for more space. Here he is under a lot of pressure."

By the end of her journals, Tayja's writing has become quite uniform. Evidence of her good qualities remains while abrupt changes become much less evident. Gone are the schizophrenic loops and the wild imagination.

The Shaman Tayja has
working very hard she has
spent many hours on he
promply to meet you. She
doing some intensive days of w
get ready for a major transfer
It seems exciting that many thin
diffrent for me. I am working t
to many days pass
I have said what I
need to say Bless You
                    cloth and much
                    friendship.
                    White Feather

Tayja rush wigen
there. I have a friend who has said
with some P.R. work. No at this point
my little brouchia to get out to the
really excited about that. No is new i.

Samples Twenty — Twenty-three

Here, after her healing, Tayja's samples show great improvement. Her writing is more normal but still shows mood changes. There is good spacing between rows indicating a lack of the confusion so often seen in the earlier writings. The wild loops are gone, indicating an imagination within reasonable limits. The generous left borders tell us she wants to leave the past behind her. The vertical slant on July 24th shows control. The upper points on the 'm's' show a quick intelligent mind, and her analytical ability shows in the 'v's' within the 'm's'.

In the Setpember 15th letter, the writing flows outward to people indicating an open caring and concern for others. This sample shows a consistent mood and a lot of initiative, a push to get out and accomplish.

The final letter consistently shows excellent concentration and good organization."

Tayja's personality shows an unusual array of qualities to choose from, and she now has the ability to make the most appropriate choice for the situation at hand.

July 9, 1984, See Sample Twenty.

Mary Rowan does not think this is White Feather's writing, but rather indicates Tayja's attitude toward the spirit channeling through her. Some fear of the future is evident in the wide right-hand margin, and the emotional slant to the writing is extreme indicating Tayja's excitement with the experience of her guide within her. This agrees with Tayja's account: "He was talking to me, telling me what to write, not channeling through me," she explained.

"It is wonderful how far she has come!" Mary exclaims.

Appendix II
Techniques for Waking the Shaman
Within You

The shamanic process is activated when a person learns to alter consciousness at will, so contacting and utilizing normally hidden knowledge and power for the purpose of helping self and others.

Tayja's story demonstrates in epic proportions the power of the shamanic forces and their potential for destructive use; then in the resolution of Tayja's shamanic potential, you have seen the coin flip from a harmful to a helpful use of power. By harnessing her shamanic (psycho/spiritual) power, she moved from hurting herself and others to helping first self, then others.

The following guidelines are designed to assist each one of you in finding your own unique growth path, the specific personal power of your own center. It is not only possible, but important for each of us to do this, for misdirected or undirected power can cause unnecessary mental and physical pain. It is through this quest that each one of us activates our potential capacity for joy, not only for ourselves, but radiating outward along every strand of the web of life, so spreading peace around us and throughout the planet.

Tayja has experienced within her being the Buddha's meaning when he said, "All that we are is the result of what we have thought. The mind is everything. What we think we become."

As Tayja expresses it, "Our future is made by the thought patterns we make for it, so not one person can predict the future for sure because those thought patterns can always change." As we wake each morning to a fresh day, we can plan that "first day of the rest of our lives," and it is within the power of our will to transform our belief system cleansing it of negative beliefs, changing darkness to the light. This transformation may be practiced as a simple, yet demanding

229

exercise beginning with the individual spark of love clearly visualized, then allowed to grow until our entire planet is seen in peace.

Tayja puts it simply: "Think positively for seven days. After seven days the brain starts to change, and only the positive can remain. But it has to be *all* positive, even when it's 'raining.' After seven days the pure thinking will start reinforcing itself, and the light that fills the mind will bring right happenings to the whole life. To help this process along, it is important to meditate at least ten minutes a day, and this will open the third eye, the eye of God within us. Then look beyond physical sight, look past illusion to the reality of all things and see the God in them. Change happens in the silence. Progress is never made until we forgive the anger and fear of ourselves and others, then leave it behind."

Although most of us have an easier time releasing anger and fear than did Tayja, it is seldom easy for anyone. Tayja's inner chaos was maintained in a chaotic home. Her inner force, although extremely powerful, remained outside her control until she took steps to harness it. Only when she was ready to take those steps did she find the help she needed. So it can be for all of us. Each of us can find our own way to erase the pain and fear from our lives. Tayja's success with this is told in her dedication of this book: "To my real mother and my real father because I love them both in spite of all the things I went through with them. I know now that it was my choice. It was the rough way, but it was the way I learned the best."

Before beginning the following exercise, select a quiet place and time when you will be free from interruptions. To prepare for meditation, lie down on the floor in a relaxed position. If you wish, play quiet, unobtrusive music. Begin by stretching first one side of your body, then the other, feeling one side relaxed while you stretch the opposite side. Next stretch your entire body, hold the tension for about ten seconds, then relax. Now breathe slowly and deeply, filling the abdomen, then expelling completely. Continue this for five or ten minutes.

Now you are ready to reprogram your limiting belief systems. To do this, it is necessary to change, not only your mind, but your total experience. I will now suggest two ways to enter into this experiential change. Read both alternatives, then choose the one that best fits you:

Step 1. a) In your mind, review Tayja's healing. If negative thoughts intrude, focus on the joy of healing, and let the unwanted thoughts drift into the background, then fade. When you are able to do this with your *mind*, move into your emotions and *experience* Tayja's transformation *within yourself*. It *is* possible; we *are One* when we enter shamanic consciousness. Do not attempt to force this technique. Allow it to happen while maintaining a loving belief in yourself. You will probably find that ten or fifteen minutes is long enough to spend for the first time.

b) Use a transformative experience of your choice, then proceed as above.

When you feel you are ready, move on to Step 2. This may be on the same day, or a day or two later.

Step 2. After preparing as for Step 1, go into your own life taking inventory of its best aspects. Experience the love, joy and peace of these aspects. Allow your deep mind to capture a feeling of transcendence, then hold this feeling as long as you are able. When you can do this with ease, move on to Step 3.

Step 3. This step may take you longer than the previous two. Don't rush it. Do a little each day until you achieve mastery. Now take aspects of your life which you consider negative or in some way harmful to you. One per session will be enough at first. You are now commencing the transformative process. Accept these circumstances within yourself—not as outside events beyond your control. See them as perfectly designed to assist you in your psychospiritual growth. See them as opportunities and be thankful for them. Peace with the past clears the way to a peaceful future.

Doing this exercise daily will take you "out on a limb" of your own personal tree of growth, and you will see higher branches toward which to climb.

If you are not already in contact with a healing or psychospiritual growth group, regular practice of the above life-changing exercises will prepare you to attract others of like mind and heart. When you are ready, look for them and they will be there. It is important to realize that change within makes change without. In shamanic consciousness the rule is unity, not only within self but with all of existence.

When the mind and heart have been cleansed, it will be easy for you to think of yourself in perfect love, joy, beauty and peace. When you and your group of three or four or more are gathered together, you are prepared to draw into your consciousness, universal energies from the cosmos and so assist the earth-healing process. As you commence this exercise, think of yourself as a fine-tuned radio or television set designed to make visible the healing energies of Earth and Sky.

Select a quiet place outside or a quiet room indoors. If you wish, use candles and/or music to set a meditative mood. Now stand in a circle, relax and close your eyes. See and feel the Earth as a part of your own body. Think of roots extending from your root chakra and growing down into the center of the Earth, passing through earth, rock, water and fire. Think of the rock as your bone, the Earth as your flesh, the water as your blood, and the fire as your energy. When your body feels rooted in the body of the Earth, concentrate on your crown chakra and breathe deeply into your lower abdomen, the center of your physical power. Think of your name for God, whatever that may be and breathe in that spirit, that energy deeply into your being. Think of the air you breathe as the living spirit which enters and activates your energy centers.

Each one of you will be able to feel your body as a light source, an energy source. See your seven chakras as the central pillar of your body, open and ready to be charged with energy. Now bring the earth current up through your feet to fountain up through the Crown and out and down to sweep in at the feet again. This will strengthen the physical aura.

Now take hands and join the individual auras as one group aura extending in through the left hand and out through the right hand, counter-clockwise around the circle. Now, step by step extend this aura spiraling outward to include the whole room, then the home, then the community, and finally out over the Land. Visualize Earth as a beautiful globe of perfect peace.

Finally draw the energy back into yourself keeping all you need for your own healing, then send the surplus back into the Earth.

In this way we can use our power to recreate with our vision the God-created universe. We then become co-creators with God, and all things can be seen in congruity. When this happens for enough people, there is peace. Peace within removes validation of fear, hate and violence without. When a light is turned on, darkness is gone. When heat is applied, ice is melted. When the God-created universe is recognized, the ego-created world vanishes.

Through regular practice of these exercises, you will come to experience a new universe.

You will find as you continue to work together that the power of the group will steadily increase just as it has done for the Blind Awareness group in Minneapolis which Tayja now helps to teach when she is in Minnesota.

Some Guidelines for Discovering Your Personal Path

We can look at ourselves as rough gems with many facets which might be polished. We can only work on one at a time, and which one that will be is up to each one of us to determine for him or herself.

The options listed below are intended as suggestions only. Your personal path may include many of them, some of them, or others which are not listed here.

Spiritual Training Organizations (The following list is suggestive rather than inclusive.)

ALOHA INTERNATIONAL
Aloha is dedicated to teaching the philosophy of Huna, an ancient shamanic system of pratical principles. Huna combines the areas of spirituality, psychic sciences and psychology and emphasizes the power of the mind.
Aloha International
P.O. Box 665
Kilauea, HI 96754

ASSOCIATION FOR RESEARCH AND ENLIGHTENMENT
The A.R.E. program promotes autonomous study groups of individuals who wish to study, pray and meditate together. Their work is based on the psychic readings of Edgar Cayce and is primarily Christian.
A.R.E. Study Group Department
P.O. Box 595
Virginia Beach VA 23451

SPIRITUAL FRONTIERS FELLOWSHIP
(For a description of S.F.F. aims and objectives, see

Chapter 11.)
Spiritual Frontiers Fellowship
10819 Winner Road
Independence, MO 64052-0519

SPIRITUAL SCIENCE FELLOWSHIP

" . . . is an Inter-faith fellowship providing spiritual services, educational programs, and pastoral ministrations for persons —regardless of religious background—who desire to understand experiences of psyche and spirit. The S.S.F. provides opportunities for personal spiritual growth and psychic development, in an atmosphere of informed free-thought and enquiry."

The principles of S.S.F. as quoted, in part, from their guidebook are as follows:

"The Spiritual Science Fellowship has no dogmas or creeds, and welcomes persons from all traditions. It is based upon higher truths shared in many of the world's great religious traditions.

Our Foundations rest upon insights from the Modern Spiritualist Movement and Classical Yoga, as well as other ancient and modern traditions for the development of human potential, including Metaphysics and New Age Thought."

The Spiritual Science Fellowship
C.P. 1445 Stn. "H"
Montreal, Quebec
H3G 2N3 (Although Canadian based, S.S.F. has branches in the U.S.)

THE THEOSOPHICAL SOCIETY

" . . . is a world organization dedicated to the promotion of brotherhood and the encouragement of the study of religion, philosophy and science, to the end that man may better understand himself and his place in the universe. The Society stands for complete freedom of individual search and belief.

Objectives of the Society:

1. To form a nucleus of the Universal Brotherhood of Humanity, without distinction of race, creed, sex, caste or color.

2. To encourage the study of comparative religion, philosophy and science.

3. To investigate unexplained laws of nature and the powers latent in man.

THE THEOSOPHICAL SOCIETY IN AMERICA
P.O. Box 270
Wheaton, IL 60187

Churches and Temples:

Individual congregations of many faiths are willing to support the perennial philosophy and the human potential for unlimited spiritual growth. Avoid congregations which validate fear and sin.

Unity Christ Church
Many Spiritualist Churches (Watch for an over-emphasis on
    psychic phenomena.)
Unitarian Universalist Churches
Kabalistic Synagogues

Meditation Techniques and Philosophies:

Buddhist Ashrams
Yoga groups
Transcendental Meditation
Quaker Meetings

Martial Arts classes: (The Eastern Martial Arts, with adequate philosophical preparation for physical realization, can lead from controlled power to absence from fear, and hence to love first of self, then of others.)

Tai Chi
Akido
Karate

Exercise:

Yoga
Dancing
Walking or jogging, especially in natural surroundings
Swimming

Possible Elements of Holistic Health: (Many doctors and practitioners combine methods. The following list is partial.)

>Acupuncture
>Biofeedback
>Homeopathy
>Kufuto
>MariEL
>Reiki
>Therapeutic Massage
>Touch for Health
>Hot tubs, Saunas, Sweats

Counseling:

Counselors are difficult to categorize. The best of them combine methods in accordance with the needs and belief systems of their clients. Variations of Transactional Analysis, Transpersonal Psychology and Yungian Analysis are often used by new age counselors, usually in harmony with intuition or psychic sensitivity.

>AA and other 12 step programs.
>New Age Book Stores (Many of these conduct classes.)

A final word of caution: Do not put yourself into a position of subservience to any person or to any system. You have been given the key to your own life, so use it to open your own doors.

Notes

The Step Forward
1) King, Serge: "The Way of the Adventurer," "The American Theosophist." Pub., 1985. p. 391.
2) *Ibid.*, p. 392.
3) Neihard, John G.: *Black Elk Speaks: The Legendary "Book of Visions of an American Indian."* Simon & Shuster Pocket Books, 1972. p.p. 152 & 173.

Chapter 1
1) Storm, Hyemeyohsts: *Seven Arrows.* Harper & Row, New York, 1972. p. 75.

Chapter 2
1) Neihard, *op cit.*, p. 36.
2) Andrews, Lynn V.: *Flight of the Seventh Moon.* Harper & Row, 1984. p.p. 45-46.
3) Tsonakwa, Gerard R., class, "Touch the Earth," SFF National Midwest Retreat, Northfield, Minnesota.
4) Halifax, Joan: *Shamanic Voices: A Survey of Visionary Narratives.* E. P. Dutton, New York, 1979. p. 91.
5) Tsonakwa, *ibid.*
6) Tsonakwa's talk at the Raven Gallery, 2/2/84.

Chapter 3
1) *A Course in Miracles,* Vol. II. Pub., Foundation for Inner Peace, New York, 1975. p. 356.

Chapter 4
1) Deer, Lame and Erodes, Richard: *Lame Deer; Seeker of Visions,* Simon & Schuster, Inc., New York.
2) Lamb, Bruce and Cordova-Rios, Manuel: *The Wizard of the Upper Amazon,* Simon & Schuster, Inc., New York.
3) Neihard, *op cit.*, p. 71.
4) May, Rollo: A.H.P. Keynote address, 1985.
5) Storm, *op cit.*, p. 7.
6) Susann, Emily: A.H.P. Newsletter. Analysis of Perception, N.Y.

Humanities, 1956, p. 70.
7) Pearce, Joseph Chilton: *The Crack in the Cosmic Egg.* Washington Square Press, New York, 1971. p. 52.
8) Storm, *op cit.*, p. 20.
9) *Ibid.*, p. 7 & 8.
10) *Ibid.*

Chapter 5
1) Storm, *op cit.*, p. 243.
2) Halifax, *op cit.*, p. 13.
3) *Ibid.*, p. 14.
4) *Ibid.*, p. 18.
5) Storm, *op cit.*, p. 7.

Chapter 6
1) Halifax, *op cit.*, p. 5.
2) *Ibid.*
3) Grof, Stanislav, M.D., ed: *Ancient Wisdom and Modern Science* ed. Grof, Stanislav, M.D., State University of New York Press, Albany, 1984. p. 137.
4) Grof, Stanislav, M.D., *Beyond the Brain: Birth, Death and Transcendence in Psychotherapy,* State University of New York Press, Albany, 1985. p. 130-131.
5) Halifax, *op cit.*, p. 169-170.
6) Grof, *Beyond the Brain, op cit.* p. 38-39.
7) *Ibid.*, p. 158.
8) *Ibid.*, p. 159.
9) Institute of Noetic Sciences Newsletter, Winter 1985-86.
10) Tsonakwa, S.S.F. National Midwest Retreat, 1983.
11) Halifax, *op cit.*, p. 13.
12) Tsonakwa, *op. cit.*

Chapter 7
1) Hurley, Thomas J. III, "Possession, Dynamic Psychiatry & Science," a Research Bulletin of the Institute of Noetic Sciences, Volume I, Number 3/4 p. 9.
2) Halifax, *op cit.*, p. 22.
3) Hurley, Thomas J. III: "The Scope of Multiplicity." *op cit.*, p. 10.
4) Hurley: "Inner Faces of Multiplicity," *op cit.*, p. 3.

5) Hurley: "Etiology of Multiple Personality: From Abuse to Alter Personalities." *op cit.*, p. 11.
6) Harvey, Youngstook Kim: *Six Korean Women, The Socialization of Shamans.* West Publishing Co., St. Paul, 1979.
7) Hurley, *op cit.*, p. 11.
8) *Ibid.*, p. 12.
9) Hurley, *Ibid.*, p. 12.
10) Hurley, "Signs & Symptoms," *op cit.*, p. 14.
11) Hurley, "Multiple Personality Disorder: Key Findings," *op cit.*, p. 4.
12) Hurley, "Etiology of Multiple Personality," *op cit.*, p. 12.
13) Hurley, "Multiple Personality Disorder," *op cit.*, p. 5.
14) Hurley, *op cit.*, p. 6.
15) Hurley, "Signs & Symptoms: How to Recognize MPD," *op cit.*, p. 14.
16) Hurley, "Etiology of Multiple Personality," *op cit.*, p. 13.
17) Hurley, "Multiplicity & the Mind-Body Problem," *op cit.*, p. 20.
18) Hurley: "Possession, Dynamic Psychiatry & Science," *op cit.*, p. 9.

Chapter 9

1) Neihart, *op cit.*, p. 148.
2) Talamonti, L.: *Forbidden Universe.* Stein and Day, 1975.
3) Davison, Ronald C.: *Astrology.* ARC Books, New York, 1963, p. 10.
4) Andrews, *op cit.*, p.p. 45, 67.
5) Storm, *op cit.*, p. 6.

Chapter 10

1) *The Course in Miracles*, Vol. II. Foundation for Inner Peace, New York, 1975. p. 443.
2) Steiner, Lee R.: *Psychic Self-Healing for Psychological Problems.* Prentice-Hall, 1977.
3) Liaros, Carol Ann: *Practical ESP.* PSI Search Publications, New York, 1985.
4) *Ibid.*
5) Harman, Willis and Rheingold, Howard: *Higher Creativity,* Liberating the Unconscious for Breakthrough Insights. Jeremy P. Tarcher, Inc., 1984. p.p. 62, 63.

Chapter 12
1) *The Course in Miracles*, Vol. II, *op cit.*, p. 470.
2) *The Course in Miracles*, *op cit.*, p. 386.

Bibliography

Andrews, Lynn V., *Flight of the Seventh Moon*, Harper & Row, N.Y., 1984.

Davison, Ronald C., *Astrology*, ARC Books, N.Y., 1969.

Foundation for Inner Peace, Inc., *A Course in Miracles*, 1975.

Grof, Stanislav, M.D., ed., *Ancient Wisdom and Modern Science*, State University of New York Press, Albany, 1984.

Grof, Stanislav, M.D., ed., *Beyond the Brain*, State University of New York Press, Albany, 1985.

Harman, Willis, Ph.D. and Rheingold, Howard, *Higher Creativity*, Jeremy P. Tarcher, Inc., 1984.

Halifax, Joan, Ph.D., *Shamanic Voices*, E. P. Dutton, N.Y., 1979.

Hurley, Thomas J. III, "Multiple Personality—Mirrors of a New Model of Mind?": *Investigations: A Research Bulletin of the Institute of Noetic Sciences*, 1(3/4), 1985.

King, Serge, Ph.D., "The Way of the Adventurer," "The American Theosophists," 1985.

Neihard, John G., *Black Elk Speaks*, Simon & Shuster, N.Y., 1932.

Storm, Hyemeyohsts, *Seven Arrows*, Ballantine Books, N.Y., 1972.

Tsonakwa and Yolaikia, *Legends in Stone, Bone and Wood*, Arts and Learning Services Foundation, Minneapolis, 1986.

Books on Related Subjects

The following categories are suggestive rather than absolute.

I. Spiritual Principles for Opening the Mind; many paths to one source.

Ancient Wisdom and Modern Science, edited by Stanislav Grof.

The Aquarian Conspiracy: Personal and Social Transformation in the 1980's by Marilyn Ferguson.

A Course in Miracles: 3 Volumes, edited by Foundation for Inner Peace.

The Crack in the Cosmic Egg by Joseph Chilton Pearce.

Death: The Final Stage of Growth by Elizabeth Kubler Ross.

Energy, Ecstasy and Your Seven Vital Chakras by Bernard Gunther.

Higher Creativity: Liberating the Unconscious for Breakthrough Insights by Willis Harman, Ph.D. and Howard Rheingold.

Journey of Awakening by Ram Dass.

Kundalini by Gopi Krishna.

Kundalini Yoga by R. K. Karanjia.

The Kybalion, Hermetic Philosophy by Three Initiates.

Major Religions of the World by Marcus Bach.

Mastering Your Hidden Self: A Guide to the Huna Way by Serge King.

The Medium, the Mystic, and the Physicist by Lawrence LeShan.

Modern Man in Search of a Soul by C. G. Jung.

Mystery Teachings of All Ages by Manly Hall.

The Psychic Roots of Ancient Wisdom by Rev. John Rossner.

The Seth Material, and other Seth books channeled by Jane Roberts.

Stalking the Wild Pendulum by Itzhak Bentov.

Superlearning by Sheila Ostrander and Lynn Schroeder.

II. Shamanism

Black Elk Speaks by John G. Neihardt.

Kahuna Healing by Serge King.

Medicine Woman by Lynn Andrews, also *Flight of the Seventh Moon, Jaquar Woman* and *Star Woman.*

The Sacred Pipe: Black Elk's Account of the Seven Rites of the Ogalalah Sioux, recorded & edited by Joseph Epes Brown.

Seven Arrows by Hyemeyohsts Storm.

Shamanic Voices: A Survey of Visionary Narratives by Joan Halifax, Ph.D.

Shamanism by Mircea Thade.

The Way of the Shaman by Michael Harner

III. Psychological Wholing

All My Children: Reparenting therapy by Jacqui Lee Schiff with Beth Day.

Beyond the Brain: Birth, Death and Transcendence in Psychotherapy by Stanislav Grof.

The Dream Game by Ann Faraday.

Imagineering for Health by Serge King.

Magical Child: Nature's Plan for Our Children by Joseph Chilton Pearce.

The Myth of Meaning by Aniela Jaffe.

Man and His Symbols: Edited, with an introduction by Carl G. Jung.

Man's Search for Meaning: An Introduction to Logotherapy by Viktor E. Frankl.

Psychic Self-Healing for Psychological Problems by Lee R. Steiner Ph.D. Illustrated with Kirlian photography by the author.

Psychology and the Occult by Carl G. Jung.

Psychosynthesis: A Manual of Principles and Techniques by R. Assagioli.

The Third Force: The Psychology of Abraham Maslow; The Science of Self-Actualization by Frank G. Goble.

Visions Seminars by Carl Jung.

IV. Physical Healing

Amazing Secrets of Psychic Healing by Benjamin O. Bibb and Joseph L. Weed.

Anatomy of an Illness: How one man proved your mind can cure your body. Reflections on Healing and Regeneration by Norman Cousins.

Getting Well Again by Simonton & Simonton.

Imagineering for Health: Self-healing through the use of the mind by Serge King.

Listening to the Body: The Psychophysical Way to Health and Awareness by Robert Masters, Ph.D. & Jean Houston, Ph.D.

The Magic Power of Healing: Learn to Heal Yourself by Beverly C. Jaegers.

Occult Medicine Can Save Your Life by Norman Shealy, M.D., Ph.D.

90 Days to Self-Healing by Norman Shealy, M.D., Ph.D.

You Can Fight For Your Life: Emotional Factors in the Causation of Cancer by Lawrence LeShan.

Your Body Doesn't Lie: A New Simple Test Measures Impacts Upon Your Life Energy by John Diamond, M.D.

We Are All Healers by Sally Hammond.

V. Multiple Personality Disorder and Channeling

Apparitions: An Archetypal Approach to Death, Dreams and Ghosts by Aniela Jaffe.

Astral Doorways by J. H. Brennan.

Fifty Years a Medium by Estelle Roberts.

The Five of Me: The Autobiography of a Multiple Personality by Henry Hawksworth with Ted Schwarz.

How to be a Medium by W. H. Evans.

Multiple Man: Explorations in Possession & Multiple Personality by Adam Crabtree.

"Multiple Personality—Mirrors of a New Model of Mind?" by Thomas J. Hurley III. "Investigations: A Research Bulletin of the Institute of Noetic Sciences," 1(3/4), 1985.

Sybil by Flora Rheta.

University of Spiritualism by Harry Boddington.

VI. Understanding and Developing Psychic Abilities

After We Die, What Then? George W. Meek.

Challenge of Psychical Research by Gardner Murphy.

Creative Visualization by Shakti Gawain.

E.S.P. in Life and Lab by Louisa E. Rhine.

Hauntings and Apparitions by Brian Inglis.

How to Read the Aura, Practice Psychometry, Telepathy and Clair- voyance by W. E. Butler.

Mind Games: The Guide to Inner Space by Robert Masters and Jean Houston.

Passages: A Guide for Pilgrims of the Mind by Marianne Anderson and Louis M. Savary.

Practical ESP by Carol Ann Liaros.

Psychic Studies by Hal N. Banks.

Life After Life and *Reflections on Life After Life* by Raymond A. Moody, Jr., M.D.

Soul Mates by Jess Stearn.

Zen Mind, Beginner's Mind: Informal talks on Zen meditation and practice by Shunryu Suzuki.

STAY IN TOUCH

On the following pages you will find listed, with their current prices, some of the books and tapes now available on related subjects. Your book dealer stocks most of these, and will stock new titles in the Llewellyn series as they become available. We urge your patronage.

However, to obtain our full catalog, to keep informed of new titles as they are released and to benefit from informative articles and helpful news, you are invited to write for our bi-monthly news magazine/catalog. A sample copy is free, and it will continue coming to you at no cost as long as you are an active mail customer. Or you may keep it coming for a full year with a donation of just $2.00 in U.S.A. ($7.00 for Canada & Mexico, $20.00 overseas, first class mail). Many bookstores also have *The Llewellyn New Times* available to their customers. Ask for it.

Stay in touch! In *The Llewellyn New Times'* pages you will find news and reviews of new books, tapes and services, announcements of meetings and seminars, articles helpful to our readers, news of authors, advertising of products and services, special money-making opportunities, and much more.

The Llewellyn New Times
P.O. Box 64383-Dept. 034, St. Paul, MN 55164-0383, U.S.A.

• • •

TO ORDER BOOKS AND TAPES

If your book dealer does not have the books and tapes described on the following pages readily available, you may order them direct from the publisher by sending full price in U.S. funds, plus $1.00 for handling and 50¢ each book or item for postage within the United States; outside USA surface mail add $1.50 per item postage and $1.00 handling per order. Outside USA air mail add $7.00 per item plus $1.00 handling per order.

FOR GROUP STUDY AND PURCHASE

Because there is a great deal of interest in group discussion and study of the subject matter of this book, we feel that we should encourage the adoption and use of this particular book by such groups by offering a special "quantity" price to group leaders or "agents".

Our Special Quantity Price for a minimum order of five copies of BIRTH OF A MODERN SHAMAN is $29.85 Cash-With-Order. This price includes postage and handling within the United States. Minnesota residents must add 6% sales tax. For additional quantities, please order in multiples of five. For Canadian and foreign orders, add postage and handling charges as above. Credit Card (VISA, MasterCard, American Express, Diners' Club) Orders are accepted. Charge Card Orders only may be phoned free ($15.00 minimum order) within the U.S.A. by dialing 1-800-THE MOON (in Canada call: 1-800-FOR-SELF). Customer Service calls dial 1-612-291-1970. Mail Orders to:

LLEWELLYN PUBLICATIONS
P.O. Box 64383-Dept. 034 / St. Paul, MN 55164-0383, U.S.A.

THE INNER WORLD OF FITNESS
Melita Denning
Because the artificialities and the daily hassles of routine living tend to turn our attention from the real values, *The Inner World of Fitness* leads us back by means of those natural factors in life which remain to us: air, water, sunlight, the food we eat, the world of nature, meditation, sexual love and the power of our own wishes—so that through these things we can re-link ourselves in awareness to the great non-material forces of life and of being which underlie them.

The unity and interaction of inner and outer, keeping body and psyche open to the great currents of life and of the natural forces, is seen as the essential secret of *youthfulness* and hence of radiant fitness. Regardless of our physical age, so long as we are within the flow of these great currents, we have the vital quality of youthfulness: but if we begin to close off or turn away from those contacts, in the same measure we begin to lose youthfulness.

0-87542-165-2, 240 pgs., 5¼ x 8, softcover.   **$7.95**

THE ART OF SPIRITUAL HEALING
by Keith Sherwood
Each of you has the potential to be a healer; to heal yourself and to become a channel for healing others. Healing energy is always flowing through you. Learn how to recognize and tap this incredible energy source. You do not need to be a victim of disease or poor health. Rid yourself of negativity and become a channel for positive healing.

Become acquainted with your three auras and learn how to recognize problems and heal them on a higher level before they become manifested in the physical body as disease.

Special techniques make this book a "breakthrough" to healing power, but you are also given a concise, easy-to-follow regimen of good health to follow in order to maintain a superior state of being.

0-87542-720-0, 209 pages, softcover, illus.   **$7.95**

THE WOMEN'S BOOK OF HEALING
by Diane Stein
At the front of the women's spirituality movement with her previous books, Diane Stein now helps women (and men) reclaim their natural right to be healers. Included are exercises which can help YOU to become a healer! Learn about the uses of color, vibration, crystals and gems for healing. Learn about the auric energy field and the Chakras.

The book teaches alternative healing theory and techniques and combines them with crystal and gemstone healing, laying on of stones, psychic healing, laying on of hands, chakra work and aura work, color therapy. It teaches beginning theory in the aura, chakras, colors, creative visualization, meditation, health theory and ethics with some quantum theory. 46 gemstones plus clear quartz crystals are discussed in detail, arranged by chakras and colors.

The Women's Book of Healing is a book designed to teach basic healing (Part I) and healing with crystals and gemstones (Part II). Part I discusses the aura and four bodies; the chakras; basic healing skills of creative visualization, meditation and color work; psychic healing; and laying on of hands. Part II begins with a chapter on clear quartz crystal, then enters gemstone work with introductory gemstone material. The remainder of the book discusses, in chakra by chakra format, specific gemstones for healing work, their properties and uses.

0-87542-759-6, 6" x 9", color plates, softcover.   **$12.95**

BEYOND HYPNOSIS
by William Hewitt

This book contains a complete system for using hypnosis to enter a beneficial *altered state of consciousness* in order to develop your psychic abilities. Here is a 30-day program (just 10-20 minutes per day) to release your psychic awareness and then hone it to a fine skill through a series of mental exercises that anyone can do!

Beyond Hypnosis lets you make positive changes in your life. You will find yourself doing things that you only dreamed about in the past:

Out-of-Body Experiences: including previously secret instructions to easily and safely leave your body.

Channeling: you will easily be able to communicate with spiritual, nonphysical entities.

Skill Improvement: you will learn techniques to improve your physical or mental abilities. Speed up your learning and reading abilities and yet retain more of the information you study. A must for students of all kinds!

Beyond Hypnosis shows you how to create your own reality. how to reshape your own life and the lives of others—and ultimately how to reshape the world and *beyond* what we call this world!

Beyond Hypnosis will introduce you to a beneficial altered state of consciousness which is achieved by using your own natural abilities to control your mind. It is in this state where you will learn to expand your psychic abilities beyond belief!

THIS IS NO FANTASY! You can do all of what has been described here *and more* by using the instructions in this book! If you are ready to improve your life, to get the respect and admiration you deserve for being the special person you are, you need *Beyond Hypnosis.*

0-87542-305-1, 202 pages. $7.95